Let Me
Explain

Let Me Explain

Eugene G. Fubini's Life in Defense of America

David G. Fubini

Foreword by **Harold Brown**

Former United States Secretary of Defense

SUNSTONE
PRESS

SANTA FE

Sunstone books may be purchased for educational, business, or sales promotional use. For information please write: Special Markets Department, Sunstone Press, P.O. Box 2321, Santa Fe, New Mexico 87504-2321.

Book design ▶ Vicki Ahl
Body typeface ▶ Adobe Garamond Pro
Printed on acid free paper

Library of Congress Cataloging-in-Publication Data

Fubini, David, 1954-
  Let me explain : Eugene G. Fubini's life in defense of America / by David G. Fubini ; foreword by Harold Brown.
      p. cm.
  Includes index.
  ISBN 978-0-86534-561-4 (hardcover : alk. paper)
  1. Fubini, Eugene G., 1913-1997. 2. Physicists--Italy--Biography. I. Title.
  QC16.F787F83 2009
  530.092--dc22
  [B]
                          2008052280

Published in

WWW.SUNSTONEPRESS.COM
SUNSTONE PRESS / POST OFFICE BOX 2321 / SANTA FE, NM 87504-2321 /USA
(505) 988-4418 / ORDERS ONLY (800) 243-5644 / FAX (505) 988-1025

This book is dedicated to my wife, Bertha, and to our four wonderful children, for whom this book was originally written: Michael, William, Anna, and Marco.

Contents

Preface

*L*et Me Explain grew out of my desire to honor the memory of my late father, and to preserve that memory for my children, grandchildren, and extended family. It's not an uncommon desire, particularly for an only son, but the aspiration was enhanced by the fact that my father had one of the most distinguished and least publicly visible careers in the modern history of United States national security: For more than three decades he was one of the key architects of the defense sector. He was essentially a shadow figure, and few people outside the Pentagon, if any, ever knew of my father's role. He was not a spy; rather, he was an indispensable counselor to numerous appointed and elected officials, as well as many uniformed military officers. The job with which they'd been entrusted—and which they, in turn, largely entrusted to my father and a handful of other people—was nothing less than overhauling America's defenses following World War II, and leading America to the fore of the digital/space age. For the rest of his life, this was the mission to which he dedicated himself wholly. He was the man in the corner who was always there to say, "Let me explain." In doing so he helped influence, guide, demand, push, and drive the U.S. defense establishment to new heights of capability and performance.

However, history is never neat or simple, and neither are people; my father was no exception. He believed that one exercised greater influence by being in the "back of the parade," giving counsel, than by being in the "front of the parade," with all its presumed glory and public visibility. This tactic undoubtedly improved the efficacy of his work, but it was less ideal in fatherhood, and left his children with, at best, an incomplete understanding of his life, work, and personality. And so, perhaps inevitably, the writing of this book quickly became a process of personal and historical discovery: What did my father do? Who was he? And what was at the core of this drive to reshape the defense of his adopted country? The answers were often surprising, frequently gratifying, and not occasionally painful.

The details about his work that were the hardest to find were often the easiest to hear. I learned that only months after emigrating from Italy during World War II, he began working to create technology that would jam German radar. I heard stories about his leadership of the Airborne Instruments Laboratory; his pioneering work in the new world of electronic weaponry; his effort with the government in the early 1960s to lay the groundwork that would allow the conception of the Internet; and his roles as the father of modern electronic warfare, as the promoter of the stealth concept, and the driver of satellite-guided weaponry. All of it was fascinating and, of course, indescribably satisfying for a son to hear about his father.

But the stories about my father that were most easily discovered—stories of advice he'd given, of his selfless commitment to the careers of others—were surprisingly difficult to hear, even as they were enriching. If friends remember fondly his brilliance, dynamism, and thoughtfulness, his family (less fondly) recalls his demanding, egocentric presence, and his volcanic anger. His demands for excellence in his children were relentless, and while the goal was laudable and came from a place of real love, the methods were maddening and at times cruel. Learning that others had known such a different Gene Fubini—one of such consistent care and sensitivity—was both pleasing and difficult.

Of course, the most significant obstacles in researching and writing this book were not emotional, but practical. To begin with, little of the secrecy in which my father's work was shrouded during his lifetime has since lifted, and the facts and substance of his career remain largely hidden to all but a few colleagues with proper security clearance (a telling compliment to the legacy and enduring relevance of his work). There is also the fact that my father died several years before work began on the book, and during his lifetime he was never very forthcoming when the subject was himself. Piecing the story together from the remembrances of colleagues and family was an enormous undertaking, but gaps remained, especially with regard to his youth. The only way to bridge these gaps was through informed conjecture based on hard evidence, personal experience, and intuition. Forming a complete picture of who he was as a man seemed to ask for a measure of subjective storytelling.

That basic lesson about history and people—that neither is ever simple, and that what is visible is often a mere hint of the whole—is not a revelation, I realize. My father's life, as I am only now able to see it, cut a cross-section through much of the last century, and seems to illuminate critical machinery in the evolution of the country he made his own. But he is also as fine an example as you can find that people hold untold and often unfathomable depths and complexities, which is, in the end, what makes us human. As difficult as it was at times to realize the dimensions of himself my father never really allowed his family to experience, in the end the process of researching and writing *Let Me Explain* has brought my father more fully into my life by helping me understand more completely who he was. If my father's life, as I've tried to tell it here, serves as a prism that usefully explains some part of the American century to other readers, then I will be pleased. Yet this is not the primary reason for this book. Rather, I hope that reading about my father's journey will serve my family and engage my father's colleagues as much as writing about the journey has fulfilled me.

—David Fubini

Boston

Foreword

by Harold Brown
(Former United States Secretary of Defense)

*E*ugene Fubini was short in stature. But in all other respects, he was larger than life: physically and intellectually energetic; voluble and imaginative; untidy in dress and gesture; by turns impulsive and thoughtful, impatient and persistent; aware of his superior talents but quick to acknowledge his mistakes. (And he made some; his driving was a menace to himself, passengers, and other drivers.) He dedicated his life to his family, to his many friends, to the pursuit of technology—and, notably, over five decades, to the security of his adopted country.

My own thirty-five years of close association with Gene began in 1961 (though we had met briefly a dozen years earlier) when he became my deputy for research and technology in the Defense Department's Directorate of Research and Engineering. Through the following decades—as he was at various times in government, in the private business sector, running his own consultant activity, and acting as an outside adviser to government agencies, we remained close friends as well as professional associates. He was a loyal colleague, a valued source of advice (on matters technical, professional, policy, and personal)—and an endless generator of ideas, projects, and anecdotes.

Fubini's experience working as scientific consultant and technical observer with the U.S. Army and Navy in the European Theater of Operations—including electronic reconnaissance and jamming for the invasions of Italy and southern France as well as combat missions for the Eighth Air Force—was central to his subsequent approach to the application of technology to military capability. He thought always in terms of the needs of the military user, and in particular about how to fit technical capabilities together with intelligence inputs and operational doctrine in support of executing military objectives. He learned to be the technologist as well as the system engineer that weaved the individual technologies into a system with ease of use and strength of result. This approach, together with his evident affection for the institutions and personnel of the U.S. armed forces, engendered a reciprocal positive sentiment from all levels, from enlisted ranks to chiefs of staff. And the same customer orientation characterized his work in the private sector, including his early advocacy of the development of the personal computer when he was at IBM and the effort to ensure that the strength and operative capability of IBM's seminal 360 machine was fully utilized.

On a personal level, Gene's high ethical standards, his broad interests, his ebullient manner, and commitment to excellence inspired all who knew him. He was quick with his opinions and had little patience for sloppy thinking, analysis, or presentations. That offended some. He was well known for a lack of tolerance of the obvious in program reviews and was a demanding personality in a debate. But Gene had at the same time an unusual degree of sympathy for the personal problems and aspirations of others, especially young people. He volunteered as a matter of course to help find positions for those he knew—and many whom he didn't, but had heard of him and asked him for help. He helped untold numbers of ex-military officers and defense executives, through an expansive network of contacts, find roles that would not only enhance their personal stature but build the greater defense infrastructure of the country. But his legacy is not limited to what he did for individuals; he helped to build valuable institutions. In particular, the intelligence organizations of the Defense Department owe much of their strength and fundamental approaches to his efforts. The influential Defense Science Board is, in its current structure and processes, largely the result of his decade as its Chairman and Vice Chairman. When I appointed Gene to the Chairman of the Defense Science Board I had hoped to raise its stature and impact on the defense community. Little did I imagine that Gene, through his strength of convictions and determined efforts, would build it to be the premier external advisory group to the Department of Defense that it is now.

Gene's breadth of interests and abilities is illustrated by the fact that he was deeply involved in drafting the conflict of interest legislation that, in modified form, still applies to government service today. (At the dinner marking Gene's departure from the Defense Department in 1965, then-Deputy Secretary of Defense Cyrus Vance joked that he, Vance, was losing his lawyer.) Gene did so recognizing that the role that he played as one that straddled industry and government was a role that would soon go away as a result of conflict and political necessity. As a result, Gene was the last of a breed. He had lived comfortably in both the service to his country and to industry. He was, in this way, also unique.

There will not be another Gene Fubini. Even if there were, it is doubtful that he could achieve similar results now. Institutions age and ossify; the Congress and the media are much less open to the idea of movement between the private sector and government (the "revolving door"). They prefer career civil servants (except when they call them "bureaucrats") and are less troubled by movement between Congressional staffs and executive branch positions. Barring a crisis severe enough to cause a fundamental transformation in the way government works, a Gene Fubini, no matter how capable, effective and admired by the military, would have a harder time today. Part of Gene's special gift was his ability to weave this understanding of industry, technology, and military need together to the benefit of all. Just as he had eighteen months after entering this county from an Axis nation and aided in the design of radar countermeasures in collaboration with others from academia, industry, and the military—so did Gene do this for the balance of his life. We will likely never see that same integrated effort emerge again.

There is another lesson, though not a new one, to be drawn from Gene's career. From its beginning, America has been built by immigrants and their descendants. It has depended on its ability to attract the adventurous, vigorous, and talented from outside, and on their dedication and devotion once here. As has happened periodically over the past two centuries, the last decade has seen a growth of attitudes and actions discouraging that process. Talents like Gene's are rare; we need more of them, whether indigenous or imported. His lasting legacy is to be found in his technological achievements that continue to contribute to our national security and our modern economy, in the many individuals who learned by association with him how to innovate and to solve problems, and from the example he provides of how one unusual individual can change for the better even so gargantuan an institution as the U.S. Armed Forces.

The country benefited from Gene's behind-the-scenes effort. Gene never sought the limelight and always felt his impact was better served through the counsel to others. His constant refrain of "let me explain" is at the core of my and many others' relationship with Gene. He always wanted to explain. Not take action for you, not make the decision for you. Rather his was the role of a counselor, mentor, and guide. Through his explanations and his questions, he showed us the path to the building blocks of a modern defense establishment. Gene did this not only in by enabling informed choices around the deployment of technologies but also in the network of talent and expertise that he brought to the task.

Joseph Alsop, the well-known columnist, once wrote to Ted Sorensen on the death of President John F. Kennedy urging him to stay the course because as JFK's counselor Sorensen had "strengthened his arm and extended his reach." Well for me, Gene strengthened my arm through his intellect, his drive, his indomitable spirit, and his humility. He extended my reach and helped me in my service to country. Gene was a true patriot and my valued counselor. We all are the beneficiaries of what he did in defense of his country.

1

Turin

$\mathcal{I}$n 1492, the year Columbus undertook his explorations of the Americas, Spain defeated the last of the Muslim armies occupying the country, restoring Christian control and ending the relative acceptance of the Jews in Spain. With the threat and expense of Muslim wars behind them, Ferdinand and Isabella were not only prepared to sponsor the westward explorations of Columbus, but they could also attend to further political consolidation and religious housecleaning within their own domain. The Inquisition was in full flower, and the king and queen indulged Spanish Inquisitor General Tomas de Torquemada's passion to expel the Jews by issuing the Alhambra Decree, which ordered the country's 200,000 Jews to leave Spain and its territories or convert to Christianity. The punishment for disobeying the order was death. All 200,000 lost the preponderance of their property, and many died in the flight that followed. Some Jews reached Portugal (where their acceptance proved short-lived). Some made the voyage to welcoming Turkey. Some made it across to North Africa. Others migrated to Sicily and Sardinia. Still others made the trek over the mountains into France and, eventually, through the Alps into Italy. This is where the story of Gene Fubini's family begins, for it was here that the Jewish émigré Ghiron and Fubini families would be joined.

Turin was, by the early twentieth century, a booming city with a robust industrial economy and a thriving intellectual community. Among the city's elite was Pacifico Ghiron, patriarch of one of Turin's wealthiest and most powerful families, and a prominent name in the Jewish community. He had begun his business career as a low-level employee of a small coal importing business. Born in 1856, he began at the age of fourteen as an employee of a small coal dealer named "Valenzano" as a warehouse keeper. Over the years he became owner and manager of the company, buying the company outright in 1913. It was a time of rapid growth for the city, and Pacifico's company had grown right along with it until it was a major force in the Turin business community.

Pacifico Ghiron: Patriarch of the Ghiron Family, Gene's grandfather (circa 1885).

Pacifico and his wife, Ida Foa, had five children: Camillo, who would die on the battlefield during World War I; Marco, who was to succeed his father in running the coal import business; Angelo, who was to work beside Marco; Ricardo, his mother's favorite, who dabbled in a variety of passing interests, but essentially lived the life of the spoiled socialite; and finally Anna, the only daughter. The sons had all gotten themselves married, but a daughter was another matter, and Ida—described as a hard, unloving woman—was eager to have Anna married and out of the house. The moment Anna turned seventeen, Pacifico was charged with finding her a husband.

Anna Fubini: Gene's mother in her early teenage years.

For all their wealth and standing, there was one thing the Ghiron family could not claim: intellectual status. As a self-made man, Pacifico understood hard work and perseverance, but what he really prized was education, something he'd had little of himself. And in early-twentieth-century Turin, if a man was looking for an intellectually respected husband for his daughter, he could not do too much better than Guido Fubini.

Mathematics may not be known as a romantic profession, but in an unexpected way, Guido might be considered an exception: small, rumpled, self-effacing, and among the most important mathematicians of his generation. In Italy at this time, mathematics was producing some of the most innovative thinkers in the world, and there was no better example than Guido. His father, Lazzaro Fubini, had been a mathematics teacher in Venice, at the Scuola Macchinisti, so it was in his blood. Influenced by his father's interests—and, presumably, blessed with his father's gifts—he entered the Scuola Normale Superiore di Pisa in 1896, and soon found his passion for geometry. His doctoral thesis, *Clifford's Parallelism in Elliptic Spaces*, was completed in 1900, and was widely praised and circulated by one of his teachers, the great mathematician Luigi Bianchi. It propelled Guido to considerable fame in the international mathematics community at an age when most mathematicians are still trying to find their voices.

After this triumph, Guido began studying the theory of harmonic functions in spaces of constant curvature, and, in 1901, began his teaching career, first at the University of Catania, in Sicily, then at the University of Genoa, and finally, in 1908, at both the Politecnico and the University of Turin. Though most mathematicians have a narrow focus of study and expertise, Guido pursued and excelled in a variety of fields, including differential geometry, analytic functions, and functions of several complex variables. During WWI, Guido applied his skills to the improvement of the accuracy of artillery shells, and moved on to work in the fields of acoustics and electricity.

Guido Fubini: Gene's father and famous academic and mathematician (circa 1925).

Like many highly accomplished men, Guido had focused on his career to the exclusion of his personal life, putting off marriage and family until such time as he had acquired the financial stability and social standing then thought to be required for a successful marriage. Now at the age of thirty—young for a leading mathematician, but rather old for a single man—he, too, was looking for a spouse.

The pairing of Guido Fubini and Anna Ghiron was perfect in many ways. From the Ghiron perspective, the family gained intellectual standing by association, and a new kind of respect in the wider community that it could not have achieved on its own. For Guido, the attraction was a lovely young wife who was social and outgoing in ways that he could never manage. There was also the attraction of a substantial dowry, and entry into the circle of Turin's business elite.

It was to be a match. In 1910, Guido and Anna were married.

Anna and Guido Fubini (circa 1915).

It's easy to imagine their first meeting: Guido, sheepish in an ill-fitting suit with his short legs and seemingly too-long arms; his big head of unruly hair; his large, somewhat unkempt mustache; and his manner shy, but charmingly deferential and undeniably engaging. Anna: young, vivacious, and slender, with long, flowing hair, and an air of moneyed refinement tempered by playful approachability. She may have been surprised, or even a little shocked, at the sight of this man, shorter than her at less than five feet, and nearly twice her age. But Anna would come to know that while Guido was a serious man, he was also kind and caring, mischievous and humble, and, above all, loving.

2

Gino and Eugenio

In their early marriage, the new couple lived in the Ghiron family home on Via Pietro Mica in central Turin, where they occupied one of the larger apartments in the home of Anna's family. The building that housed the family apartments was one of the larger on the avenue, with servant's quarters in the basement and the first floor given over to elegant retail shops. The interior was heavy with marble and had, as its centerpiece, a beautiful sweeping staircase that led to the upstairs apartments. Later, an interior elevator would be added, easing access to the eight floors of apartments.

Anna was a natural homemaker and went about acquiring the inlaid furniture, sculptures, and pictures that would decorate the homes of Fubini families for generations to come. She had the refined taste and sophisticated eye one would expect of a young woman with her elite education and social training, and the complete disregard of expense one would expect from the same.

Both Guido and Anna understood that decorating their home was both Anna's responsibility and her pleasure; it was not something for which Guido had any aptitude or enthusiasm. Guido may have reached the point in his life when he was ready to begin a family, but that did not mean his work had become secondary. Quite the contrary: He was usually to be found in his office at school or in the classroom, and even on his rare visits home he would continue his work, either in his study or "in his head," as he described his thought processes. Always focused on his latest explorations, he would litter the apartment with scraps of paper scribbled with equations, notes, and theories. He seemed to live in a world of his own thoughts, and Anna found it difficult to get him to focus on the present and the practical.

Yet, Anna and Guido grew to love one another. He provided the intellectual underpinning of their marriage—a sort of intellectual validity—and she provided the means to live a regal and privileged life. As was the Italian custom of the time, Guido—who, though not classically handsome, nonetheless wielded an undeniable charm—continued the affairs of his single life. And Anna, as was also the custom of the time, neither questioned nor objected to his frequent absences and the fact that they were sometimes not to tend to work, but to other women.

Instead, Anna turned her attention to the social side of their lives. She had always enjoyed parties, and now, with a home of her own and her adulthood fully realized, she became an accomplished hostess, entertaining frequently and eagerly. Anna was already used to occupying the highest stratum of Turin society, and now she found her status enhanced (just as Pacifico had expected and sought) by her marriage to a respected intellectual. This new position and the social functions that went with it were, in fact, new to both her and Guido; she—legally a child less than a year prior, and thus generally excluded from most of her parents' parties—and he—a distracted, socially disinterested workaholic—had had little experience with serious socializing.

Anna's cousins, the Foas, lived in the apartment above the newlyweds and came to figure largely in their lives. Though always busy with work, Guido could not resist a request that he serve as mathematics tutor to the charming Anna Foa, then in the later stages of elementary school. She was a bright child, and strongly interested in literature, and not a bit interested or naturally skilled in mathematics. Still, she was eager to please her much older tutor, a goal which consistently escaped her. Anna Foa tried to break the tension of what was an inherently difficult situation—the earnest but inept pupil and the patient but ineffective teacher—by teasing him. She said that as soon as she outgrew him (which would surely not be long) she would do the teaching, and he would have to learn the poems she loved so dearly. Every time she came downstairs, she would warn him, "It won't be long before the poems." He would give her problems, explain concepts, and offer gentle correction, and she would struggle to understand. If Guido left the room, her attention would wander, and he would come back to find her writing a poem among her math exercises. When the frustration became too much even for the patient Guido, he would walk out onto the balcony of his study and call up to her parents, "Anna Foa is a beast!" But the rupture would never last, and was never serious.

Anna Fubini kept a social attachment to her family's Jewish faith, but agreed with Guido—who disdained religion, and offered its banishment as his only major contribution to the state of their household—that there would be no Bar Mitzvah for their sons. Religion was, of course, central to the cultural and social fabric of Italy at this time, and their decision caused a number of awkward moments and situations in their lives. The Foas would later recall that Guido would often join them for Passover meals, and would make it a point to smoke while everyone else prayed.

Anna Foa's grandfather had been a rabbi, and her father was prominent among Turin's religious Jews, so there were admonishments and debates among the friends and extended families. But Guido was steadfast in his views.

Guido, like many men of reason, believed that the intellect was the only thing upon which one could be truly rely. Indeed, he believed intellect defined individual character. The things he wanted to know about a person—the only things he felt he needed to know in order to understand him—were: Are you smart? Are you driven to succeed? Can you aid your family in doing this? Everything else, Guido believed, was extraneous. This attitude would soon form the core of his attitude to raising children.

In 1910, after one year of marriage, Anna and Guido welcomed their first child, Gino, into their lives. Gino was a beautiful baby (which must have been a relief to Anna, given Guido's physical disproportions) with a sweet disposition and a mild temperament. This was despite the fact that he had been a breech birth, and during a complicated delivery had suffered an irreparable leg injury; he would have a slight hitch in his step for the rest of his life. He was also born with one arm that was slightly longer than the other.

Three years later, on April 19, 1913, a second baby arrived. It was another son, Eugenio, this time physically perfect and delivered uneventfully. But where Gino was agreeable and easy to manage, Eugenio proved to be a demanding and difficult baby. He was only happy when in motion. His crib was a place of restraint, and when he was confined to it he expressed his displeasure without subtlety or hesitation. Most of the memories of him as a baby involved his screaming, kicking, or striking out at anyone who curtailed his freedom in the slightest.

Pacifico Ghiron and baby Eugene.

Baby Eugene (on left) and brother Gino Fubini (1914).

Anna relied, as many of that era and class, on the aid of nannies to raise her two boys. She had become an effective and respected household manager, and she approached motherhood as another task to be directed and managed. Parental warmth was not her strong suit, and that sort of affection came, instead, from Guido; the irony being that he was rarely home. Still, he was thrilled to have two sons to play with and he delighted in their presence for the short intervals that he took away from his studies, classes, and academic pursuits. The boys settled into a routine, directed by Anna, with care provided by a succession of nannies, and the occasional visits and roughhousing with their largely absent father.

The characteristics the boys exhibited at birth continued into childhood. Gino was quiet and thoughtful. Eugenio was loud, demanding, precocious, and difficult to control. Anna despaired over Eugenio's seemingly inexhaustible energy and combativeness. The one person he seemed to almost always get along with was Gino, although the siblings also showed the natural competitiveness common to most brothers. Eugenio's early emergence as a gifted child would come to have a clear effect on Gino.

One afternoon when Eugenio was six and Gino eight, the story goes that the two brothers went together to buy bread for everyone and the Sunday newspaper for their father. Gino was a supportive older brother, and let Eugenio carry the paper home. But at some point he realized Eugenio was no longer walking along beside him, and when he looked back he saw his younger brother standing on the corner, apparently reading the paper. Eugenio was only four, of course, and Gino assumed he was playing a game. Gino joined him, also pretending to read, but Eugenio didn't laugh. "I'm reading about the war," he explained. When they returned home, their mother asked what had taken so long, and before Gino could answer, Eugenio began to recite the news of the day.

That same year their multilingual parents began speaking German when they didn't want Gino and Eugenio to overhear their conversations. Eugenio, ambitious and curious as ever, said he was going to learn the language so he could understand what his parents were saying. Their governess at that time, who was German, helped Eugenio learn. He made a game of sneaking as close as he could to his parents to make out what he could, and running back to his governess to consult on words he hadn't understood. Gino, who always loved a new game, would play it, too, but he picked up only a few words of German in the process. Eugenio, on the other hand, soon proved his quickness (not to mention the value of intelligence) when he correctly understood his parents' conversation about the new skis the brothers were to receive. They arrived a few weeks later.

These were among the first times that Eugenio's brilliance made Gino feel like the younger brother, a theme that would persist for the remainder of their lives.

Two years later, Eugenio started classes at the Giberti School (exact name uncertain), and from the start he seemed to be perpetually in trouble with both the students and the faculty. Like most gifted children, his perception of the world was simply different from that of others, and he had little time for or interest in the social dynamics of the schoolyard. Not surprisingly, this made him a frequent target, at least early in his school career when his intelligence was perceived as simple oddness. His older brother protected him as best he could, of course, but in any event being an outcast did not seem to affect him too strongly, perhaps because he was moving too fast for anyone or anything to touch him: Not long after starting school, he was moved up, first one grade, then another, putting him in the same class as his older brother. Inevitably, Eugenio skipped up again, moving ahead of Gino. Indeed, even the school's principal seemed powerless to discipline him: One threat of suspension was met with Eugenio's unperturbed response that if he was suspended, the school would be at a serious disadvantage in the upcoming academic contests with rival schools. The threat was withdrawn, suggesting that in the end, perhaps he wasn't an outcast at all, but had cannily understood the role he played in the broader social structure, and the latitude he'd be accorded as a result.

A note from the principal of the Giberti School illustrated the challenge of dealing with Eugenio. The note urged Guido to speak with Eugenio, because as the principal put it, "Eugenio is not interested in rules." When Guido confronted his son about the note, Eugenio said, "This is not true. I am very interested in rules. I am interested by what is on the other side of them. Rules seem to keep people away from what they need to or could understand. I am smart enough to understand, so for me the rules are a barrier." Guido, recognizing the beauty of his son's answer, simply kissed Eugenio's forehead, and went back to his study; this would become a familiar response.

Anna recalled this as a time when Eugenio was in a constant state of exploration. She would send her son to the market, and a simple errand would take hours. When he returned, he would explain that he'd stopped to read or talk with someone about some new topic, and that he had lost track of time. He was a forever curious, blissfully undisciplined, and perpetually forgetful child.

Throughout this time, the Fubini family had grown ever closer to the Foas. Anna Fubini regularly consulted her older cousin, Lelia Foa, for advice on mother- and wifehood, and Lelia—who was Anna Foa's mother—insisted that the Fubinis vacation with them at their house in Diano Marina on the western Italian Riviera. The house had been a wedding present from Lelia's father, and though the Ghiron wealth far exceeded that of the Foas, Lelia wanted Anna and Guido to consider it their second home. Later, Lelia found the two families a mountain house to share in Courmayeur, a perfect escape from the Turin summer heat and chance for the children to hike and climb in the summer, and ski in the winter.

Eugene and Gino Fubini at the family's mountain retreat in Italy (circa 1920).

These homes offered Anna a retreat from the full-time job of managing Eugenio's seemingly boundless energy. In Turin, the boys took fencing lessons, had their schoolwork, and were sent on endless errands, but this was not enough to slow down Eugenio. In the mountains or at the seaside, however, there were innumerable opportunities for an energetic boy, and Eugenio took to both locales. He loved the challenge of climbing and skiing, and spent many days in the mountainside. As early as nine he was with guides exploring many of the smaller slopes and summits of the western Italian Alps. At Diano Marina, he would sail and row, and it was here Eugenio cemented his friendship with Anna Foa. By this time she'd given up any pretense of mastering Guido's mathematics and instead had given herself over fully to literature. Her fondest memories as a young child were of making Eugenio row out onto to the lake as she read Dante aloud to him. He would memorize these works of literature as she read, and when they reached the other side, recite them back to her.

But Anna didn't need this display to know that Eugenio was gifted. Living upstairs from the Fubinis, she had seen firsthand how relentlessly active his mind was. He seemed to be in perpetual motion, a whirlwind of discovery and wonder, always examining the contents of any rooms, pulling things from shelves, perusing books, and investigating the workings of the world around him. While he was consistently in trouble with any and all authority figures, he wasn't antagonistic, but rather he was guided more by his own experiments and explorations than by any adult rules that might constrain them. The governess got tired. Anna got tired. Even Guido got tired. But Eugenio never seemed to tire. It seemed in everything he did, he was always watching, learning, imitating.

Eugene Fubini as a young boy (circa 1926).

Eugenio was always small, but as he grew older, he became strong for his size. That was what mattered when he went to the mountains. For dangerous climbs, he always went with one of the alpine clubs or a guide. He challenged himself to climb higher and faster than anyone else, especially those who were bigger. He was a daring, aggressive climber who treated the group climbs as a competition. As for skiing, he was more determined than skilled, but again, he focused on results.

He prided himself on his ability to ski any slope, any terrain, and he was strong enough to ski all day. Skiing with a wide base, skis apart, he would fearlessly tackle any slope, no matter how treacherous. As he would later tell his own children, "It is not the manner in which you ski which matters. What matters is the terrain you can ski." For him, ability was defined by where you could go, and what you could accomplish. Style counted for very little.

Eugene Fubini on one of his many Italian climbing expeditions as a young man (circa 1933).

Eugenio liked people, but struggled to understand why forming friendships was hard. Because he had skipped several grades, he was surrounded by children of greater social and emotional maturity, but this inferiority likely never occurred to him. Instead, he tried to make his intellect and learning the natural basis of friendships, little realizing that in grade school, intellect—or anything else that sets you apart—is far less important socially than the things that make you the same. Wouldn't anyone who lived near mountains or enjoyed skiing be interested in the particulate conditions before an avalanche? Wouldn't anyone be interested to hear about his father's work, which Eugenio had by this time begun to understand? Bafflingly for Eugenio, the answer was no. But Eugenio was no conformist, and he was as incapable of changing his approach as he was unwilling to do so. He was born to be what he was, and in the face of social frustrations, he only became more of that thing: He spoke up in class as much as he could, argued with teachers, pointed out the things others missed. Only at exam time was his input really sought. With so little social interaction at school, he relied on Anna Foa for friendship and companionship; she was, at least, an intellectual, even if she only wanted to talk about literature. The two of them, along with Anna's younger brother, Vittorio (who was smart, but little interested in his studies), formed the core of Eugenio's social group throughout his adolescence.

Mathematics was, of course, Eugenio's father's domain, and perhaps as a way to be or feel close to Guido, Eugenio had first applied his considerable talents to the same work that had been his father's first love for all of his adult life. But as his intellect blossomed further and his secondary education loomed, Eugenio found himself drawn increasingly to physics. There were many things to recommend the field of physics at the time. First, of course, was that Eugenio found it perfectly fascinating. It also allowed him to maintain a connection with his father's work while charting his own course. Then there was the fact that physics was then exploding as the most important field in science; if, for Guido's generation, mathematics had been the field that had captivated the brightest minds in the world, the coming generation was to belong to physics. The University of Rome, Eugenio's father would soon learn, was building a new physics department around a brilliant new professor, Enrico Fermi, who was then opening new frontiers in physics. Surrounded as he always was by important thinkers, Guido was in a unique position to understand completely the intellectual trend toward physics. Mathematician and theoretical physicist Henri Poincaré, once a student of Guido's, often came to visit his old professor, and the talk was all of physics. Renowned mathematician Luigi Bianchi was another frequent visitor, increasingly in the company of his colleague, Albert Einstein, who would become a close friend of the Fubinis.

So, with his father's contacts, Eugenio was accepted for his two college years at the Politecnico di Turino, in the fall of 1929, when he was seventeen years old. Anna Fubini thought he was too young, but his father didn't think about young or old, and neither did Eugenio. For them, what mattered was ability, drive, and results. It was an attitude that would serve Eugenio well when, in the spring of 1931, he left his parents, his brother Gino, his close friends and cousins Anna and Vittorio Foa, and whatever childhood he had ever known, and went to the University of Rome. There he was to take his Ph.D. in physics, studying under the already-legendary Fermi. He was nineteen years old.

3

Rome, Fermi, and Revolution

The emergence of the new physics was unquestionably its own event, and just as unquestionably a revolution. Its foundation was 200 years of Newtonian mechanics, which were now being driven in a sudden and distinctive direction, focused on the fundamental geographies of matter. It was only in 1913, the year Eugenio was born, that Niels Bohr presented his model of atomic structure, and not until 1919 was relativity corroborated with practical measurement. The University of Rome's fledgling physics department had only just begun to gain momentum under Fermi when, at the 5th Solvay Conference in 1927, the principles of quantum mechanics were the critical matter of debate. There were twenty-nine invited physicists—of whom seventeen were or would be Nobel Prize winners—and they gathered to do nothing less than lay the foundation for this new branch of science. Those twenty-nine physicists formed the core of the first generation of this revolution in science.

Physics was then and continues to be a small field, and there was shared excitement about the new horizons being opened. That excitement would last for much of the century as the exploration grew, as more and more scientists were drawn to the work, and as applications and ramifications of the work became more apparent. Within ten years of the 1927 Solvay conference, fission would be looming. Within just five years, Fermi would be well into the slow neutron work that would enable him to lead the application process from Rome to Chicago to Los Alamos and, finally, to the atomic bomb.

Outside this small, sheltered community of scientists, world events moved towards their own, no less revolutionary irruptions. In 1919, as relativity was finding corroboration in observable nature, Benito Mussolini was rising and fascism was taking hold in Italy. As in Germany, the social and political climate in Italy made it vulnerable to aggressive, brash leaders who spoke loudly of returning the country to its rightful place among world powers—no matter the methods. This vulnerability existed in large part because of World War I, which had been a disaster for Italy: The country had entered it unprepared and suffered terribly. In 1917, at Capporetto, the Italian army lost 300,000 men, and by the end of the war had lost 300,000 more. After the war, nearly a million Italians were left wounded, a quarter of those severely crippled, and they returned in anger to a decimated civilian economy. Compounding the shame of the country's enormous losses during the war were the disproportionately paltry spoils the country received from the other victorious Allies. People were hungry and out of work, crime was on the rise, and Italy seethed with political unrest fed by resentment and disaffection. In Turin, one of the few cities with substantial manufacturing, fascist forces loyal to Mussolini—and preceding his dreaded Blackshirts—attacked and killed leaders of socialist workers' organizations. By 1922, Mussolini had staged the "march on Rome," consolidated various elements into the Fascist Party, and installed himself as the country's leader.

All of this was a none-too-inconspicuous backdrop to Eugenio's life.

He was only nine when Mussolini came to power, so certainly fascism would have been his political reality. But for Eugenio, who was so focused in his academic and intellectual pursuits, political considerations were surely peripheral, at best. He was sheltered in the way of the intellectual elite, and lived a life blissfully insulated from the turmoil roiling around him. In 1931, with world events marching toward another inevitable conflict, Eugenio left home to travel to Rome to join the only revolution that concerned him, the one led by a professor named Fermi.

In Rome, in the old, modest building on Panisperna Street, the University of Rome had established its new Department of Physics. Giants like Edoardo Amaldi, Franco Rasetti, Ettore Majorana, and Emilio Segrè were the older generation of the department and would later be seen as the founding fathers of the modern era of physics. Eugenio came in with the so-called "puppies" of the field; being interviewed years later, Eugenio said they included Ugo Fano, Leo Pincherle, someone named Sapienza, and Bruno Pontecorvo. Pontecorvo was as young as Eugenio, but Eugenio seemed the youngest because he was so small and so youthful. He made up for his height with his voice.

Arriving in Rome, and counting as his classmates some of the brightest minds of his or any other generation, must have been a great balm to whatever boyhood wounds Eugenio had suffered as a social outcast. Here, his curiosity was matched. Here, his brilliance and insight were the norm. If he had been a big fish in a small pond before, he was now in an unmistakably large pond, and it suited him. In his letters home, he said that the first time he entered the Panisperna building, he felt that truly at home.

"The Panisperna Boys," as this first generation of students was to become known, soon developed their own internal structure. It was the famous and respected Rasetti who coined the term "puppies" to refer to the youngest of the team; Eugenio was the puppy of the puppies, but he took it as a compliment and wore the label with pride; indeed, Rasetti's other nickname for him—"Golden Fubini"—made the compliment overt. Fermi, meanwhile, was "the Pope"; Rasetti himself was "Cardinal Vicar"; and the forbidding, brilliant Majorana was the "Grand Inquisitor." Rasetti was the tallest in the building, and slender as a reed, and because Eugenio was the shortest and still carrying his baby fat, together they were an amusing study in physical contrasts. In class and group discussions, the contrast was fully realized as Rasetti—older, more sedate, and largely silent—allowed Eugenio, his younger and more boisterous student, to verbalize his solutions to the toughest problems Rasetti could present. Eugenio spoke quickly when he was excited, his voice getting louder and higher as his excitement mounted, as if he could spread that excitement aurally. He moved constantly as he spoke, gesturing wildly with his arms and hands to illustrate his ideas.

At the heart of the team, of course, was Fermi. Corbino (the head of the department, but not himself a scientist) actively advertised Fermi in promoting the department's reputation, which was already growing well beyond Italy. Many of the best German physicists came through Panisperna, and although in part they came because of the German political situation, mostly they came because of the electrifying work that Fermi was doing. Fermi, in his rumpled and too-small suit, didn't seem to care about his individual reputation. Rather, he brought everyone together and held them together, orchestrating the work among them in a way that leveraged the strengths of the individuals on behalf of the entire group. From the first time Eugenio met him, Fermi treated Eugenio as if the two of them were near intellectual equals, two scientists in pursuit of the same lofty goals.

Most of the department kept Fermi's hours: From nine in the morning until twelve-thirty, and then from four in the afternoon until after eight. Eugenio, of course, worked through the early afternoons and late into the night, as well. When Fermi taught, it was in his room and the style was informal and effectively Socratic. Fermi would probe deeply substantive issues in the form of everyday questions—"Why is the sky blue? Why do waves break on a beach?"—and, despite his casual manner and patience in waiting for a response, he wanted serious, scientific answers. The work became more structured when each student was asked to help in solving every other student's problem. On many days, too, Fermi brought his own work to class, posting it on the board and thinking out loud as he puzzled it out, inviting the younger students to discus the issue at hand, and the best approach to solving it. A layman peeking into the classroom might not have guessed from the style of Fermi's teaching—relaxed, open—and the atmosphere in the classroom—pleasant, calm—that this was some of the world's preeminent physics work. It was a testament to Fermi's brilliance as teacher, as well as scientist, that he understood an unassuming generosity was the best method with which to inspire the best work. Everybody followed in Fermi's thought process as if they were an extension of his own intellect, even when they could not fully comprehend its depth.

In the classroom, Eugenio simply could not contain himself. Still reveling in the freedom to be himself, ever more spurred on by the towering intellects that surrounded him, he became a serial interrupter during Fermi's lectures, picking up the master's solutions even as Fermi himself was working them out. Fermi recognized in Eugenio a mind at last unbound, and could only laugh. Indeed, Fermi and his wife, Laura, often took Eugenio and the others on lengthy Sunday strolls—a practice which became known as Fermi "taking his puppies for a walk." They were, of course, not really leisurely walks as much as classes in the open. "Why is the snow white?" Fermi would ask his students. "Why is the grass green?" The eager puppies would answer, and simple answers wouldn't do. As long as there was another "why?" to be asked, Fermi would ask it, probing deeper and deeper into the issue, peeling away layer after layer, until at last the truth was revealed; truth was what they were all after in everything they did. Eugenio savored these walks, and yearned to be asked the questions. But, of course, even if he hadn't been asked directly, he felt no hesitation in giving the answers.

Physics, in ways as plain or as complex as one chooses, is a window into the world in all dimensions. The nature of the physical world and everything about it, seen and unseen, is the business of physics; its aim is to illuminate, to reveal. On those walks in the gardens of the Villa Borghese or on hikes out into the country, Eugenio was able to feel physics come alive the way mathematics had for his father. Eugenio began to understand how far he could take physics and, in turn, how far physics could take him. Others must have felt the same way about their futures, but none of them would likely have said so aloud, and neither, likely, did Eugenio. It may have been the only thing, in fact, he ever left unsaid at this time in his life; his classmates frequently offered him a penny for every minute he could remain silent. Eugenio was strangely proud that nobody ever had to pay.

On holidays there were longer hikes in the mountains and there were trips skiing in and around his home in Turin. Eugenio returned often to the Alps to climb and ski, tackling tougher and tougher climbs. Eventually he would climb nearly all the major peaks in the area.

In the spring of 1933, at the age of twenty, Eugenio finished the two years of study for his Ph.D.; he was no longer a "puppy." He had gotten the highest marks in every course, and had written his thesis for Fermi, who had long since become more than a professor to him, and now was as much a friend and a mentor. He received a summa cum laude on all but one of the exams for his degree: Only Fermi held back the summa honor, awarding him instead the lesser magna cum laude.

Spring in Rome comes on quickly; the heat rises and the sky goes to a summer's glare with seeming prematurity, the palms turn brittle, and the city begins to empty, its inhabitants making their way to the relative cool of the mountains and the seaside resorts. Eugenio wanted to be among these vacationers, but he had untended business. He found Fermi in his classroom and asked the question that had nagged at him: "Why didn't I receive a summa cum laude? I don't understand. I made no mistakes."

Fermi said, "You do not earn a summa simply by avoiding mistakes."

"How do you earn one?" Eugenio replied. The motivating issue for Eugenio was not pride or thirst for acclaim but was, as in most things, curiosity. If a perfect answer did not earn the highest mark, what could?

Fermi understood Eugenio's question, and answered it in his frank, uncompromising way. He stood and walked to the board, the same board in the room where Eugenio had learned to truly think; where he had watched Fermi working out the details of his early exploration into the nucleus; where, in short, he had grown from a bright, eager boy full of potential to what he now thought of as a real scientist. Taking chalk in hand, Fermi said, "In solving one of the biggest problems I put before you, you arrived at your answer via the familiar path, never realizing that there was a better path, a more elegant path." He wrote it out on the board.

Eugenio studied what Fermi had written.

After all his time in this room with the great physicist, after all the progress Eugenio had felt he'd made, after all of the explorations of the blue sky and green grass and floating ice, Eugenio saw that he still had a great deal more to learn. When Fermi approached a problem, Eugenio saw, he stood back from it, examined it from every angle, distilled its essence, and then dismantled it systematically. There was, Eugenio realized, value and meaning in the method as well as in the result. This was the definition of original thinking.

It was only a summa to a magna. It was only one grade, and still a very good grade, the second-best grade a student could earn. The issue meant nothing.

And yet to Eugenio, it could not have meant more. That point was brought home to him as he stood in that silent, sweltering classroom on that late spring day. He didn't want to be the second-best anything. He wanted to honor his father. He wanted to honor Fermi. He wanted to join Rasetti, Segrè, and Amaldi, as well as Fermi himself, as giants. Eugenio wanted and expected to do work that mattered, work that would further the discipline of physics. He expected to become, as the rest of them were becoming, internationally important in physics, just as his father was in mathematics.

No one else could have shown him this, only Fermi. Eugenio had always been the smartest, and he'd always had the energy and the will to use his gifts. But now Fermi—no one but Fermi, in perfect silence—had delivered the question in a way that distilled it to its essence: Could Eugenio be a physicist of the highest rank?

4

Return to Turin, Engineering, and Gia

$\mathcal{E}$ugenio faced a dilemma: Should he remain in Rome and try to succeed in the shadow of Fermi and his team, or should he move on? To this point, he had assumed unquestioningly that his work would be in physics; Bruno Pontecorvo, alone among the "puppies," had stayed on with Fermi's team, and that option was open to Eugenio, as well. Likewise, Eugenio's exceptional credentials and ability, his notable youth, and his unflagging energy put other positions in physics easily within his reach. But Eugenio had been a prodigy. He had grown up in the home of a world-class mathematician. He had trained at Panisperna with Fermi. In short, he had always been the best, always striven for the highest position in whatever he had done, always treated every endeavor the way he treated those climbs in the Alps. If there was a higher peak to be reached, Eugenio wanted to stand upon it. The highest peak in the field of physics was the work Fermi was doing. If he couldn't reach it—and Fermi's reasoning in the matter of the magna cum laude grade had by this time convinced him that he could not—then, he reasoned, he needed to find another mountain range altogether.

The heady atmosphere of constant intellectual stimulation and growth—not mention the romantic allure of being at the very vanguard of all the sciences—surely exerted a powerful pull for him. Turning his back on all that must, at times, have had the flavor of needlessly self-imposed exile. But the prospect of conquering a new field and being closer to his father must have been equally alluring, and in 1933 he simultaneously became lecturer on radio engineering at the Royal Institute of Technology, and won a position as a research and development engineer in non-linear acoustics and high-frequency measurements at the National Electrotechnical Institute; both schools were part of the University of Turin. He did not work with his father directly, but Guido's mark was everywhere at the university and in the field. Returning to his father's university, he must have felt the older man's presence in nearly everything he did.

Back in Turin, the Foas were living in Guido and Anna Fubini's old apartment, which they had vacated when they relocated to the Ghirons' elegant building on Pietro Mica. By the middle of the 1930s, the Foas' had become home to a Friday night gathering of artists and intellectuals, with Anna Foa as the hostess and some of the city's more famous literary, academic, and up-and-coming political figures as eager guests. Among the participants in these gatherings were the painter Carlo Levi and his sister Natalia (a writer, who would become Natalia Ginsberg when she married another of the Friday crowd, the literary critic Leone Ginsberg, a Russian Jew from Odessa).

For a time, Anna Foa's father had pushed her aggressively to marry a much older man. But she was an educated woman and a modern woman, and considered herself above antiquated notions of old religion and social rules; arranged marriages certainly fell into this category for her. Further provoking her father, she had a total disregard for devout Judaism. Her father, furious, took her out of school when she refused the engagement, but she did not relent. Left without a formal or structured context within which to study her beloved literature and poetry, she was forced to pursue them on her own, and her personal network of friends and family—of which these Friday night gatherings were a large part—enabled that pursuit.

Art and culture were the pretense for the gatherings, but the focus quickly shifted to politics and the growing problem of fascism. But these were not casual conversations. Eugenio may have spent his life to this point largely oblivious to Mussolini's rise and its implications, but others were paying close attention. Anna Foa's brother Vittorio, along with Carlo Levi and Leone Ginsberg—as Anna Foa would learn only later, when arrests began—had become deeply involved with the anti-fascist organization, Giustizia e Libertà. With the Friday night gatherings as a pretext, they'd begun plans to assist the anti-fascist underground and organize resistance. Carlo and Leone were named codirectors of the Italian branch of Giustizia e Libertà and had begun, by the time Eugenio had returned to Turin, an intense and clandestine anti-fascist propaganda campaign.

The anti-fascist movement by this time had a strong and growing voice in Italy. In the Piedmont region particularly, where the Italian Unification Movement had began in the early nineteenth century, there was a deep feeling for Italian pride and civil liberties, making it a natural bastion of anti-fascist support. The Organization for Vigilance and Repression of Anti-Fascism (OVRA), Mussolini's secret police force, was laughably inept, but nobody had forgotten the violence of the early 1920s and, perhaps with the more vivid example of Adolf Hitler's crushingly effective political control in Germany as an example, public fear of the government rose as arrests and subversion of individual rights became more evident.

Every Italian male was required to serve in the military, and Eugenio entered his service early in 1934, scheduled to serve until the middle of 1936. While the slow neutron work came to fruition in Rome and the gang on Panisperna Street—a group that had seemed eternal only a few years before—began to disperse, Eugenio was assigned to the military with a rank of sub-lieutenant. He served in the conscripted staff bureaucracy of what he considered to be a pathetic army unit, and fought at the Brenner Pass. He later participated in what he called Mussolini's "absurd war" with Ethiopia, a war that alienated everyone but Germany and led Mussolini into a more subservient relationship with Hitler.

While Eugenio was in the army, fascist oppression grew. The OVRA intercepted anti-fascist literature being smuggled into the country from France and the state-run newspapers loudly reported a Jewish conspiracy. Leone Ginsburg was among those arrested in the ensuing campaign against the organizations thought responsible. While he was later released for lack of hard evidence, it was a sign of the pressure that would be increasingly applied to anyone connected with anti-fascism, particularly if that person happened to be Jewish. In May 1935, while Eugenio was between tours of duty, many more arrests were made in Turin. Most of those arrested were Jews, and they included Anna Foa's brother Vittorio and their father Ettore Foa. The pressure on the Fubini/Ghiron/Foa families, as well as most other Jewish intellectuals, was undeniable. Ettore was released almost immediately, but Vittorio was not. It became apparent that whatever roles or positions one held in Italy at this time, no matter the scope of one's contributions to the wider society, being Jewish was simply the only thing that mattered to the fascists, and that single characteristic rendered all other points moot.

Eugenio had seen Anna Foa infrequently due to his military service and his prior work in Rome, but upon his return he went to the Foa family apartment for a Friday night gathering. He found that he was the only visitor. Others who had frequented the Foas' home and been active in the weekly gatherings now stayed away for fear of retribution. Fear, of course, was a central tactic of the fascist forces, and it had begun to work powerfully in Turin. Eugenio and others were shocked when Beppe Foa, Anna's brother, was arrested. They were soon able to secure his release, but the fear clung to them all.

In the midst of the political turmoil, Eugenio, like his father before him, was forging an unlikely way with women. Just as his father, he was physically small, and relied on his intellect, confidence, and natural charisma to charm women. He was deferential and courteous to them—without, of course, surrendering his position of intellectual superiority—and he was, in a word, a flirt. For the first time he was less than totally consumed with and encumbered by his work, and the small amount of room this created in his life soon began to be filled by his socializing and romantic pursuits.

Chief among Eugenio's romantic interests was Gia Cova. She was not a new arrival in Eugenio's life; quite the contrary. Though Turin was a geographically large city, its social circles could be quite small. Gia, whose father was a highly regarded member of the Mussolini administration and whose mother was a close friend of Anna Foa's mother's, had always been around, moving about the edges of Eugenio's life. He had never taken any particular notice of her. But now Gia, as girls of her age often do, had suddenly turned beautiful and charming, and she and Eugenio spent increasing amounts of time together. It wasn't long before they began to share the easy comfort of lifelong acquaintances who had begun to build their casual relationship into something more. Gia would tease Eugenio about his height and his need to ceaselessly talk, for imagining himself important, for his delusions about being handsome, and for his habit of dressing carelessly, as all intellectuals seemed to. Eugenio, for his part, would meet it all with a sheepish grin, charmed by this beautiful creature and seeing it all for what it was: expression of a growing fondness, and real love. Gia's family, though connected to Mussolini and not Jewish, did not object to Eugene's family. Eugenio's mother, Anna, already thought the world of the Covas.

Despite the building political pressures, life settled down for the Fubini family. Eugenio began his lecturing and academic career in applied engineering. Guido continued his work at the same university teaching and furthering his work on probability theory. Anna Foa entertained and lunched with her friends. Gino, meanwhile, had become an engineering professor and had also received a position at the university. He did not teach at Eugenio's level, but Eugenio rightly suspected Gino was, in fact, a better teacher, displaying greater patience and taking time with all the students, not just the brightest. In the classroom, Eugenio was known to aggressively challenge his students in the same way Fermi had challenged him, but Gino—true to his calmer nature as a baby—was patient and calm, fine qualities in any teacher.

When he wasn't teaching, Eugenio's research continued and he placed several papers on non-linear acoustics and high frequency-measurements with leading academic publications. These papers not only began to establish Eugenio as a force in the academic engineering community, but also demonstrated his growing stature and future prospects to Gia's father. He was moving ever closer to a discussion of marriage with the Cova patriarch.

Meanwhile, Mussolini became more accommodating to Hitler and the fascist pressure began to increase yet again. The stream of German scientists that had passed earlier through Panisperna, fleeing the early constraints in Germany, now turned into a flood of people of all sorts fleeing Germany. Jewish families all over Turin had begun to accept the open-ended visits of German relatives and friends who had fled their homes. The growing concern was that if the trends continued, a similar migration out of Italy might soon be required. Eugenio, who had never distinguished Jewish households from any other, observed that within all Jewish households no discussion seemed to take place that didn't involve mention of passports, work papers, secret police, and preparation for war.

Anna Foa's brother Vittorio, who remained in prison, told Anna that she and the rest of their family must plan on leaving the country soon. Indeed, soon lower- and middle-class Italian Jews began to lose their civil service positions simply for being Jewish. Nonetheless, few believed Hitler's crusade against Jews could ever truly reach Italy. The elite of Turin had always lived politically, religiously, and economically comfortable lives; the descent into anything such as what Germany was experiencing seemed inconceivable.

In hindsight, of course, the trend seems all too inevitable. The fascist thugs who had murdered people in the streets of Turin after the end of World War I were succeeded by the Blackshirts. The newspaper editor and political rabble-rouser who had once been thrown out of school for stabbing a fellow student had become Benito Mussolini, a dictator of near-imperial power. And the closeted anti-Semitism of Europe was becoming overt, aggressive, and poised to be a defining characteristic of Europe's next decade.

If the Great Depression hadn't savaged Italy as severely as it had most of Europe, it was only because so much of the country was still agrarian. Mussolini, however, instituted tariffs and price controls that did considerable damage not only to the agrarian economy generally, but to farmers and the rural population specifically. It was a weak economy and a weak country and, just as those same conditions had helped enable Hitler's rise in Germany, in Italy they lead to widespread unhappiness, confusion, violence, and the opportunity for demagoguery. When Mussolini's ill-advised war with Ethiopia once again proved Italy's military weakness, and when Mussolini's petulant defiance of the country's former allies put him in thrall to a Germany where institutionalized violence had already identified the Jews as scapegoats, the descent became rapid.

At least one person saw what was coming, and quietly prepared. Anna Fubini's brother Marco met with Eugenio and Gino one day to tell them that for some time he had been leaving accounts receivable in the coal importing company's banks in England and the United States. Now, as discreetly as possible, he was also transferring his and Guido's personal capital out of Italy, as well. Marco further suggested to the two brothers that the time to flee was rapidly approaching. Thanks to his foresight, the Fubini family was spared many of the hardships and losses that other families endured in the coming years.

For Eugenio, the shock of realizing that his family would have to flee Italy was like the nightmare of a mountain climber losing his guide ropes in mid-climb. How was it possible? His father was a great mathematician. He himself was a respected professor. They were among the most admired families in all of Turin, visited by international colleagues as famous as Einstein and Poincaré. Eugenio and his family had led a life of importance and relevance. And here Eugenio's reaction shifted from terror and bafflement to plain rage. He hated stupidity, and Mussolini's stupidity deserved all his fury. He allowed himself this moment—which may have been a long moment—of pure emotion, before his scientific mind took over. This was the reality, and there was little time to stew over it. What was called for was rational planning and quick action.

They would certainly go to the United States. Marco had already insisted that Eugenio's father, Guido, offer his name out to American universities, which would be eager to have the internationally respected mathematician. Eugenio himself, being younger and much less established, might have a harder time finding his place in America. But according to Anna Foa, Eugenio had become exhilarated at the prospect of building a new career in America, and he felt undaunted by the challenges.

Despite the circumstances, Eugenio felt sure that the time had come to propose to Gia. He had no doubt that his family's standing and financial resources would make their relocation successful, but he knew he would need to convince Gia's father of this. Following a trip to Milan to hear the opera *Tosca*, Eugenio asked Gia to marry him. To his surprise and disappointment, she counseled patience. Everything, she said, was changing, and it made more sense to wait and see how things developed than to make a rash, reactionary decision. Particularly, she expressed concern for her family's safety if she, the daughter of a high-ranking member of the Mussolini administration, were to marry a Jew. For his part, Eugenio hardly saw himself as Jewish—indeed, hardly considered religion at all—but there was little he could do besides accept her decision.

5

Escape to Paris

*M*arco was an adept businessman and, like his father Pacifico Ghiron, had managed the family coal business very successfully. He also proved to be the most analytical and cool-headed among the male Ghiron-Fubini family members. Possibly his role dealing with businesses throughout northern Italy and neighboring countries allowed him to have a more comprehensive understanding of the emerging political and religious situation. Or possibly, because he had contacts in the U.S. and dealt with businessmen who asked the hard questions about the stability of the country, he was simply less insular. Whatever the reason, Marco saw what others refused to see: the reality of fascist rule, and the absolute necessity of leaving Italy.

Marco, like his father, had never invested more capital in the stationary physical infrastructure of the coal import business than was absolutely necessary; he made sure that the business remained highly liquid. At the time of his death in 1936, Pacifico had significant and active accounts in Scottish and English banks. These were partially a result of forward-thinking joint ventures with an English firm, the Brownlie of Glasgow. Marco now used these accounts to establish ever-increasing amounts in permanent deposits in a Philadelphia, Pennsylvania bank. If the wrong people had been paying attention to what Marco was doing, of course, he would have been arrested instantly. But the fascists were essentially bullies and opportunists, and the right amount of money helped them forget their ostensible political and ideological principles. He spread bribes around liberally, and his questionable accounting practices and large, unauthorized money transfers were ignored. Bit by bit, the coal company was "hollowed out" and the family wealth was

Marco Ghiron (1954), older brother to Anna Fubini and uncle to Gene Fubini. The architect of the Fubini/Ghiron family's flight from Italy and long-term overseer of family finances.

moved out of the country. Such actions were necessary but expensive, and a great deal of the family wealth went to making these transfers happen. Nonetheless, they would be leaving with more than enough money. In future testimony to a Senate subcommittee approving his appointment to the United States Defense Department, Eugenio—who by then had Americanized his nickname to Gene—testified that the family's total net worth when they left Italy had been in excess of $400,000, a substantial sum in the late 1930s.

In order to preserve the family heritage as much as possible, Marco also arranged for Italian citizens with no Jewish connection to be put in control of what remained of the coal company and the family residences, most critically the large apartment building on Via Pietro Mica. At the time it may have been a simple attempt to continue to control family assets, but it would prove an important decision, as it allowed nearly a quarter of the extended Fubini family to return to Turin after the war.

Others in the family with less financial acumen than Marco also tried to aid in the transfer of funds out of the country. For example, his brother Angelo's wife, Elsa, arranged for a set of a dozen demitasse cups to be made with what looked like gold plating and shipped to friends in the U.S. Little did anyone outside the family know that, in truth, the demitasse cups were made of solid gold and represented a neat nest egg for the family, if and when they were retrieved.

Out of necessity, Eugenio had not told Gia of his family's preparation, but as the time of departure approached, he finally explained it all, and asked her to join them. This was where his considerable, inexhaustible powers of speech served him well. He outlined their plan, explained how much money had already been transferred out of the country and, most of all, emphasized his complete confidence that what lay ahead of them would, in the end, be far better than what they were leaving behind. But again, Gia saw only complications for her father and the rest of the family. And again, caution was urged, patience was requested, and decisions were deferred.

It was a busy, stressful, and chaotic time for the family. Guido, Gino, and Eugenio all held university posts that were stable and prominent, but under increasing attack by fascists who considered Jews essentially ineligible to hold them. Eugenio had to maintain his teaching schedule, aid in the planning for the upcoming flight, deal with his relationship with Gia, and, perhaps most importantly, quickly build a body of work that would open doors for him at American universities. In all ways, he heard the ticking of the clock, and he drove his research as quickly as possible, aware that his university position, along with its laboratory and assorted other scientific facilities, might vanish at any time. He wrote papers more rapidly, focused on the most significant topics (his research at this time was concentrated heavily on very high frequency waves, which were then called microwaves, and were a relatively unexplored part of the radio spectrum), and he assembled a resume that would do for him in America what reputation alone had done for him in Italy.

Anna Fubini was confused by most of what was happening. She didn't fully understand the politics of the situation, and didn't grasp the seriousness of the consequences of staying. She perceived the move as she did most things: in terms of their impact on her material comfort. She loathed the idea of leaving behind her clothes, her jewelry, her furniture, and of course, the social standing that went along with them all; these were the things that defined her. And while she hoped that the people Marco selected as caretakers of these things would be trustworthy, she felt it more likely that they would be left behind forever. She retreated into her position of elegance (and a bit of ignorance), and that seemed to be all the comfort she needed.

By now the family was certainly psychologically prepared for the departure, but many details had yet to be settled, and Marco continued to move family wealth out of the country. Still, the walls were closing in. In Italy and Germany, the pressure on Jews seemed to be growing ever greater, and violence against Jews seemed to be increasingly endorsed and even orchestrated by the governments. On November 7, 1938, a young Jew named Herschel Grynszpan, whose family had been forced out of Germany, walked into the German Embassy in Paris and shot a German diplomat, Ernst vom Rath. When Rath died a few days later, seemingly spontaneous anti-Jewish violence broke out across Germany—violence that was, in fact, carefully planned and executed by the Nazi government. More than 7,500 Jewish shops were destroyed and 400 synagogues were burned down in a single evening. Ninety-one Jews were killed and an estimated 20,000 were sent to concentration camps, which had to this point been primarily used for detention of political prisoners.

In Italy that same year, Mussolini delivered his racial laws, which prohibited miscegenation between Jews and "Aryans," and placed Jews, as defined by racial criteria, under further restrictions. These laws were part of a comprehensive racial system that included the banishment of alien Jews, the expulsion of Jewish students, and the elimination of Jewish teachers from the school system. It also enacted severe economic constraints on Jews.

When the *Manifesto of the Racist Scientists* came in the summer of 1938, it was, for the Fubinis and others, the final blow. It held as follows:

1. Human races exist.

2. There are great and small races.

3. The concept of race is purely biological.

4. The population of modern Italy is of Aryan origin and its civilization is Aryan.

5. It is a myth that other peoples have mingled with the Italian population during the modern era.

6. There now exists an Italian race.

7. The time has come for Italians frankly to proclaim themselves racists.

8. It is necessary to distinguish between European Mediterranean people and the Africans and Orientals.

9. Jews do not belong to the Italian race.

10. The European physical and psychological characteristics of Italians must not be altered in any way.

What had dwelled in the darkness for so long was now emerging fully. The Fubinis and Ghirons were not yet in physical danger, but that would come in time. Marco moved the family's funds faster than ever; Eugenio's lab work was redoubled. The whole family readied itself.

Marco's insistence that Guido seek an invitation to a U.S. academic institution appeared to have been another piece of wise counsel. Marco's foresight was rewarded when Guido received an offer from the Institute for Advanced Study at Princeton University. This invitation would prove critical for the Ghiron-Fubini clan: It allowed the political cover for an exodus, provided a base of operation for the family in the U.S., and would be essential for securing visas. Guido's friendship with

Einstein, who was firmly in place at the institute by this time, had surely been essential in securing the post because Guido's now failing health would have cast doubt on his ability to contribute as a professor. In fact, Einstein, who'd fled Europe shortly before Hitler became chancellor in 1933, wrote many affidavits throughout the 1930s and 1940s recommending visas for Jews fleeing European persecution. But at a time when the atmosphere in Europe was becoming so poisonous for Jews, there were certainly other professorial candidates available to Princeton who might have offered more robust service. Einstein's recommendation made the difference.

It was late in 1938, when Eugenio, then twenty-five years old was finally discharged from his teaching position at the University of Turin under the new racial laws. He was relieved of his research position, too, but was able, for the moment, to maintain access to his lab. He pushed even harder on his microwave research knowing that this alone might mean the difference between success and failure in the U.S. In later years, he would often say that the only money one could really count on was "that which was still remaining in your head." He knew that the capital Marco had managed to send abroad was a good starting point, but that ultimately his intellectual abilities and accomplishments were going to determine his future.

Other members of the family were affected by the new racial reality, as well. Gino was discharged from his professorship at roughly the same time as Eugenio, and he worried that without Eugenio's resume he would have few prospects in the U.S.; he must have approached the upcoming journey with considerable anxiety. A short time later, Guido, too, lost his academic position, but because of his reputation and standing in the global math community, his department allowed him to resign to avoid the shame. The plain fact that the shame actually belonged to university officials was lost on no one, probably including the officials themselves.

Others in the extended academic community of friends had also began to flee. Segrè had already left Panisperna and was making arrangements to leave the country. Rasetti was already in Canada. Pontecorvo was on his way to America, and so was his brother, Paul. Amaldi decided to stay and hoped that by doing so he could keep physics alive in Rome.

Finally, a deadline was established: The Ghiron-Fubini family decided that if they stayed beyond the fall of 1938, arrest was likely or even inevitable. In fact, around the time they made this determination, Guido himself was briefly arrested after an associate, eager to curry favor with the fascists, accused him of secretly transferring funds out of the country. Perhaps the associate had gotten wind of Marco's activities and simply confused the situation, but to anyone who knew the professor, the very idea of the oblivious, distracted professor cunningly manipulating finances was laughable. But no one in the Ghiron-Fubini family was laughing; it served as a chilling reminder that in Italy's increasingly hostile environment, you simply didn't know whom you could trust. Internally, the family resolved to depart at the first available opportunity.

The plan was worked out over a series of family dinners. The two families would break into five separate groups, none large enough to arouse suspicion. There would be a separate car for each group, each car would have at least one of the six men, and each car would follow a different route over a different border crossing into neighboring Switzerland. It was possible that one or more cars wouldn't make it, but chances were that at least one car would. In order to support their official story of traveling on a day trip, they would travel with no money and with no luggage.

With all the details of the escape planned, only one issue remained unresolved: Eugenio's relationship with Gia. He knew, of course, that none of the objections from the previous conversations had been addressed: her father was still a member of the Mussolini administration; she would still be leaving her entire family behind; and no matter how vividly Eugenio could imagine his new life in the U.S., no matter how overpoweringly determined he was to make himself a success in his new life, none of it was assured. Still, he was a talker, a man who could take complex ideas and make them understandable. He saw the situation scientifically: identify the problem, apply the solution. He said to her, "Let me explain."

But of course love isn't science. He did explain, and she did listen. He described his father's position at Princeton, and the family connection to the influential Einstein. He outlined the work he'd been doing so feverishly in his lab before being removed from his university post, and how it would enable him to secure a teaching position in the U.S. He told her about the family wealth that had been safely moved, and even the specifics of their plan for escape, coming now in only a few days. But in the end Gia wanted that most scientific thing of all: proof. Proof that the life he described was the life they would lead. Proof that her family would be safe even after it became known what she had done, which might even be construed as treason. And of course Eugenio could offer no such proof. Gia revealed, too, that her father would never allow her to marry a Jew, and Gia, for her part, would never confront or defy her father. And so they had reached an impasse.

Eugenio was bitterly disappointed. But how long was it before the realist in him took over? It must have felt like the final conversation he and Gia would have on any matter (though, in fact, he and Gia would be in touch even after his leaving Italy, and talk fruitlessly of her coming to America). Like his work with Fermi, like his life in Italy, the subject was settled, and dwelling on it served no purpose.

Marco had not yet secured visas as the families' five cars left for Switzerland one morning in September 1938; he feared the paperwork would bring further attention to his financial maneuverings. Everything else that could be done, had been done. The plan was complete and the family was on the move. At every checkpoint the story was repeated: We're on a day trip, the passengers of the cars told the guards. They forced smiles, affected an attitude of nonchalance, and hoped the guards noticed their carefully selected casual clothes. And at every checkpoint the guards would look them over, circle the car and peer through the windows, pause, discuss the situation, and then wave them through. Anna Fubini had managed to bring some of her most treasured jewelry, which was sewn into the lining of her coat, and she felt for it frequently, her fingertips discerning the hard, hidden shapes of brooches, pendants, and rings. They passed checkpoint after checkpoint, guard after guard, until, suddenly, it was over. They were in Switzerland, and behind them was Italy, the only life they'd ever known, finished now, without ceremony.

All five cars had made it through, and as planned they met in Sion. From there they drove to Montreux, where the next day they boarded the train for Paris. By evening they were all in the St. James and Albany Hotel, where Marco had arranged rooms. The next step was simple waiting for the documents that would allow travel to the U.S.

With their escape complete and the panic and anxiety receding, the families' anger began to rise. Their stature in Turin was not happenstance; it had been earned. The coal business had helped drive the booming industrial economy. Pacifico had very conspicuously condemned war profiteering during World War I when, during the hardest times, he literally gave coal away; for that, the city government had erected a plaque in his honor. Guido, meanwhile, had covered the city and the university in honor and glory with his intellectual achievements. In short, the family had been as central to the cultural and economic life of Turin as any family. It was a familiar story in Europe, of course, but that didn't ease the pain of it. For Eugenio, it was a hard lesson in the temporality of nearly everything.

During this surreal time of emotional, financial, and political limbo, the family members occupied themselves as best they could. Guido seemed the most at ease. He told everyone he was on vacation, and that's how he treated the situation. He became a familiar sight to the other guests at the hotel, shuffling along the corridor, moving slowly because of his weak heart. He spoke to everyone with his quiet humor, and treated the hotel as his home. Casual bemusement was his typical manner, but he was also secure in the knowledge that his resume and contacts would allow the family to endure. He sat up deep into the night with his chess set, and left his equations, scribbled on scraps of hotel stationery, laying all around the hotel.

Eugenio was his usual active self. He and Marco haunted the American consulate, constantly inquiring about the prospects for visas; they booked passage on ships when they thought the visas were forthcoming, only to change the reservations when things were delayed. Eugenio kept up correspondence with academic journals, finished papers he'd been working on, and did what he could to make influential contacts that might speed along the visa process. He also set himself to the considerable task of learning not just a new language, but a new culture. He sought out American guests at the hotel and listened to the unfamiliar cadence of their speech, and watched their body language and the way they carried themselves. He went to every American movie he could and read every American newspaper he found. And all the while, as he looked ahead to his new country, he burned with hatred for the fascists and what they had done to his family and innumerable others. And he thought distantly of how he would exact his revenge.

6

Columbia Broadcasting, New York, and Betty

*I*f the escape from Italy was full of last-minute planning and high anxiety, the time in Paris was an agony of waiting. Ship passages were booked and cancelled; letters were written—to colleagues, to friends abroad, to relatives—and letters were received; meals were eaten, clothes were pressed, and laundry was sent out and returned. The days spun slowly through their monotonous revolutions, but no word came about the visas. Marco, growing weary of the confines of the hotel, took his family down to Nice, where he had personal connections and his young children could attend a local Italian school. Everyone else remained in Paris, waiting, waiting. And then, all at once, it happened: The family secured the visas that would allow passage to the U.S. Eugenio and Gino booked the family first-class passage to New York on the SS Ile de France, and they departed in March 1939, arriving in New York a little more than a week later. From the New York waterfront, they traveled by car to New Jersey, arriving at their new home on Naussau Street in Princeton. The family had arrived.

Among the first guests in their new home were Albert Einstein and fellow Princeton faculty member John von Neumann, who came to welcome the family to America and to safety. Von Neumann, a mathematician who would go on to work on the Manhattan Project and help produce the first atomic bomb, was then nearly as celebrated as Einstein himself. Guido was sixty—a more advanced age in 1939 than it is now—and his heart was failing. But he was thrilled by the visit, and even more thrilled by Einstein's request for his consultation on a number of projects. Eugenio—who had adopted "Gene" as his Americanized first name when he landed—watched with pleasure as his father partnered with the two great thinkers, happiest, as he always had been, when he was able to work. The other family members may have been suffering through their adjustments to a strange new land, but for Guido, the work was the common cultural language.

Gene knew that his situation would be more of a struggle. In Italy he'd had a bright future ahead of him; everyone knew it. But in America, he had no reputation, no network, no colleagues to help guide him. The Depression was still gripping the country and the war was looming, making both job and social prospects slim. The culture was strange to him, he had not yet mastered the language, and to any of the nearly innumerable American faces who passed him on the street—open, inquisitive, but not necessarily friendly faces—he was just a short, oddly dressed man with a thick, perhaps impenetrable accent. But before long, his practical, scientific brain took over.

Fermi was by this time teaching at Columbia University. Gene thought briefly of contacting his old mentor for a position, but he never did. Perhaps he was mindful of putting himself back in the great man's shadow, but more likely he began to realize that academics generally were not the right path. With Guido's health in decline and his capacity for work diminished, Gene felt it was up to him to be the breadwinner for the entire clan, and to secure the highest-paying job possible. That alone ruled out academics. He turned his attention, instead, from the theoretical to the applied sciences, specifically electrical engineering. Not only were private sector jobs more secure and more lucrative, but they were generally more egalitarian, ensuring advancement to those who worked hardest and were most deserving, and providing, along with that advancement, access to ever-larger amounts of research funds. Gene set his sights on the Columbia Broadcasting System, which was then developing the new technology that would make television possible, and was also doing fascinating radio spectrum research.

Nonetheless, he faced the same trio of challenges here as he did everywhere else: a lack of contacts, a shortage of reputation, and an abundance of more connected and experienced competitors for the few positions available—and most of those competitors were native English speakers. But when it came to CBS, he was undeterred. Why? Gene was a rational thinker above all else, and it's likely he was led to CBS by research that told him it was the place most suited to his skills and needs; having found it, he pursued it relentlessly.

From the beginning, he sought out any individual related to CBS in any way. He met them for drinks and asked them to lunches, cornered them in lobbies, caught them exiting buildings, and followed them across busy streets. And from these people he extracted whatever information he could about the work CBS was doing. His tactics in questioning these people were familiar and effective: the old Fermi method of asking series of questions, peeling away layer after layer. What were they investigating? What was their approach to the questions at hand? Why did they choose this approach? Had they tried other methods, and what had come of those efforts? He would point out where he thought the work could be improved, and why he might be the one to help drive it in a new, better direction. Later, he would counsel many others in this manner of job seeking: Never allow yourself to be interviewed, he would say. Have more and better questions than the people with whom you meet, and you will display your knowledge, intelligence, and aptitude. But, try as he might, no offer presented itself.

One day, after yet another fruitless interrogation of some unsuspecting CBS employee, Gene left the CBS building in a driving rainstorm. Despite the scarcity of cabs in bad weather, he managed to hail one at the curb and told the driver to take him to Grand Central Station, where he planned to catch the train back to New Jersey. Just then another man rapped on the cab window and asked if he might share the ride. Gene agreed. As they crawled through the congested, rain-soaked streets, the two men fell into conversation, as happens under such circumstances. The man soon revealed that he worked at CBS (he may have been the only CBS employee, by this point, that Gene had never met) and Gene produced his usual battery of questions. As it happened, the man helped oversee research at CBS, but Gene, as usual, didn't temper his questioning or his judgment of the network's research. And little by little, the man began to see how much thought Gene had put into work that was not even his, how many innovative ideas he had about it, and how formidable his mind was. Curious about this randomly brilliant man in this random cab in the middle of a Manhattan rainstorm, the man asked about Gene's background; it must have been a shock to realize that this short, thickly accented man had been a student of the great Fermi. The next day Gene had a meeting with executives overseeing the CBS development labs, at which a classic "Fubini bargain" was struck: Gene agreed to work that was, by his standards, rather menial: monitoring the radio broadcasts for the big band concerts that CBS then broadcasted in the evenings from the Rainbow Room atop Rockefeller Center, and from other venues around New York City. It was, essentially, a technician's job. In exchange for this effort, however, and in addition to the modest income it yielded, Gene would be allowed, on an informal basis, to participate in the ongoing exploration of ultra high frequency (UHF) and microwaves; he was also permitted to conduct some independent lab work of his own. When one considers Gene's lack of leverage, the bargain seems a testament to his perseverance, an awesome piece of luck, or both.

The evening job running the radio broadcasts was a dull and thankless task. Gene monitored microphone placements and oversaw the radio equipment necessary for the network broadcasts. He picked up the necessary equipment at six o'clock, took it to the hotel ballroom where the band was playing, installed the equipment, established the connection with the radio network, and managed the equipment while the various bands were announced and the commercials were inserted. For some, it would have been the opportunity of a lifetime, if only for the music: The broadcasts included some of the most popular and most significant bands of the era, including those led by Benny Goodman and Duke Ellington. But Gene, no jazz fan, was indifferent to the music and benumbed by the work, which he found as crushingly tedious as the work under Fermi had been relentlessly stimulating.

In September, after five months of commuting from Princeton, Gene decided to take an apartment in the city. The less time he spent on the train, he reasoned, the more time he could spend in the lab. The timing was not ideal: His father's health had continued to decline, and being even as far away as Manhattan meant taking the chance of being absent during a crisis. But the work, as always, came first. If anyone would understand this, it would be Guido. Gene found a modest room at the International House at 503 West 121st Street, which shared a building lobby with the Fairholm College Club, next door at 501 West 121st Street.

———

Meanwhile, in Northampton, Massachusetts, in the spring of 1938, as the young ladies in their graduation attire walked through the main quad and settled into their lawn chair seats under the graduation tents at Smith College, one would have heard this graduation song:

Thanks for the memories
Of English 111
Shakespeare under Dunn
Angora mittens
Harlow writes
Scott Roof in the sun
How lovely it's been
Thanks for the memories
Of ski boots in the rain
Hoods of cellophane
Autumn's haze
Of mountain days
That were not giv'n in vain
O thank you so much
Many the times we've cut classes
And many the movies we've seen
Without our knowledge time passes
So that somehow we're seniors now

And thanks for the memories
Of symphonies in tune
Skiing 'neath the moon
The Grécourt Gates
And fancy skates
And caps and gowns in June
O thank you so much

Elizabeth "Betty" Machmer was one of the singers, and sang with her head tilted back and her eyes bright and earnest. This ceremony marked the end of her college years. She was not one of Smith's wealthy, urbane young women; she was known around the campus as the "local gal" who'd somehow found her way into the elite school to learn with the privileged daughters of the gentry. Her father, William L. Machmer, was not a bank executive or a diplomat; he was the longtime dean of Massachusetts Agricultural College, or "Mass Ag," which had recently become Massachusetts State College, and would later become the University of Massachusetts. If Smith, Harvard, and Yale were the natural destinations for the children of the monied elite, Massachusetts State was where everyone else went. Though it produced innumerable graduates who went on to occupy some of the highest and most important seats in business and government, its reputation was not, to be sure, anywhere near that of the Ivies.

Despite her obvious qualifications for Massachusetts State College, Betty Machmer chose nearby Smith. She was a scholarship student but, because of a Depression-induced shortage of students who could pay the highest residential rates of the school, Smith placed her in one of the most expensive residence halls at the college. This—along with the more famous names and haughty attitudes of many of her classmates—left Betty feeling profoundly out of place. She did not have the right clothes or the right shoes or the right tones of voice. She was just young enough to still believe such things mattered, and certainly no one in her class would tell her any different.

Betty Machmer at one of her early preschool teaching jobs.

But Betty was bright and earnest, and most of all she cared. She graduated with a B.A. in early childhood education, and then worked as head counselor at a summer camp near her family's cottage on Cape Cod. The following September she became the teacher in charge of the three- and four-year-old group at the MacDuffie School in Springfield, Massachusetts. The following year, in 1939, she worked one last summer as a counselor on Cape Cod, and at the beginning of September, as the Nazis invaded Poland, she moved to New York City to begin her new job as head teacher of the two-year-old group at the Manhattanville Day Nursery. Her new address, as it happened, was the Fairholm College Club at 501 West 121st Street, and she entered and exited her building every day through the shared lobby.

Edwin Armstrong—who had invented the super heterodyne circuit and, more recently, the wideband frequency modulation system—managed the Columbia University labs. Naturally, Gene approached him and asked how he might join the work of the lab. Armstrong, in order to test this unknown man, gave Gene a problem to take home and work out overnight. Gene worked out the problem on the spot. Armstrong gave him a more complex problem to bring back in a week; Gene brought it back the next day, complete. As Gene would later say: "When one would suffice, do three." Armstrong took Gene into his lab, again on an informal basis.

The Armstrong lab work made the big band work more bearable, and gave Gene his first inkling since leaving Italy—perhaps since leaving Fermi—that his decision to leave physics and theoretical science behind had been a sound one. He was contributing again, and engaged in stimulating work, as he'd known he could. In his spare time, he continued to improve his English and, in fact, kept a dictionary open beside him almost always, browsing for new words and memorizing tenses. At nights he went, as he had in Paris, to as many movies as he could, a challenge because he had little patience for the films themselves, and cared only about learning the language, the cadences, and the accent. Little by little, he was building the life he'd envisioned during those long months awaiting departure from Italy.

Betty Machmer, meanwhile, settled into her new life somewhat less certainly. Work, to be sure, was not the problem. Smith College had given her the tools and training to succeed at her career, and in teaching children she had found her true passion. Her social life, however, was another matter. The feeling that she'd had in college—that she simply didn't belong—persisted, and, perhaps, her trouble fitting in at Smith had left her without the beginnings of an adult social network. For her, there was work and there was her humble home at the Fairholm College Club, and there was not much else.

Office of the Dean
Amherst
October 17, 1939

My Dear Betty,

More than a month has passed since you began your work at Manhattan. Apparently you are finding conditions new but not too difficult. The great difficulty you have, if I read your letter correctly, is to adjust yourself to New York City life and social conditions. That is a problem for almost every person not accustomed to metropolitan conditions. There are plenty of people, but they do not appear to be interested in each other. Each one goes his or her own way. They do carry on projects in an organized way, but it takes time to learn the ropes.

When I was at Columbia there were thousands in the Summer School and scores in my own classes, but very few that I learned to know real well. Naturally most of my time was spent in study, but when I did go out I usually went by myself. So do not be discouraged if it takes a little time until you cultivate friendships. Attend to your work and keep up the habit of reading. By all means attend church services on Sundays. There are so many excellent opportunities to hear good sermons and listen to exceptionally fine music. By going quite regularly to young people's meetings you will soon meet some nice congenial people.

I am a bit worried about your losing weight. Be sure to eat regularly and at good places. You will feel better and have the energy you need to do your work well. As to changing your living quarters. Of course I have never seen your room, but Mother thought you were conveniently located and in a reasonably good room. I can understand that you see many things that are not elevating. There may be drinking and careless living. But sooner or later you will have to meet such people. Just pass it up as long as they do not involve you. Their conduct leads you to have more respect for yourself and your standard of living.

There is an Education Conference at the Hotel Roosevelt in New York City next Thursday and Friday October 26 and 27 which I am attending as a representative of the New England College Entrance Certificate Board. I expect to leave early Thursday morning so that I may be on time for the 10:30 meeting. The afternoon program does not interest me very much, but I will have to go to an important dinner at eight o'clock in the evening. This means that I will come to see you at the King's College Club soon after four o'clock on Thursday afternoon. That will give us a few hours on Thursday. We will have more time on Friday.

I am glad you like the radio. Do you continue to get good reception with it? The key adjustments can be made rather easily. If you were not successful in making them, I will attend to it when I get down

We had our first frost on the fifteenth and since then it has been very cold here. I have brought in all the vegetables except the beets and carrots. The next job will be to put on the storm windows. Since cold weather we have changed our mind and allowed Krag his usual place in the laundry. He loves it there but hated the garage.

With much love until I see you Thursday. As ever.

Lovingly,

Father

Gene, growing weary of his big band broadcast job, took an unusual step considering the state of the job market: He wrote an operator's manual for the broadcasting equipment used on the radio shows, thus allowing anyone with the slightest technical skill to perform the task. For Gene, it killed two birds with one stone: it allowed an equipment stock boy he knew, who wanted to get ahead, to move up; and it allowed Gene himself to escape his jazz-tinged purgatory and spend more time on his lab work. Together, he and the stock boy did their studying in the late hours as the band played on.

Gene also went to CBS and demanded more challenging work. By this time he had sufficiently impressed his bosses and associates with his skills to make such a request valid; as a result, Ed Cohan, the CBS director of engineering at the time, put Gene in charge of engineering for the all the music programs on the network. Gene was installed in an office at 485 Madison Avenue, and he quickly streamlined operations by upgrading the UHF link between the buildings within New York, and the linkage to the high frequency transmitter and antenna farm on Long Island. Soon he began working with the international division to set up connections between New York and Europe. As the work became more demanding and challenging, Gene became happier. His lab work continued, but was pushed back into the night to allow for his busier and more interesting daytime workload.

On Sundays, Gene would take the train to Princeton to visit his father and mother. Einstein and others from the university were frequent lunch guests; mathematics, physics, and of course the war were the topics of conversation. Germany had invaded Poland on September 1, 1939, and Europe was at war. The battle of Britain was under way, and it was clear to all that the departure of the Fubini family had been none too soon. All their worst fears about fascism and anti-Semitism were being realized.

News soon came that Austrian physicist Lise Meitner had split the uranium atom, and now the concept of fission was no longer an academic theory. It was a watershed moment for the scientific community and the world, but not, perhaps, in exactly the way anyone would have expected. For quick on the heels of the excitement surrounding the accomplishment came an understanding of just how this advancement might be used: for a bomb more deadly than anything ever conceived of before. And the information was in German hands. Einstein and Leó Szilárd drafted and delivered the now famous letter to U.S. President Franklin Delano

Roosevelt warning of the danger, and urging him to expend whatever resources were necessary to develop an atomic bomb before the Nazis did. This letter would lead directly to the formation of the Manhattan Project, America's full-fledged effort to develop atomic weaponry. Before long, it would draw Fermi and almost every other leading physicist of the day. Almost overnight, casual discussion of nuclear fission—once so common around Princeton and the Fubini household—ceased.

As the war churned on, Gene, as others, continued with their daily routines, attempting to maintain a sense of normalcy. One day in late winter, 1940, Gene entered his building and trudged through the shared lobby. It was either very late or very early, depending on one's perspective. For Gene, it was the end of a long night at the lab; for the attractive young woman who caught his eye, it was the beginning of a ski weekend with friends, and she was getting an early start. Perhaps distracted by the girl, or possibly impaired by his exhaustion, he managed to run into her, knocking her skis to the floor. Apologies were offered, and Gene quickly scooped them back up, bowed to the young lady, and introduced himself.

7

Countermeasures and a Death

With the war raging in Europe and pressure growing for the United States to become involved, it became clear that the scientific community would play a key role in any war effort. In 1940, Vannevar Bush, along with fellow scientists Karl Compton, James Bryant Conant, Frank Jewett, and Richard Tolman, put together the National Defense Research Committee (NDRC) and then its successor, the Office of Scientific Research and Development (OSRD). These federal agencies were tasked with organizing academics and industry scientists who had deep expertise in selected disciplines. The goal was to harness America's best and brightest for the benefit of the Allies' war effort.

Richard Tolman was a mathematical physicist and graduate dean at California Institute of Technology. He undertook oversight of the working groups that were focused on development of armor and ordnance. He later became science advisor to General Leslie Groves, who was the military director of the Manhattan Project. James Bryant Conant, president of Harvard University, dealt with bombs, fuels, gasses, and chemistry, and he also later helped to get the Manhattan Project up to speed. Frank Jewett, physicist and president of Bell Labs, had the lead for communications and transportation. Karl Compton, president of Massachusetts Institute of Technology (MIT), had detection, controls, and instruments, and as part of that work assembled the radar groups. Vannevar Bush oversaw the entire effort. Bush was a respected scientist, an accomplished academic administrator, and an organizational genius with a gift for defusing academic egos. Perhaps most importantly, he was also (alone among his scientist colleagues) adept at navigating government bureaucracies, deftly maneuvering through native power struggles, and emerging intact with his agenda satisfied.

World War I had been fought with revolutionary and hideously successful methods for killing, but the technology developed since then promised to make mustard gas and the machine gun seem like quaint anachronisms—but only if the technology could be applied. For in truth, little of the Allies' scientific breakthroughs could be said to have had a tangible effect on their military efficacy by 1940. The Germans, on the other hand, with access to largely the same science and technology had, for ten years, been building and equipping what had become, by a good margin, the most technologically advanced military in world. Now, with Hitler's aggressiveness and intentions so nakedly on display, the Allied nations were stricken to realize they'd been forced into a ghastly game of catch-up, with the fate of perhaps the entire world hanging in the balance. Thus, the army of scientists and engineers that Bush and his team assembled was unprecedented in scope. Teams from universities and industry across the country, and from almost every imaginable field, had to be recruited, organized, and tasked with the charters necessary for the staggering challenge now at hand.

But for all the size of the undertaking and the importance of the work, it would happen almost entirely outside of the public eye, and even outside the scope of the main war effort. During the 1930s, physicists such as Fermi, Ernest Rutherford, and Meitner had pushed one another toward fission without fully realizing the implications of their work. Fermi, in fact, had gotten to the origins of fission and not even recognized the ramifications of his discovery. Moreover, the work was so new, so contained within a growing but still tiny population of elite scientists, so far from public consciousness, so initially without apparent practical use, that this work never became part of the general war effort. The main effort was focused on conventional weapons, communications, and logistical support. The race to harness nuclear fission, on the other hand, was conducted in the shadows.

Other new technologies were reaching full realization, too, however, and radar was one of the most important. With its origins in fundamental physics, it had first been developed by the British in the 1930s, in anticipation of German aggression. But the Germans—as in so many areas—were by the 1940s employing much more advanced radar than what the Allies possessed, which was part of what allowed the German Air Force to rule the skies of Europe and led the Axis powers to their dominant position: By June 1940, France had fallen and England—the blitz of London raging nightly—was in serious peril. If the Germans were to be turned back, radar would have to play a key role, and in November 1940 the NDRC set up a lab at MIT—the Radiation Laboratory, or "Rad Lab." It soon became, outside of the Manhattan Project, arguably the most critical scientific endeavor of the war.

The crisis in Europe dominated American headlines at this time, but it was still possible for Americans to carry on largely undisturbed in their daily lives. Betty Machmer was intrigued by her encounter with Gene in the lobby that winter morning, even if she had too much sense to believe in love at first sight. A charming encounter became a date; one date became regular dates; and by spring they were seeing each other seriously. At concerts and plays, over coffee, and during walks in the city, she told him about her students at the Manhattanville Nursery and he spoke in vague terms about his research and his life in Italy. He avoided the topic of his family's departure, except to depict their border crossing, focusing on the seeming romance and adventure of it all. When talking with Betty, Gene initially employed the same aggressive style of questioning he had used with students and still used for nearly everyone, a style that must have seemed condescending when transferred from the classroom to a candlelit dinner. Betty let him know she wasn't impressed with his approach. But much about Gene did impress her. His determination to succeed, his focus and enthusiasm, and his intellectual prowess all struck Betty, who herself not only came from an intellectual family, but was also (having elected to attend Smith rather than Massachusetts State College) no stranger to ambition.

Without going into too many unnecessary details, she told her parents in correspondence that her social life had indeed improved.

If Gene had spent his youth in Italy largely oblivious to Mussolini's rise and other political events, he was now acutely aware of the situation in Europe. In early 1941 Gene was speaking anxiously about the war effort, specifically the scientific component, and he longed to contribute. Gene was certain that America would soon enter the war, and he set about preparing himself by reading everything available in both the mainstream and scientific presses. One of the subjects that caught his attention was the Rad Lab and its work. He made it clear to the executives at CBS, as well as Columbia, that he was one of the few scientists in the world who had been working for some time, and at significant depth, in the research and measurement of very short radio waves—expertise that would be instantly relevant to Rad Lab's work.

Whatever his qualifications, however, he was a realist, and understood completely those things that would weigh against his selection: He was a recent Italian immigrant, a former member of an Italian fascist organization (most student organizations at universities in Italy and Germany were classified as such, regardless of circumstance), and he had served in the Italian army. Though he considered himself, even then, utterly an American, it seemed likely that some would question his loyalty.

As fighting progressed in Europe, the Germans quickly demonstrated that they understood how to use radar to full advantage: The air war over Britain and the early success of the German Luftwaffe demonstrated the increasing importance of sophisticated radar. Vannevar Bush saw that developing better radar was essential, but he saw something even more interesting: the idea of using the enemy's radar against them.

In order to understand how radar can become a detriment, it's necessary to understand the basics of how radar works. Radar sends out radio signals that echo back to the receiver after those signals strike a specific target, such as a plane. From this echo, information about the plane, such as its location and speed, can be inferred. But, of course, the signals sent out don't only echo back—they also travel past the plane, and with sophisticated search-receivers and direction-finders, the presence of the signal sender, and even the exact location, can be discerned.

Those outgoing radar signals can also fall prey to intentional disruption of the signals, and the information those signals provide. For instance, countersignals sent from beyond the echo's reach can "drown out" the echo. Another tactic is to send disruptive countersignals from within the range of the radar to distort the echo and create false information.

All of this required significant technological improvements, and that meant significant resources had to be allocated to countermeasure research and development. Of course, the Rad Lab had hardly been created to *counter* radar. The work was taken seriously, but it would always be second-fiddle to the work on radar itself, work which was already absorbing most of the minds best equipped to tackle the problems. Nonetheless, as soon as the Japanese bombed Pearl Harbor and America's involvement in the war became official, there was news in the Columbia Labs of a stepped-up effort around radar countermeasures and the formation of a group within the Rad Lab at MIT to pursue the developments of such devices. For at least one person, the secondary status of the countermeasure work was a boon. Though he would have preferred to work on the radar project, Gene saw the countermeasure work as his opportunity to overcome whatever bias against him may have existed, and begin contributing to war work.

Gene pursued the assignment to the radar countermeasures effort with considerable and, at that point, wholly typical vigor. He was sure his name had surfaced from Armstrong's lab and had come to the attention of Vannevar Bush's recruiters. He also expected his name would have come up at CBS in a different context, as broadcasting engineers were also a valued war resource. He haunted Armstrong, dogging him daily with requests to talk, to state his case, even to suggest how the work should be conducted. He went to Ed Cohan to ask CBS to endorse him, and he pushed his new but evolving network of colleagues to find a way into these efforts. Through these channels, he learned that Fred Terman, who had written the essential textbook on radio engineering, was going to run radar countermeasures at the Rad Lab, and that the program was to be called the Radio Research Laboratory (RRL).

By July 1941, the RRL had moved out of the Rad Lab and a mile north to the Harvard University campus. Increasingly, Gene saw scientists at both Columbia and CBS leaving to join the work on the now-expanding countermeasure program. Armstrong was recruited to head a large portion of the work; John Dyer, a colleague of Gene's at CBS, who had been a radio engineer on an Antarctic expedition and then done television research at CBS, was also going. Every day, it seemed, another CBS or Columbia peer was invited north to Boston for the project, and Gene was jealous, angry, and determined to join them.

Gene was never one to let anger, or any other emotion, cloud his judgment or hinder his focus. Whatever his frustrations at the continued resistance to his involvement (and given his background and the delicacy and importance of the work, even he must have understood that resistance), he pressed on, soon managing to secure an interview with the RRL. His uncle Marco, meanwhile, contacted his lawyer, Sylvan Gotshal (an influential man, and a saint to Italian immigrants), who wrote an important, and what proved to be critical, recommendation. Gotshal cited Gene's patriotism, his intelligence, and his commitment to the defense of his new country. This independent endorsement, combined with the support Gene received from Columbia and CBS, began to open the door: Gene received an invitation to join the lab at last. But his fight was not over yet.

Despite the invitation, Gene was still considered a possible security risk, and he had to clear his status with the draft board, the F.B.I., and both the Army and the Navy, before he could be approved to work in the labs. He summoned all his patience—something that was never in great supply for Gene—and proceeded to work the system. Soon he had all the different groups talking to each other, and eventually the concerns were put aside and his clearance to join the group was granted. In the second week of August 1941, a large group from CBS went up to Cambridge, Massachusetts, and Gene—finally—was part of it.

His relationship with Betty, meanwhile, had grown serious, but he wasn't the only one pursuing his career and his passions. As he was making arrangements for moving to Boston, Betty was securing a year of study and work at a nursery school at the University of Iowa. They parted under somewhat artificial circumstances, neither eager to leave the other behind, but each putting their work first.

Gene got a room at 114 Brattle Street in Cambridge, close to Harvard Square. It was an old house with brick ends, clapboards front and back, and nicer rooms than what he'd had to settle for in New York City. He was thrilled to finally be working directly on the Allied effort, but troubled to be leaving his parents behind in New Jersey. Guido was still in poor health, but still active in his work. The Princeton University community was supportive, and Gino was close at hand to tend to their father's needs, but Gene knew that his visits home would be spread out, the time between would be lonely, and he would lose touch with the day-to-day details of his parents' lives.

Still, Gene attacked the RRL work with the hunger of deprivation. When he was not sleeping, he lived at the RRL on Divinity Street, to which he could walk from his room in ten minutes. The RRL had had floors built for it on top of the old Harvard biology building. There was ample laboratory space among the administrative offices and there was a first-class machine operation, a woodworking shop, photography facilities, and a transformer shop.

Gene joined a team building a new countermeasure receiver. The initial work went forward despite the fact that the design engineers did not have detailed knowledge of the capabilities of the German radars they were seeking to jam. Speculation and informed thinking guided the group's initial efforts; when German Wurtzburgs and Freyas were captured and analyzed, the work became more focused on the specific capabilities and frequencies of the German radars. Operating frequencies, their characteristics and signals, how much power they used, what type of antennas—these details directed the work and dictated how the Axis radar would be attacked. But even with this information, the ability to apply countermeasures was still more art than science. The Germans had built effective radars and deployed them widely to great effect. The science of radar countermeasures was new, even in theory. In a way, the radar countermeasure work was two kinds of scientific work—the theoretical and the applied—happening simultaneously.

Jamming the enemy's radar was only half the work, of course. Gene also applied himself to the effort of locating the enemy radars. Airplanes or ships with countermeasure receivers would take two directional cuts on enemy radar and find the radar where the cuts intersected. Accuracy depended on the ratio of the size of the German antenna to the wavelength of its signal. With the Germans operating mainly at UHF between 400 and 600 megacycles, the RRL had to build antennas sized to several meters and capable of measuring frequency instantaneously, as well as measuring pulse repetition frequency and the width of the pulse. It would then be able to locate the radar source, counteract it, and put in on a "strike list" for bombers.

Fred Terman established three areas of focus for the RRL as a whole. One group carried out components design, a second group assembled those components, and a third group determined how to operate the system in practice. Gene's extracurricular interest in locating enemy radar involved him, as he had hoped, across all three groups. Deciding where to put the antenna in the plane, and how an operator might get to it, required assembling components to fit uniquely constricted spaces. Controlling the function of the antenna, and determining where to aim it, were operational concerns. Because there were so many variables, including the many possible signals to edit, there needed to be a continuing functional liaison between the design group and the other two application groups to ensure an operational system. Gene hoped to be that liaison.

Gene soon familiarized himself with all the systems and issues across the three groups, and he immediately understood that managing the technologically sophisticated components into a working integrated system was going to be a challenge. Someone had to help make all the tradeoffs between design, functionality, delivery, and ease of use. If he could do so successfully, it would be the hallmark of his contribution to the effort. It also occurred to him that if he played this role well, he could reprise it on other projects for other engineering and technical efforts. He went from group to group, assembled a comprehensive understanding of their roles, and informally made sure that channels of communications were open between the groups. Because it was a role he had not been asked to take, and because he worked with no official authority, it was a delicate position. He dispensed with diplomacy and used what was becoming his trademark blend of impatient rudeness and self-effacing charm.

He was a small man among Americans, and he was thirty years old while many of the men in his grade—the lowest grade—were far younger. Without these advantages, he simply ignored his size and age, and assumed the persona of the seasoned veteran. He spoke loudly—as loudly as he needed to speak to get people's attention—and he spoke passionately, which was, in fact, his default manner of speaking at nearly all times. His voice, in moments of pique, was high and penetrating, the same voice that had allowed him to feel an equal in Fermi's group during his days at Panisperna. If others were intelligent, he was eager to listen; but he did not suffer fools, or even foolish comments, easily. Balancing all this bluster was his ability to make people laugh, often using himself (his accent, his size, his tendency to talk not just with his hands, but with his whole body) as the butt of the joke. On occasion, he stood on a bench while loudly making a point, or screamed down the fourth floor hall, just to be heard. Love him or hate him (and most responded to his crude, unique ability to lead), everyone in the lab knew who he was.

His sole distraction from his work was his family and Betty.

Betty was in Iowa for a full year from September 1941 to September 1942. When she returned, she took a position in New Britain, Connecticut, where she'd been offered a chance to start a new center for small children, and she and Gene resumed their relationship as best they could, given the distance. Both busy, they would often meet halfway in Shippan Point, a neighborhood in Stamford, Connecticut, where a friend of Gino's had a house.

Gino, who had graduated from MIT and was now working as a civil engineer, often joined them on these visits, and they proved as important to his romantic future as to Gene's. On one warm day in 1943, Gino took a break from tinkering with his car out in front of the Shippan Avenue house to get a cool drink. On his way in he saw a beautiful young woman rushing from the door of the first floor apartment. She was Gaby, whose parents lived there, and she was in a hurry to catch the bus for a movie in Stamford. But looking in her purse, she saw that she didn't have the quarter she needed for the ride. Gino offered her one from his pocket. She smiled. "Don't worry," she told him, "I'll give it back." Gino knew then that he would marry her.

Meanwhile, Gene, glad to be reunited with Betty after her time away, was doing his best to make sure they would never be parted again. Betty was an attractive young woman, often compared to Katharine Hepburn. Despite their many differences in backgrounds and personalities, she and Gene seemed natural together. Regardless of their differences, they balanced each other well: Gene was always full of energy, impatient to move forward, determined to succeed, and move on; Betty was calm, disciplined, measured, and understood that sometimes being still was the best way to achieve a goal. Gene was often negative, relentlessly skeptical, and always looking for answers; Betty was positive, always seeing the opportunities in even the darkest situations. Gene was passionate and expressed his emotions plainly; Betty was quiet and introspective, and kept her own counsel. She had a way of quietly calming Gene, a gift for saving him from his own manic energies and spiraling intensity. Few would ever have this effect on him.

The uniqueness of their match wasn't lost on either of them and soon things turned—as they tend to, and as they almost always did in those days—to talk of marriage. But before it could be seriously considered, there was the significant matter of each partner meeting the other's parents.

Betty was proud of herself, of the life she'd made and her professional accomplishments. Amherst, where she'd been raised, wasn't exactly the middle of nowhere, but she recognized that, when compared to New York or Boston or, certainly, Turin, it was hopelessly provincial. She loved her family, but she worried that Gene—multilingual, highly educated, worldly— was too starkly unlike her parents and the people back home to accept them or be accepted by them. And she didn't imagine his occasionally difficult personality would help matters.

Gene, meanwhile, was worrying about bringing Betty home to meet his parents, and his concerns were along the same lines. Would his parents, who valued social standing so highly and who were, to be fair, still in the process of coming to understand their new home country, be able to accept Betty, no matter how far she'd come from her small-town roots? His mother was not known for her welcoming spirit or generous warmth with her own children—how could she be expected to embrace Betty?

The young couple went to visit Gene's parents in late 1940 at their new Manhattan apartment at 88 Central Park West, where they'd moved when Guido's health had finally forced him into retirement. If the meeting was not a disaster, neither was it a great success. Betty enjoyed Gino (and was fascinated to find that any brother of Gene's could be so quiet and contained), and, of course, Guido was gentlemanly and abundantly kind. But it was Gene's mother who made the most distinct impression on Betty. As expected, Anna Fubini was distant and cold. Always focused on the superficial and what she felt it revealed about a person's character, she sized up Betty's unsophisticated dress, her plain manner of speaking, and her reserved politeness, and she simply saw an unremarkable, small-town girl who wasn't good enough for her favorite son. Inevitable comparisons to the beautiful and elegant Gaby, who Gino was now seeing regularly, only made matters worse.

Gene's meeting with Betty's parents was equally mixed. She took him home to Amherst in the spring of 1941, where he was introduced to her parents (though not to her sisters and brother, who were all away). Clearly, Gene understood the weight of the situation: He showed his calmest demeanor and plied Betty's mother, Olive, with cosmopolitan, urbane attention. Betty was disappointed to see that her mother responded with strained graciousness—a sure indication that her mother simply didn't care for Gene. Fortunately, her father did. If Betty had worried that Gene would look down on her father, she soon saw that there was no need. Gene treated her father with exactly the respect he should have, both as his girlfriend's father and as the head of a major academic institution.

During the trip they spent a great deal of time exploring the town where Betty had grown up (perhaps inspired to spend time outside the house by Betty's mother's reaction to Gene). The neighborhood on Amity Street was lively in the way of a college town, crowded with students and professors and thick with an atmosphere of learning and curiosity— something Gene could always appreciate. The barn where Tar Baby, Betty's beloved pony, was once housed was gone, but Betty and Gene walked the trails where Betty had ridden in her youth, up through woods and into the Amherst Cemetery, where the Machmer family plot was already planned. The family vegetable garden, where the family tried to compensate for wartime food shortages, was below the large ridge in the backyard where Betty and her sisters had gone sledding during the long winters. Betty wanted to work in the garden and Gene, his intentions good, insisted on helping. But, having been raised in a city and confined to classrooms and labs for most of his adult life, she spent most of the time trying to keep him from stepping on things.

The issues facing the radar countermeasures effort were daunting. What seemed, at first glance, to be simple concepts quickly became complex when they moved from the theoretical to the applied. One of Gene's great strengths was that he could very quickly grasp the complex nuances of most technologies and translate them into practical engineering. The secret was to distill down, as Fermi had taught him, to fundamental principles. Gene may not have thought he could match Fermi's genius in physics, but as an engineer he was a powerhouse. "Let me explain," he liked to say when he had to elucidate the work of one group to another. And he would, indeed, explain, helping two separate groups with seemingly conflicting needs find the solution that worked for everyone. He could take two opposing viewpoints in his hand, play with them, deconstruct them, find the common ground, the shared border, the natural place where compromise could live, and put them back together into one harmonious whole. When he explained, his voice would naturally be raised (as it almost always was), but when volume wasn't enough he would climb up on a chair and, as promised, explain. You could only do that if you were right, and you could only do it if everybody understood that all you wanted was to get things done. Soon, it became apparent to everyone that this was Gene's singular goal.

Gene's standing within the RRL began to rise. To be fast and right and dedicated and able to talk across disciplines, to be able to do your assigned job and several other jobs at the same time—these were skills that got you noticed. And, the pressure to catch the Germans being as great as it was, it was a skill that was soon rewarded with more authority. After all, when someone shows the will and the talent to get things done, he will generally be given the power to do so.

But as Gene gained credibility in his work, he suffered a long-expected loss: In June 1943, Guido Fubini passed away in his sleep at the age of sixty-four. He would be remembered as one of the great academic minds of his generation, as well as a kind, humorous, and engaging man. He would always be known as one of the most luminous and original minds in mathematics during the first half of the twentieth century.

After his long decline, his death was not a shock, of course, but the loss for Gene was complex and multifaceted. The two men had been close, but despite this, Gene would speak little in later life about his father. This may be the strongest indication that their relationship (as is so often the case between fathers and sons) was nuanced and intricate. Guido was a genuinely loving and kind man, but he hadn't risen to the upper echelon of the international mathematics community by brilliance alone; like most highly successful men he was, beneath his exterior, also a highly driven and competitive man. In a professional environment, this was completely appropriate, but when his son entered adulthood and became, in effect, a competitor, the relationship took on another dimension. Was Gene deserving of his love and patience and guidance? Or was Gene a competitor, another tiger in the intellectual jungle, to be either avoided or dominated? These questions were never really answered.

Gene, for his part, was no less determined to be the best at whatever he did, and was no more capable than his father of holding back. This tension was at the core of their relationship and perhaps explains why, ultimately, they probably had more respect than love for one another. Given their personalities, however, a relationship based on mutual respect might have been more precious than any other.

8

Fighting for the Allies

$\mathcal{G}$overnment officials assigned to Draft Board 37 on the Upper West Side of Manhattan in the early 1940s dealt in bulk. They were paper pushers, by and large, and most men of draft age (and there were many) were easily classifiable as one of two things: eligible or not. And the guidelines by which these men were judged were usually clearly defined. But every once in a while a special case came along, and none was more special than the odd case of one Dr. Eugene Fubini, also known as Dr. Eugenio Fubini-Ghiron, also known as Gene Fubini.

He worked for the government, but was not a naturalized American citizen; rather, he was a citizen of Italy, a country with which the U.S. was officially at war. As a resident of Manhattan under the jurisdiction of Draft Board 37, he was eligible for the draft—despite having served in the Italian military. Even more perplexing was that while he was on the payroll of the Columbia Broadcasting System, he also evidently worked for a laboratory at Harvard University and physically lived in Cambridge, Massachusetts. And then there was the fact that he was doing government work that was so highly classified no one on the draft board could learn a single thing about it, besides that it was presumably connected to the war effort. Draft boards during wartime wield considerable power, but in this case the best they could do was issue six-month deferrals and bring it up again for further consideration. It was yet another wrinkle in the unique case of Dr. Gene Fubini.

For security reasons Radiation Laboratory (Rad Lab) engineers—the scientists working on radar—could not be involved with the RRL radar countermeasures work. In one of those paradoxes that always seem to find their way into government work, however, the RRL needed information only the Rad Lab possessed in order to fully complete its work. The solution, Fred Terman felt, was Gene, whose background in physics and his now-very-evident engineering ability made him the ideal, tight-lipped go-between who could gather and disseminate the necessary information. Thus, only four years after leaving Italy, he began to be the bridge between two of the U.S. government's most sensitive and important projects. His unique, demanding style of engineering, combined with an intellect that even his harshest critics had to admire, had placed him at the very core of the U.S. war effort.

His new position also gave him leverage to push his involvement even further, and Gene—never shy—was ready to use it. In late autumn of 1943, RRL material began shipping overseas in preparation for the assault on southern France. The radar countermeasure equipment was to first be used to establish an Army Signal Corp site on Corsica that would seek to jam German radar in support of the invasion. The installations were critical to the mission, naturally, but they were also considered the first real, applied test of the radar and radar countermeasure work thus far. The placement and usage of the equipment required knowledge of the technology and skill in operating it for maximum efficacy. Gene bluntly asked to be sent overseas with the equipment. He made the point that because he had worked on both radar and radar countermeasure projects, he was uniquely qualified for the trip. He further pointed out that he spoke German, French, and Italian. Terman, who questioned whether language made much difference for the endeavor, could not so easily dismiss Gene's aptitude or his skill as a team leader. He would be more able than most men to ensure that the countermeasures equipment was appropriately installed and properly operated, and if there were difficulties, he would be someone who could effectively communicate with a broad range of military and technical elements—even if it was only in English.

Gene Fubini as he prepared to go overseas in World War II (1943).

As Gene shifted overseas, he did so with little concern about his family. Anna Fubini was now in New York City and Gino was there to supplement Anna's growing network of friends. Gino had been rejected by the armed services because of his arm and leg, which had been slightly impaired since birth, so he looked after the two Manhattan buildings that he, Gene, and Marco had invested in together. His path, to this point, had been rather meandering: After spending time in Boston, where he received his master's degree in electrical engineering, he moved back to New York, where he lived with his mother and took a tedious job with a utility company in Manhattan. Uninterested in his work, he and Gaby began to consider buying Long Island property and putting up houses for servicemen as they started their families after returning from the war.

Marco, savvy as ever in the ways of their new adopted country, proved a wise and insightful investor of the family wealth. He (for himself as well as Gene and Gino) purchased lucrative interests in the two residential buildings, while also buying significant amounts of American savings bonds and instructing Anna, Gene, and Gino to do the same. He further instructed his lawyer, Sylvan Gotshal, to arrange for all of the family members to give to prominent private charities. This was an example of both his enduring humanism and his shrewdness. Given the circumstances of the family's departure from Italy, bitterness and a general turning away from generosity would have been understandable; the family had given so much of their time, money, and energies, only to be forced to flee Italy. But the lesson for the family wasn't that they'd been driven from their home by the worst of human nature; rather, they were focused on the things that had made that probably life-saving flight possible: the generosity of Einstein and the others who'd made their transplant possible, the chances they'd been given by their new countrymen, and, above all, the principles of a country that made it possible for them to find safe harbor and opportunity. And that was where the emphasis on charitable contributions was doubly telling: Marco knew that, come the end of the war, the contributions would reflect well on the family and make possible the citizenship they needed for their residency to become permanent.

In the fall of 1943, as Gene prepared to go overseas, Betty went back to live at home in Amherst while she taught the four-year-old group at the Elizabeth Morrow Morgan Nursery School at Smith, in Northampton, Massachusetts. She would rather have stayed in New Britain, but the New Britain Teachers College, under whose auspices she had started her day care center, took over the center as a demonstration project. Probably it was for the best. Gene would be gone, and she could help her parents.

As Gene shipped overseas his thoughts were of Betty.

> My dearest darling,
>
> I am in Newfoundland for a short stop. It was so wonderful to receive your letter; it did what you wanted it to do—give me the best possible farewell. This, darling, intends to be shamefacedly a love letter, purely a love letter—repeating things you have heard already.
>
> When I miss you as I am missing you now, there is only one thing I have to tell you: I love you more than anything. I will never change, you will be loved, made love to, day after day, until you'll get tired of it. You will be near me always, you will help me, support me, share everything with me.
>
> Now the bus is leaving for the plane.
>
> My love, dearest darling,
>
> Gene

Dearest Sweetheart,

I have just mailed a letter to you. Now we are off. Flying over Newfoundland offers a unique view. An endless agglomeration of islands, big and small with land-locked patches of water; the land is covered with small trees (pines?)— I tried to count the islands and had to stop at 100. They are interlaced in such a fashion that one has to look carefully to find out what is land, what is island, what is in communication with the land and what is not. It is altogether an impressive view. Once in a while you can see a solitary steeple or a village, but it seems that most islands of this archipelago are not inhabited.

This ship is one of the former Clippers. I'll try to describe it to you. It has two floors. On the lower one, starting from the tail, a wide luggage compartment. From there, a corridor has at the right a closet, the ladies lounge, and at the left small compartments. Farther along, two more small compartments—then three "rooms" at the right of the corridor each room has seats for 6 persons (or 4 bunks), at the left, seats for 4. Then the main lounge where I am with 3 tables and 14 seats. Then one more "room" with 4 bunks (for the crew) and 4 seats, then another room with 4 more bunks at the right, a pantry at the left. Then the men's room, the kitchen and a room on the nose that I have not seen yet.

On the upper floor is the bridge, radio room, engineer's room and so on but I haven't seen this yet. The "basement" has gas tanks and cargo space—

I can't help it. I must give a parenthesis and tell you that I love you very very much, that I like you, everything that you do, and then when I will be married to you I will be very happy indeed.

I will try to make you happy in all possible ways. I may not be perhaps a good husband, but I can become good because I love you and will always love you.

People in the plane are not too interesting. There is an OWI crowd and one man from something like OSS—all civilians because people in the Armed forces can not travel in here. It looks like we will have a tail wind and we may go fairly fast. It's now 4 PM NY time and, if everything works all right, we will be in UK tomorrow night. Now the plane is on the open sea— flying much lower than the C 54's of my previous crossings. Some people here are getting slightly sick but I can't see any reason for it, the ride is very smooth, no bumps, the sky is blue, ocean is calm; darling I am thinking of you. Please do tell me when you are not sure about us. I worry but it is proper that I should. Don't try to hide feelings—you are too nice, too sincere, too honest. And your effort would show. Let me worry. If, in the end, everything will be all right (and it will) I will more deeply appreciate the value of what is being given to me.

I love you
Gene

He flew to Corisca in an Army Air Force transport plane, landing in Marrakech, a gorgeous city that he barely had the time or attention to notice as he passed through. Two days later he traveled on to Algiers, and from there, after a brief delay, onto Foch Field in Tunisia. When he got there, he had a chance to look out across the blue waters of the Mediterranean, which borders Tunisia on the north, and it finally hit him: Somewhere out there, well out of sight range, was Italy. Standing on that shore, he was less than 600 miles from Turin, and well less than 400 miles from Rome. And all of it, of course, sat under the control of Mussolini and the fascists.

Gene and Howard Zeidler, who was also from the RRL, were attached to the Army Air Force without being officially part of the military effort. Zeidler was a technical observer. Gene was a senior technical observer, which gave him a starting rank equivalent to that of a lieutenant colonel. This allowed him to move freely between operating units and theater commanders. He could also bunk wherever there were officers' quarters. Most importantly, he could board airplanes. The invasion of France was looming (Sicily had been re-taken in the summer, and the combined armies of Patton and Marshall had just invaded southern Italy), and Gene and Zeidler were sent to Corsica, along with a platoon of soldiers from the Signal Corps and a detail of Army engineers, to build a countermeasures operation for the southern Mediterranean theater.

It wasn't a simple setting up of equipment, however. Gene and Zeidler oversaw the layout of the site as the Army engineers hammered and blasted into the top of Cima allo Stillago above Olmi Capella. The crest of the mountain had to be leveled, and holes needed to be hollowed out for bunkers. Gene and Zeidler advised on equipment installation, pinpointing the spot that would provide the clearest lines of site to the full field of coverage from Toulon to Viareggio. Once the site was properly oriented, Gene flew back to Foch field and helped with the routine conversion of Mandrel units that had been flown in from Malta for use on Corsica.

In the days before flying to Corsica, Gene had been in one of those military limbos, waiting in airports and hotels for his journey to resume. Never one to sit idly by, he sought out whatever company he could and, striking up conversations with a variety of regular and Army Air Force officers, he offered his services as a translator (his earnest explanation that he spoke Italian amused his conversational partners, because his accent was hard to miss). And sure enough, this proved to be time well spent, for soon after reaching Corsica he was contacted by the military to act as a translator. Allied soldiers had captured radar sites and operators on southern Italy, and Gene was asked to find out what they knew. Unfortunately, the Germans had taken their equipment and their own operators with them in retreat, and the Italian equipment was of little interest. But the Italian operators had seen something of the German equipment and its operation, and, apparently ecstatic at having surrendered, were happy to reveal everything they knew. Gene was able to uncover bits of information that would be useful to the RRL, and also came up with odds and ends that contributed to military intelligence there on the ground. The bulk of what he learned simply reaffirmed what the Allies already knew: Namely, that the Germans had not had much radar coverage in southern Italy; it had been successfully jammed for the Allied Italian landing. But the Germans had extensive radar coverage along the arc of shore that was to receive the major invasion of southern France—this would be more difficult to jam.

Regardless of information gleaned from the enemy, Gene and Zeidler had their work cut out for them on the mountain. Seven direction-finding units, seven jamming radar sets, fourteen antennas, and the attendant common circuitry came up the mountain in component pieces that had to be assembled. And then there was the considerable matter of training signalmen to operate equipment that was new to everyone concerned (though many of the signalmen had been on the original "Beaver" radar location and jamming mission in the Aleutians, and were at least familiar with the basic operation of radar).

More than anything, Gene and Zeidler stressed that the jamming radars must not be activated until the moment of Allied attack. Jamming would send out a signal the Germans could pick up, identify, locate, and eliminate. The goal was listen to the Germans, pick up, identify, and locate their signals, and prevent them from doing the same.

As the equipment began to be assembled and installed, the signalmen began intercepting signals from all the German Coastwatcher radar sets, from the variously sized Wurtzburg tracking and fire control sets, and from the early-warning Freyas. Before long, they'd identified between seventy and 100 radar stations, broken out the frequencies and pulse repetition rates, and recorded changes in frequencies and in the cessation and resumption operation. Before long, the installations had become rote, the signalmen more than capable, the routine smooth. In short, it ceased to be challenging for Gene, and, with no sign of an imminent invasion, he began to look for something new to do.

In synchronization with the signal corps, he began alternating forty-eight hour rotations with Zeidler, and during his rotation off, he wandered down to the airfield and talked himself onto the Ferrets: the B-17s equipped with countermeasure listening devices tuned to the Wurtzburgs and Freyas. The Ferrets flew at night, when the German radars were most active, skimming as low as possible along the coast. They picked up signals and got D/F cuts on them which, when combined with the cuts from Corsica, pinpointed the locations of one German radar after another. Night after night, Gene would watch through the small window as his former home, visible under moonlight, rolled slowly by. If he was shot down and captured in Italy, he knew, he would certainly be shot as a traitor. He found that amusing.

With typically unrelenting focus, Gene pinpointed every enemy radar location from Toulon to Viareggio, in the process becoming the only individual who knew precisely where every German radar was located in the southern theater. But before long, this project, too, had reached its end, and he began to look for more to do. At the airfield, he discovered that the Free French Forces, for some reason, had in their possession a group of English Spitfires, one of the superlative fighter planes of World War II. But the planes were always sitting on the tarmac. Why? Gene wanted to know. The French replied that they simply had no targets. Gene smiled. He said, "I have the whole chain of German radar from the Spanish border to Italy." Gene shared the coordinates for the pilots to confirm, and they woke him two nights later to give him their report: The Spitfires, which were equipped with cameras, had taken clear pictures of radar stations. Gene had the right coordinates.

The French asked for more coordinates, and set about confirming more radar stations. One night they woke Gene and brought him to the airfield. One of the pilots had passed over land and flown so low he'd hit a flagpole, which had cut halfway through the wing and become lodged there. Incredibly, the pilot had successfully flown home and landed with the flagpole stuck in the wing. They took the luck as an encouraging sign, and continued to pursue destruction of the radar stations. Spitfires, unfortunately, were only equipped with machine guns, useless against receivers, the functioning of which was unaffected by bullet holes. They returned with heavier weapons, but the Germans had detected them and were ready with anti-aircraft guns. In the end, the Spitfires were never able to fully eliminate the radar stations, but, at the very least, the French were glad to have had some use for the Spitfires.

In any event, as they all awaited the start of the invasion of southern France, D-Day arrived—the massive invasion of northern France. All the preparations for the southern invasion were useful, but it became apparent that it was no longer going to be a central focus of the war. Instead, emphasis was shifting rapidly to England. Gene, upon realizing all of this, put in an urgent request for transfer to the British Theatre.

While Gene pushed his request to go to England through channels, he kept himself from going crazy by getting down off the mountain and around to the coastal town of Ajaccio, the capital of Corsica. What might have been a chance for relaxation was, for Gene, just another opportunity to get more involved in the war effort. His position—attached to the military and possessing a certain amount of authority, but not under anyone's direct command—was unusual and, for Gene, advantageous. Stationed in Ajaccio, Gene found a squadron of PT boats commanded by, of all people, the actor Douglas Fairbanks Jr., who, it would only much later be made public, was in fact a brilliant naval tactician who would, by the war's end, be a highly decorated officer. The squadron was searching out anti-ship batteries, which Gene proposed might be positioned with the anti-aircraft radar stations. Gene suggested that if he could use his equipment to locate these radar stations, he could help Fairbanks and his PT Boats find more productive targets. Fairbanks invited Gene to come aboard as a guide.

The PT squadron, while out on patrol, would also attack German patrol boats when any were sighted. One evening, the PT boat behind the boat Gene was riding in, fired a torpedo at such a German boat. The torpedo misfired and managed to circle the PT boats and return to imbed itself in the bow of Gene's boat. Despite the fact that the torpedo did not explode, the boat went badly down in the bow, and the PT boat took on considerable water. The forward compartments were sealed, and no one was injured. In examining the torpedo, the crew saw that the small propeller on the front of the torpedo was still spinning; aside from function as the torpedo's propulsion, the propeller acted as a timing device to prevent premature detonation; after a certain number of revolutions, the torpedo would explode. Gene, being the smallest, was hung over the bow and was able to stop the propeller with his hand. The crew tied one end of a rope to Gene's feet and the other end to a railing, and there Gene hung, suspended upside-down, hand plunged into icy water, for the hour-and-a-half it took the injured boat to limp back to Ajaccio.

When they arrived, other sailors swarmed the PT boat and Gene was relieved of his duty. The torpedo was secured and disarmed. As it turned out, only seven more revolutions would have detonated the torpedo, likely killing them all.

Not every day was a bore.

By the time he left Corsica, Gene had learned two important things. The first was that he functioned well in a military environment; soldiers, after all, were good at following orders, and Gene certainly excelled at giving them. It was all right for him to be short, to have a thick Italian accent, talk too loudly and too quickly, and to think he knew everything. As long the officers knew he was in charge, and as long as he produced results, he was accepted. And by the rank and file men, he was more than just accepted—he was both trusted and admired. They saw that Gene, with his unabashed patriotism, simply wanted results. In contrast to some other senior uniformed officers in the command structure, he had a total disregard for recognition.

The second thing he learned was that in the armed forces (and, for that matter, in the United States) "everything not forbidden is permitted." His efforts on behalf of French pilots, his contributions to the PT boats, the desire to help on prisoner interrogations, all showed that someone without a portfolio, someone willing to stretch beyond the expected, who operated with the broadest interpretation of what was allowable, could have an impact that was far-ranging and highly valued. This was to be a lesson Gene would return to, time and time again, in his future endeavors. It was a truth that suited him perfectly.

Soon, Gene's reassignment to the British Theatre came through. He was to be sent to the American British Laboratory (the Radio Research Lab's British operation, headed by John Dyer) in the town of Great Malvern in Worcestershire, England. Dyer, a former colleague at CBS, had been leading the efforts in support of operations in this theatre of operations, and he welcomed Gene back. Nearby were British labs including Armament Research and Development Establishment (ARDE) with the physicist John Cockroft, and the countermeasures outfit Telecommunications Research Establishment (TRE), under Sir Robert Cockburn. Cockcroft and Cockburn were physicists of the very first rank—still more evidence of the extent of talent now shaping the new defense strategies of the war.

Gene had read enough history as a boy to understand what was happening, and that it was just the latest in a historic pattern: If war had begun in the darkest ages of man as a test of physical superiority, the advantage had soon begun to shift—and would always continue to shift—toward the combatant with superior technology, intelligence, and planning. He was now a critical part of this latest wave of experimentation and deployment, which constituted a great leap forward in the efficacy of war technology. Gene could only hypothesize what lay ahead, but he must have seen the influx of scientists and engineers, establishing their positions of importance alongside the generals and admirals, as a trend that would produce a sea change in the nature of war. The scale and nature of technology that collectively the scientists and engineers were generating was going to reshape all future defense strategies for generations to come. He had known, when he was accepted into RRL, that the move represented a major shift in the direction of his life. Whatever disappointment he may have nursed over his abandoned physics career, he must increasingly have understood that he and the men around him were doing work that would prove just as revolutionary as that of Fermi and his colleagues.

Despite its location, the war did not feel as close in Great Malvern as it had in the Mediterranean. In Algiers, there had been large movements of troops in and around Corsica. Gene had looked across to the enemy-held French Riviera, and flown alongside the enemy in the dark night skies, and been on the water in the PT boats. In comparison, Great Malvern was bucolic, a quintessential English country town. To further drive the contrast home, Gene learned, just as he was arriving at Great Malvern, that the Allies were finally invading the south of France. Of course that invasion, for which Gene and the rest of the team had worked so hard to prepare, was a sideshow compared to Normandy, but Gene was later gratified to learn that the signalmen and equipment on Corsica both performed brilliantly.

Gene settled into the Great Malvern work, bringing himself up to speed with the latest wrinkles in the countermeasures instruments and with the installation and operation in airplanes (as opposed to the fixed facilities he had worked with in Corsica), specifically those on the B-17s and B-24s. Soon Gene was assigned to work with the Eighth Air

Force Headquarters to facilitate the countermeasures operation of the American bombers now flying constantly in support of Allied troops on the continent. After the success of the Normandy landings in June, the threat to the bombers from the Luftwaffe had been largely neutralized, but the German anti-aircraft guns were still shooting down large numbers of planes.

The situation could be improved, of course, if their radar countermeasures could be improved. The common method when Gene arrived was the use of Window—foil strips strewn from a formation's lead plane, which would confuse enemy radar. As evidenced by the number of planes being shot down by the Germans, it was only modestly effective. But when Window was complemented with carpet jamming from the planes (which was the transmission of Cockburn's random noise into the frequencies of the German radar), the German radar would, they theorized, be largely negated. Those frequencies had to be monitored, because the Germans changed them regularly and the transmission frequencies had to be changed accordingly. Also, the Germans were expanding their range of available frequencies and the American instruments had to be able to adjust to that greater range. These things were part of Gene's charge.

The Eighth Air Force was headquartered in a requisitioned girls' school called Pine Tree in High Wycombe, outside London. Gene was in operational analysis, tasked with understanding the variables so critical to effective jamming processes. He received frequent reports from the Ferrets that patrolled the channel and monitored the frequencies of the German radar. As the frequency reports were sent in, Gene would relay appropriate adjustments for carpet transmission (onboard jamming frequencies) out to the bomber groups for what carpet units they possessed.

Gene Fubini at Pine Tree Air Force base in England receiving the "proper military rank" commensurate with the manner he "exercised" his civilian role (1945).

Gene had been given a Jeep, and he often drove out through East Anglia to the American airfields. At every field, every squadron had lost men. He heard firsthand the stories of the German anti-aircraft guns and the havoc they wreaked: men who would not return to their families, friends and comrades lost. It was the first time the reality of the war had really reached Gene. Corsica had felt in the thick of things, but, truly, it hadn't been: it was, after all, designed to stand apart from the real combat and contribute from afar. The Ferrets had been in no real danger, and the Free French pilots had had the option of simply abandoning their self-appointed mission when the Germans fielded their more effective anti-aircraft guns. The torpedo in the PT boat had been, for as close as they had all come to being blown up, exciting. Even in London the blitz was past, and the assault that had caused the jaw-dropping destruction Gene saw seemed remote, abstract, and hard to imagine. But at the airfields, it was different. Gene heard of the many planes that did not return, and saw planes that did return, damaged, the cockpits and cargo areas covered with blood, the wounded and dead soldiers carried off. The men who were stationed at the airfields did not speak of death; it was taboo. But they knew—and Gene came to understand—that every time a plane took off and disappeared into the distance, there was a very real chance it would not return.

Gene began to analyze the various losses across the various air groups, seeking to understand the effectiveness of the countermeasures and searching for correlations between usage patterns of countermeasures and survivability of aircraft. Initially, he took his findings to Thorpe Abbotts and the "Bloody Hundredth" Air Group and that had lost so many men. His early analytical efforts showed that the two air groups lost planes at the same horrific rate, regardless of the countermeasures being employed. Concerned by these findings, Gene went to the airfields at Rattlesden, then to Old Buckenham, then Molesworth, Polebrook, Lavenham, Grafton, Underwood, Deenethorpe, Bury St. Edmonds, and Alconbury, with its Pathfinder unit and operational radar development functions, to see if the rates varied, and if so, why. When he went to Tibenham, for instance, he found that twenty-eight of thirty-seven B-24s were lost in the first month of his posting. Eventually, he went to nearly every airfield and major air unit providing support to the invasion and subsequent European battles.

At every airfield Gene gathered data from the planes that returned from missions. Planes were going out in all weather using the British ground direction radars, and the Germans were shooting them down even through cloud cover. The improvement that should have resulted in formations equipped with carpet (and there were more and more of them) simply weren't materializing. Gene calculated and re-calculated, and he knew he was right to predict reductions, and yet the losses continued. General James Harold Doolittle, who was commanding the Eighth, wanted answers. Gene had none. He knew he had to work harder, faster, and better.

Gene expanded his data set and had men at each field who took meticulous notes for every plane, on every mission. It was a considerable undertaking at a time when the data from as many as 2,000 bombers was done by hand, and calculations were made by slide rule. Gene continued to collect and correlate the information brought back to him by the American and British Ferrets, and from that material he figured even more carefully the frequencies that bombers were likely to encounter as they flew through the German fire-control radar.

He sent out weekly histograms to all the bomber groups so they could adjust their carpet units to the appropriate frequency range and be ready to jam the extent of the range. At the airfields, he saw new men replace those who had been lost, then new men again when the replacements were lost. They listened to their equipment for the snarl of enemy radar and for the flushing sound that meant the carpet jamming had found and overwhelmed the enemy's frequency.

He did his operational analysis from every possible angle using all the data at his command, and he was certain that his bombers, the ones with carpet (which was now most of them), were engaging and disabling enemy radar. The rate of loss among the planes should have been a small fraction on any given mission—yet, the rates of loss continued to run higher. Gene was by now as confounded as he was distraught.

Gene knew the data could only tell him so much. He was limited by his ignorance of the German equipment, how it was used, and how the Germans responded to the countermeasures. There had to be something that he did not understand, some assumption that was incorrect, a variable for which he had not accounted. Only someone who knew the German method could fill that void. Gene demanded that American intelligence officers capture German radar operators with whom he could speak. He demanded the same thing from British senior officers at Government Communications Headquarters (GCHQ).

The British were first to respond with captured operators. Among their German prisoners were two soldiers who had been operating fire control radar during American raids.

Gene was allowed to talk in person to the German soldiers. He asked their names, how many children they had, where their wives were. He told them that if they gave him addresses, he would get the Red Cross to convey messages to their families. Then he told the men he was in charge of the equipment that was supposed to jam them, and he asked them what he was doing wrong, how they were getting around the jamming.

One of the soldiers said, "My God, it was terrible."

"Yes," Gene said. "But why?"

The other said, "We can't use our radars."

The first one said, "We can't use our radars because of your jamming."

Gene was baffled. "Then how can you kill so many of our airplanes on every mission?"

"You don't understand," one of them said.

"Understand what?"

It was the Germans' chance to explain: "Our officers don't get judged by how many American planes they shoot down. They get judged by how much ammunition they use. You defeated our radar, so we just fire as many of our shells as possible as soon as we hear the planes approaching. We know when your planes are coming. You have to fly at certain altitudes and there is usually only one direction from which you can approach the target. So when we know you are coming, we throw up a huge barrage. We fire up a solid wall of flak. Your airplanes cannot avoid flying into so much flak."

He went back to Pine Tree and fed all his data into the simulation of a flight going through the blind barrage from the Germans' seventy-five millimeter and eighty-millimeter guns—good guns, effective guns. He came up with loss estimates that matched the actual figures.

So the countermeasures had rendered the German radar useless. Would all the work of Gene's team accomplish only that?

Gene communicated his new insights to Doolittle, John Dyer at ABL, and the British. He saw to it that altitudes were more widely varied. He also insisted that the air wings institute more evasive action on the approach to targets, and more deception as to targets. The rate of losses fell.

Gene worked his data to discover whether countermeasures had saved any lives at all. What he found from a statistical analysis was that, in fact, countermeasures had likely saved nearly 500 aircraft with crews in excess of 4,500 pilots, gunners, and others. If the Germans had been able to target entirely unimpaired, the losses to British and American forces would have been much greater—perhaps great enough to have changed the course of the war. Gene did not advertise this success anywhere near the airfields, where the loss of life was felt most keenly. Favorable statistical analysis had no place on a battlefield. But privately, it gave him some comfort.

The flaw in the Germans' strategy of firing randomly and incessantly into the sky was simple, of course: Before long, they ran out of ammunition, and the barrages ceased. The Allied bombers flew out from their East Anglia fields, delivered their bombs, and returned. The bombers punished the Germans at will. The ground war following the invasion was not over, but it was making steady progress, and with the Russians fighting successfully from the east, a sense of inevitability about the end of the European conflict was beginning to take hold. Gene began pulling strings to be sent to the Pacific to fight the Japanese.

There is a series of old pictures of Gene Fubini on a small knoll surrounded by an assortment of military colleagues in what appears to be a sort of ceremony. Gene is wearing a civilian suit and tie, but being pinned to the suit are uniform shoulder boards, each bearing what appears to be six stars. Gene is laughing during the mock presentation and is seen in another photograph formally saluting his "troops." Throughout, Gene is grinning in cocky amusement. John Dyer remembered the occasion:

"Throughout my time at ABL, Gene Fubini had been working at Pine Tree—the Eighth Air Force Headquarters just outside London—passing us the latest information on what the Germans were doing, and pushing the countermeasures side of things there. Immediately after the war in Europe had [effectively] ended, an Eighth Air Force general called on us at Great Malvern. In a simple but moving ceremony, he presented Gene with the shoulder bars of a six-star general. This was before the rank had been officially introduced, when even the chief of staff of the Army wore only four stars. At Pine Tree Gene had gained the reputation of ordering everyone around, so they figured it was time to make it 'official.'"

What Gene and most others didn't know was that Fermi and the others in the Manhattan Project had by now succeeded in creating the atom bomb. It was both a destination—the inevitable endpoint of the scientific revolution that had been underway since the 1930s—and beginning—the first universally undeniable example of the profound contributions science would be making to warfare and, by extension, foreign policy. On a more pragmatic note, the bomb drew the war in the Pacific theatre to a quick close. Neither Gene nor anyone else was going to be transferred to the Pacific.

It was time to go home.

Dear Betty,

I should send you a lot of "best wishes" and "congratulations."

I want only to tell you that Eugene could not make a better choice and that I am very happy that you are going to be a part of our family.

Very affectionately yours,

Gino

PS. I am warning you that Gene since he has come back from Europe throws the ashes of the cigarette all over the floors and picks up crumbs from the table with his finger nails. From now on you'll have to take care of him.

Gene and Betty were married in Amherst at the Presbyterian Church on May 5, 1945, shortly before VE Day. At the time Gene had only been back in the country two weeks, and he already had orders to go to Washington. Betty's older sister, Gretchen, was her maid of honor and her bridesmaid was her sister Kay—not only her younger sister, but also her best friend. Gino was Gene's best man and his ushers were Paul Pontecorvo and Sylvan Gotshal. Paul was a friend from Italy whose brother, Bruno, was an important physicist. Sylvan Gotshal was the older, New York business associate and attorney of Marco's whose recommendation had been so essential to Gene's hiring at Columbia.

Betty Machmer shortly before her engagement to Gene.

Gene and Betty's wedding, from left: Betty's younger sister Kay, Betty, Gene, Betty's mother Olive, older sister Gretchen (May 1945).

Gene and Betty had decided to keep the wedding small, in part because of the constraints of war rationing, and in part because it was meant to be more of a family affair than a coming-out party. And Betty proved ever-mindful of family politics: she kept her mother and Gene's mother mostly separated, worried that they wouldn't mix easily; she had a hand in seating arrangements; managed the expectations of her Amherst friends (many of whom didn't understand Gene, but all of whom, owing to the feeling of the day, at least grudgingly accepted his validity, given his work during the war); and, of course, monitored the behavior of the groom. In all, she demonstrated why Gretchen had always called her "Baby Betty," the middle child and the one who always wanted everyone to get along. She'd been doing it for years in the Machmer family—bridging the gaps between the quiet, antisocial Gretchen (who would later have to be committed to an institution for depression and severe dementia), and the rambunctious Kay, between the disciplined mother and their warm but somewhat forgetful father. Her sisters foresaw (correctly, it would turn out) that this would be her role in the new family she was about to start, as well: the mediator.

To Gino, the wedding was a beautiful if baffling experience. He was delighted to have been the best man, but to him, Gene seemed to make no distinction between his marriage, the war work he'd undertaken, the job he'd been offered in Washington, and the lab work he was interested in—they were all so many projects to the frenetic, restless Gene.

Betty, if she hadn't already noticed Gene's inexhaustible energy, certainly came to understand it over the course of the honeymoon. If she'd been expecting Gene to surrender to a swooning romanticism over the whole affair, she was disappointed. Driving to the Poconos he nearly killed them both, he was so tense and erratic behind the wheel. In upstate New York he worried and talked incessantly about the war and the job in Washington, and it was a full week before he began to resemble in any way a man on a relaxing vacation. He and Betty hiked, which he still enjoyed, and she made him take a canoe trip—potentially a disaster, given his awkwardness and lack of physical precision and restraint. She also forced him into a horseback riding expedition, something he had no knack for, but which she told him he might as well "get used to," given her love of horses.

Gene and Betty traveled back to Boston and spent two days at the Copley Plaza Hotel before they took the train through to New York and on to Washington, and she had further opportunity to observe her husband's peculiarities. She saw that he always behaved in his same busy way, was usually too loud, and was frequently too demanding. She could tell that some people didn't care for him, but she also saw that he didn't care. The flip side of this, of course, was that he had an undeniable magnetism, and aura that drew people to him. If he noticed the opulence of the hotel or felt in any way inhibited by what she found to be an air of stifling pomposity, it certainly didn't show.

Gene and Betty took up temporary residence at the Wardman Park Hotel on Connecticut Avenue in Washington and began to settle into both married life and the post-war employment of the U.S. government. On May 27, just three weeks after being married, Gene (a newly minted American citizen) reported to his new assignment with General Harold Mark McClelland, the commander of the Air Communications Office in the War Office in Washington. For McClelland, Gene would be working with a new plane, the B-29, on tactics for present and planned operations, and on the role of radar countermeasures in those operations. He learned the Japanese means of countering the American air offensive, and the American countermeasures currently in place. He developed recommendations about how to improve RCM and how its use could and should evolve.

It was a unique time to be in Washington, and in U.S. government work. The war had ended the Depression, and the country was entering what would be a prolonged run as the most important—and at times the only—economic, military, and cultural superpower on the planet. The city was full of men who'd been involved in the war effort and had returned to breathe in the new atmosphere of American dominance and harness their new aspirations. Pioneering scientific work initially funded by the government took on a life of its own, as entirely new industries sprang up around it in the private sector. Many of the youngest echelon of scientists and engineers migrated to these new private sector opportunities; so did more than a few more senior men. Airborne Instruments Laboratory (AIL) was one small but typical example of just such a new opportunity.

When German U-boats were decimating Allied shipping in the Atlantic, the Vannevar Bush hierarchy at NRDC and OSRD started a project under the auspices of Columbia University to develop a magnetic method of detecting submarines from the air. The work began in 1940 at MIT with five men, and in 1941 moved to hangar number one at the Naval Air Station at Quonset, Rhode Island, where a core of twenty-five men developed a successful magnetic anomaly detector (MAD), which is used to detect changes in the earth's magnetic field and can be used to locate submarines. In the spring of 1942, the operation moved to the TWA hangar at La Guardia Field outside New York City, and then in the fall moved out to leased buildings along Old Country Road in Mineola, on Long Island. At that point the project became known as the Airborne Instruments Laboratory and by the end of the year employed 160 people. By the end of 1943 it employed 350, and the U-boat menace was under control thanks to convoys, sonic buoys, and the new MAD, which had evolved into a magnetic direction finder set into the nose of a bomb carried under the wing of a submarine search plane.

With U-boats under control, the AIL had worked itself out of a job. However, by this time the Radio Research Lab needed to develop jamming capabilities to counter the German guided bombs and the V-2 rockets. RRL annexed AIL to do that work, and subsequently expanded the work to include jamming electronic proximity fuses in anti-aircraft munitions.

By the spring of 1945, the war in Europe was ending and the Allies were closing in on Japan. War workers of all kinds began to cast around for post-war jobs. Hector Skifter, who directed AIL through the last years of the war, and who was as successful a businessman as he was a radio engineer, thought the AIL could flourish as a private company when the war came to an end.

During the summer of 1945, the idea came together. Columbia would be willing to sell the lab; Skifter would stay on as president; John Byrne, RRL's VP for engineering, would become director of research and engineering; John Dyer was to be a supervising engineer, bringing along a dozen of the other RRL men, as well as a number of men from the Rad Lab. He wanted Gene to be one of these men, and Gene happily said yes.

It would mean a move from Washington to Long Island. But this was just one of the major changes to Gene and Betty's life together: they also learned that Betty was pregnant.

Betty loved being pregnant, and physically it seemed to agree with her. She found the couple an apartment on William Street on the far side of Brooklyn, convenient to both his work at AIL, and his mother's new home, a smaller apartment Gene and Gino had found for her after their father's death. As the dust settled from the war's end, word had come from Turin that the family's home on Via Pietro Mica was indeed still intact and in the family's possession, thanks to the friends and associates Marco had put in its care. Anna Fubini was eager to return, and it was arranged that she would split her time between New York and Turin. Of course, without her husband or children in tow, the original apartments were much too large for her, so Gene arranged to have a small upstairs apartment in the Turin building converted for her use. Between the income of the building's other apartments, which would be rented out, and the income from the apartment buildings Marco had purchased for her in New York, she was able to once again live the life of leisure and privilege she so valued.

As a new wife with a baby on the way, Betty began to prepare herself for the domestic life to come: she planned meals, kept house, began to decorate the nursery, and got herself to her steady stream of doctor appointments. She also began to build her social network, which she knew would be useful when the baby came. The families she most enjoyed were those of the Skifters and the Dyers. Additionally, Gene's brother, Gino, married Gaby in June 1945, in a ceremony at the couple's apartment at 41 West 96th St., and it was presumed that babies would be on the way. These were family men and they were all, Betty believed, good examples for Gene to have on hand. What she liked most about them was that they seemed to have managed to find harmony between career and parenthood, letting neither overshadow the other. As she stood on the precipice of her life's new chapter, and regarded her impatient, ambitious, and unquiet husband—her partner in one of life's great adventures—she must have hoped he might learn the same balance from his older colleagues.

9

Babies and the Golden Era

AIL had started as a public company with debt of $150,000, capitalization of $1,000, and with old buildings and old equipment leased from the Navy. At AIL, radar countermeasures, quickly and appropriately, became known as Electronics Countermeasure (ECM). Gene started at AIL in October 1945 as senior engineer, and ECM was his field. He immediately began promoting a broader vision for the arena, expanding the opportunity set, and in so doing creating a more prominent role for himself. Much as he did at the Rad Lab, Gene also began learning more about what AIL was doing in other product and research arenas. He came to know the work with Moving Target Indicators (MTI), and spent time understanding the latest thinking in air navigation and traffic control. Gene and others had deep concerns about the concentration on air traffic control for civilian airlines, and urged diversification into other product arenas.

This main airline radar work was being led by John Dyer and was largely staffed with former Rad Lab engineers who had worked on all-weather, ground control approach radar during the war. Gene felt strongly that he could best contribute by knowing about all of the capabilities at AIL and finding new opportunities across the various engineering disciplines. Gene immersed himself in the efforts throughout AIL.

AIL quickly developed a wide portfolio of engineering programs. A team at AIL, under Joseph Petit, built on the initial wartime RRL onboard jamming system designs to develop the APR-9 airborne receiver, which would prove to be the foundation for such receivers for years to come. Additionally, to get around the large and heavy noise jammers used to prematurely detonate enemy proximity fuses, a group at AIL, under Walter Tolles, designed and built re-circulating loop repeater systems which were lighter and more functional. This kind of research and development required AIL to build its own prototype instruments for testing, and soon outside firms, learning of these design capabilities, sought to contract with AIL for this prototype. As a result, AIL set up a division to manufacture and sell prototypes and finished products. Other engineering divisions were organized around antennas, receivers, transmitters, and radar and navigation. As would be expected from a small company largely staffed with those who had emerged from R&D efforts during the war, most engineers were multi-skilled and wanted to work across disciplines. Collaboration was the norm. This style of work was suited Gene's preferences, and it allowed him to have an impact helping across various systems. He first worked on antennas and receivers, but he was soon involved with much more. He, of course, continued to be the one who stood out with his demanding personality and frequently raised voice. "Let me explain" became a familiar expression in yet another setting.

In March 1946, Betty and Gene's baby arrived, a girl they named Sylvia. Betty's sisters, Gretchen and Kay, came to help Betty, as did Gaby, who lived much closer. Betty was determined not to miss a beat and initially shunned any recuperation period, but Gene insisted she rest.

In her own way, Betty was as averse to idleness as Gene. She had always approached her work tirelessly, and, as she saw it, her work was now to be a wife and mother. It was a role she felt prepared for, and that was a good thing, because for all his confidence in most other areas, the sudden presence of a baby baffled and unsettled Gene. Having been raised by a governess, being the youngest in his family, and never having had a sister, this was an entirely new experience in every way.

Gene couldn't have been too daunted, however, because soon Betty was pregnant again, and the apartment in Brooklyn, they realized, would soon be inadequate. Betty found a house on Chestnut Street in Garden City, near Mineola and AIL. It was small, compact, and modest. There was no room for horses, but for the time being she was content that there would be ample room for the babies.

If horses were Betty's eventual wish, Gene's seemed on a career track to be able to one day provide them. He advanced quickly from senior engineer to supervising engineer, joining Dyer, Petit, Tolles, and Clark Cahill, who had been associate directors of ABL. Gene now reported directly to John Byrne, RRL's VP for engineering. The reputation of AIL was growing, as well. After the war there were still few companies doing military electronics. Some others, like Raytheon and Honeywell, were older and more diversified, but the word was spreading about the young comers at AIL.

The work at AIL was largely classified, of course, so there was little in the way of public recognition of its excellence, but engineers in the field, military personnel, and other industry players were becoming more aware of AIL's capabilities. And with an improving reputation, recruitment became easier; month-by-month, the ranks of first-rate engineers eager to work at AIL seemed to swell, and excitement within and about the firm grew, as well. For Gene, his life was becoming close to ideal, with work providing inexhaustible challenges, his family taking shape, and his home and office close enough that he could go home for lunch. In fact, Gene and his co-workers fell into the habit of doing just that: Making their way to Gene's home and invading the small kitchen for lunch, taking as much relaxation as one could in a small Long Island kitchen in an hour with a newborn close at hand, and then walking back to work, talking all the while, of course, about their work. Gene was constantly occupied with the challenges and delights of his work.

Sandra, Gene and Betty's second daughter, arrived in October 1947, a little more than two years after Sylvia. Betty was thrilled to have two girls, and Gene, too, was happy, although he harbored some disappointment over not having produced a son. Thanks again to the proximity of home and work, Gene was able to supplement Betty's total immersion in child-rearing duties, making sure to be home as often as possible in the evenings, and helping out to the best of his meager (but growing) abilities.

AIL faced a major shift in the market when the government took over all responsibility for air traffic control. With air traffic of all kinds growing, various government agencies realized that the air space over the U.S. had to be controlled and monitored by the government for both safety and security. With this decision, the airlines needed to contract individually with AIL for their own air traffic control equipment. This was where Gene's push toward diversifying AIL into military and government activities paid off: such diversification was now essential to its ongoing work. AIL turned its focus almost exclusively to the work on defense and the military. Indeed, as Fred Terman said in his 1946 book *Administrative History of the Radio Research Laboratory*:

"The experience of WWII makes it clear that if there should ever be a future war, its weapons will be built around technology—rockets and planes guided by radio and carrying bombs of amazing types that are dropped by radar, shells exploded by vacuum tubes, radar waves that hunt out everything that moves, etc. In such a war, about the only effective defense is to employ radio and radar countermeasures."

AIL embraced this inevitability and focused much of its efforts in these arenas, which Gene knew so well. Efforts on radar, ECM, and other communications equipment became the centerpiece of the company, and the focus of both recruiting and capital. Gene now headed the Special Devices Section, which borrowed from all the other engineering disciplines to help design and build a range of different equipment, most of which was "black:" that is, highly confidential and used for intelligence-gathering and specialized countermeasures. With his background at Harvard and the Rad Lab, field experience in the Mediterranean, support to the air groups in Pine Tree, and his short stint in Washington before joining AIL, Gene was in a unique position to be able to integrate across a wide range of "customer needs" with a deep knowledge of the underlying engineering and related science. He had the credibility of direct application experience so as to drive many new major product development efforts. Gene was aggressive in pushing to ensure that his section was at the leading edge of thinking in these domains, and stayed very close to the needs of the various constituents that impacted both the use and the purchase of programs as well. Gene was spending more and more time in Washington in front of key decision-makers.

One such trip (at the invitation of eminent electronic warfare expert Howard Otto Lorenzen) was to speak to the Navy Research Lab about the latest science development associated with antennas. Gene was stunned to see the huge growth at NRL since his last visit. The lab had been a busy, but not especially large, place during the war. Now it was on the way to becoming huge, industrial research complex. This, Gene came to learn, was all part of the massive and permanent growth to the Navy's needs in ECM as a result of the Cold War. And it was certainly not limited to the Navy: The Pentagon and every other part of government related to defense, intelligence, and the military were continuing to grow in importance, stature, and budget, as well. The Cold War, the Korean conflict, the Russian threat, and the spread of nuclear weapons were redefining forever the role of the military in society. At the center of all this change was the scientific community, which was coming to have a profound influence on the post-war world. Gene realized he was in the midst of it.

The pace of efforts at AIL were increasing and the success of the defense side of the business became more substantial. AIL's government contracts rose in volume and value, even as many other companies began to crowd into the ever-growing field of military electronics. Gene himself ran projects in excess of $1 million, including development of a new generation of search receivers using mostly transistors. The capital structure of AIL was also readjusted to match the new realities of what AIL had become: a company focused now exclusively on the government and defense. The airlines sold their AIL stock to a Rockefeller Investment Group as well as to many of the senior AIL employees, including Gene.

Gene, anxious to continue his many dialogues, took advantage of AIL's proximity to his Garden City home and now began taking potential customers, recruits, and other military personnel home for lunch and dinners. Betty was a confident homemaker and somehow managed the two small children, her third pregnancy, and the constant schedule of these lunches and dinners. Gene preferred, as he always had, a casual setting for discussing work: in the woods, on a ski lift, in his dining room—these would be the places where he had some of the most important conversations of his career, and forged some of his most significant relationships. However, when Betty and Gene's third daughter, Carol, arrived in June 1949, Betty put her foot down. Now with three little girls all under age four, Betty famously told Gene, "I married you for better or worse, but I didn't marry you for AIL at lunch." The lunches at the Garden City house ended.

After Carol, Betty's doctor encouraged her to take a break from pregnancy. For Betty, the demands were more than just physical, of course, and it was all the encouragement she needed to put on hold any plans for more children, and focus on just managing her and Gene's busy life. Gene—perhaps surprisingly, considering his own absent father, self-involved mother, and stern German governess—proved to be an attentive and doting father to the three girls. It was, in many ways, the golden era for the Fubini clan: Gene's manageable work/life balance allowed him to be a good husband and committed father. He made a point of dining alone with his wife after the children were asleep. On the weekends, he gave the children their baths, read them stories, and put them to bed. By the standards of the time, he was unusually involved.

Before long, Gino and Gaby bought a lot in nearby Great Neck, Long Island, where they built a house at the end of a cul-de-sac. It was a modest and comfortable home and it fit Gino and Gaby's needs and tastes. On weekends, the two families often came together for dinner and to listen to classical music and watch Gene and Betty's three girls play with Gaby and Gino's daughter, Nancy. Gino was speculating actively in the real estate market by this time, having bought and developed property in East Islip on the south shore of Long Island. The houses he built there sold for $7,800 each. Building costs being more than Gino had planned on, the venture was not lucrative and he failed to make much money. But Gino was undeterred, and bought more land and built more houses; still, few of them ever made money. The best return Gino would ever see from these ventures was the resale of empty lots, land that had appreciated more than the homes that Gino had been building.

Gaby and Betty did their best to strike up a friendship, and while theirs was a cordial relationship, they were never close. The difference in backgrounds and the lack of a shared language may have been to blame, or perhaps they were simply incompatible. Since they shared a common problem—the dominant and demanding mother-in-law, Anna Fubini—they might have found enough common misery to bond. But, in fact, Gaby was closer to and spent more time with Anna, and so Betty found it difficult to consider her a confidant. Gaby, for her part, felt some resentment toward Betty that Gene's success eclipsed Gino's, and that everyone, explicitly or not, acknowledged this. No matter where the family gathered—at Gino's, Anna's, or a neutral third party's home— Gene seemed to command attention the moment he walked through the door. He was always excited, always seemed to know everything, and always in a hurry. He had things to say, he said them loudly, and everyone paid attention. When he left, it was almost worse, because everyone felt the absence. Anna didn't make matters any better, showing her younger son, just as she always had, unabashed adulation and preference.

The irony of the situation was that, whatever Gene's social blind-spots and indelicacies, he was, during this period, more relaxed, more balanced and more approachable than he had ever been. Betty was in many ways the perfect match for Gene's energies, and her calming influence was undeniable. His involvement with his girls played a large role in calming him, as well: they forced him to slow down to their speed. But none of it was to last. With the defense industry booming, there was always more pressure to deepen his commitment to AIL; indeed, his work was effectively insatiable, always demanding more of his time, energy, and attention, never less. Work had always been what had driven him, and it always would be. His family would soon bear the brunt of this commitment.

10

Committees, a Son, and the USD-7

*M*ore than perhaps any other war in the country's history, World War II drew the U.S. together around a common cause. At the time of its entry into the conflict, the country was in the grip of history's most severe economic depression, riven by labor strife, and socially splintered. The Great American Experiment, it might have seemed at the time, was at an impasse or even, some must have felt, at an end. Despite the severity of conditions—or perhaps because of them—World War II became a cause around which there was, for a democratic country of such size, a remarkable coming together. And when the war ended, and victory over an enemy of such unspeakable malignance was secured, the sense of pride and, above all, the feeling of righteousness was more than deep: it was profound. For the vast majority of Americans, the conflict had been superior military might in the service of a superior moral position. And this, in the years before Vietnam and Watergate, taught Americans to trust the government and the military, putting what Eisenhower would later call "the military-industrial complex" at the heart of most Americans' idea of what made the country great. Indeed, there was a near-universal presumption that a strong defense, an active military, and constantly improved armaments were essential deterrents to the monstrousness of fascism and other tyrannies. And such a defense was now a core responsibility of the government.

It may have been that some of the legion of scientists and engineers who had served in complete safety during the war felt a responsibility to continue serving more than other men and women who had been closer to battle. Or it may simply have been that the country's and the military's need for the scientists and engineers continued at a high level after the war. It was certainly the case that in the interest of national security, the government and the military were sponsoring an enormous amount of the best scientific and technological research, which would naturally have drawn the best minds. But whatever the reason, scientists and engineers served with increasing frequency on increasing numbers of government and military committees and panels after the war. The Cold War and the Korean War, and then the escalations that heightened Cold War tension, all posed long- and short-term defense-related questions that involved the rapid evolution of technology. Men who had worked in various aspects of defense technology during the war were asked by the Defense Department or the military to study these issues and help the country maintain a posture of optimum security.

The committees and their panels became a constant for able men who worked in a broad range of academic and industry defense technologies. These were not professional or fraternal organizations, though to a degree they functioned as such. They demanded serious commitments of time, and they gave serious advice on weapons, communications, and surveillance. To be recruited for a committee or a panel was an acknowledgement of ability, but it was also a demanding type of service, and a service that rarely encompassed only one term on a single committee.

Gene worked actively to remain current with the full range of electronic warfare advances by both extensive networking and voracious reading. Increasingly, he was at the center of efforts that surrounded this evolving science of so-called electronic warfare, and effort to keep technological and, therefore, military pace with Russia and the other Cold War competitors. For example, as the Navy considered Russia's newest electronic equipment, Gene was asked to devise possible American defenses against, and responses to, that equipment. In this case, as in nearly every other, he said yes and dove into the work wholeheartedly. He knew associations with these committees and the men who ran them would expand his network, enhance his value to AIL, and bolster his stature and reputation. Naturally, this benefit came at the cost of his schedule, which was now so full that late nights and weekends spent in the office became routine.

One West Coast trip around this time was representative of the demands this constant committee work placed on his time. Initially, Gene made the trip to see Bill Rambo, who was at Stanford University and was leading a Lockheed "skunk works," or a group within the larger organization that was given a high degree of autonomy to work on a sensitive, advanced, or top-secret project. Shortly after arriving in California, Gene was invited to the Navy tests off Point Magu of new electronic countermeasures equipment, an invitation he naturally accepted. But as long as he was on the West Coast, he thought it best to also swing down to Los Angeles for a visit with the Air Force. What had been a one- or two-day excursion quickly and easily turned into a veritable tour of California.

At AIL, sales passed $4 million, with Gene's division accounting for more than a quarter of that total. The company's staff doubled between

1950 and 1955, so it built the first building of its own—which it promptly outgrew. AIL was becoming a small but powerful force among the large electronics giants in the industry: Raytheon, Sperry, Sylvania, and others. At the core of this success were the engineers who were at the leading edge of theory and application. Gene was one of the most prominent of the group.

Another daughter, Laurie, arrived in March 1952, a little more than three years after Carol. The four girls made two "sets" based on their ages, with Laurie and Carol close enough to form a pair. The two older girls had already become a handful around the house. With their brood growing again, Gene's salary increasing regularly, and the AIL stock climbing, Gene and Betty had both the need and the means to find a home larger than their Garden City house. And Betty had her heart set on not only a larger house, but also a larger parcel of land—one that would finally allow her to keep horses. With the four girls in tow, Betty went in search of a new home and soon found one: a handsome white colonial in Brookville, New York, deep in horse country. There was a rambling main house, along with a ready-made barn for the horses, an external garage with room for guests, enough land for a pasture, and, later, a swimming pool (a luxury Gene would come to enjoy, possibly more than anything else about the home). The living room was large and perfectly laid-out for the numerous AIL parties Gene and Betty would have, the kitchen was spacious, and the setting overall was bucolic. Betty and Gene had gone in one move from far too little room to far more than they really needed. But it was a wise move, because they hadn't been settled in Brookville for long before Betty found she was, once again, pregnant.

Gene adjusted to the new home quickly and happily. To deal with their meadows, he bought a small tractor with a mowing attachment and began what would be a small but valued refuge: mowing the grass for hours, row after methodical row, lost in thought. During the winter he found a ski club based in Garden City that ran buses on weekend days up to ski areas in Pennsylvania. They were small areas, hardly the Alps, but he was still thrilled to return to one of his favorite childhood sports. He and Dick Close, from AIL, would make regular weekend pilgrimages to the slopes, skiing enthusiastically in every weather imaginable.

Gene and Dick's first skiing trip together was a classic Gene Fubini performance. When they were outfitted with their skis, Dick remembered, Gene headed away from the lift, skiing instead up a rise, arduously but efficiently working his skis and poles on a steady, crabwise climb. He had a good head start when he called back for Dick to follow. Dick was considerably younger than Gene, and in good shape, but Gene wanted to show him that he knew a thing or two about the slopes. When you learned to ski in the Alps, he seemed to be saying, you really learned to ski. By the time Dick got to the top of the rise, Gene was waiting for him, pretending to be bored. "What took you so long?" he asked Dick, his statement having been made.

Gene skied well if not spectacularly, like a reliable old car. He didn't win many points with his style, but he could ski any trail and always stayed on his feet. One had to admire him, and "not just for his brains," Close would later say. They skied together for years to come.

At the end of January 1954, Betty finally delivered a son, David. Gene loved his girls, but those who knew him well were relieved that he finally had the son he'd always wanted. Harold Hechtman, now at AIL, circulated a cartoon strip entitled "The Final Edition…?" that showed Gene holding a baby. After four identical panels that showed a buoyant Gene exalting that "It was a girl!" the final cartoon showed Gene holding a boy. The caption read, "Who does he look like, you or Betty?" Gene's handwritten response reads, "We don't know yet. We haven't looked at that end yet!"

Gene on the slopes in Italy—"never stylish, always stable" on the slopes.

Anna Fubini maintained her residence on Central Park West in New York City, where she continued her privileged lifestyle. She wore hand-tailored clothes, collected antiques, and busied herself with the opera, museums, and ballet. She was an accomplished cook and she and her maid, Emma, found their outlet with countless dinner parties and lunches, given with old world flair. Every winter she would return by ocean liner to Turin for half the year, residing in the apartment on San Pietro Mica in the home the family had fled when they left Italy. Anna still had many old friends and family members who had returned to Italy after the war, and socializing was what she lived for.

In the autumn of 1954, John Van Vleck, chairman of the Physics Department at Harvard, invited Gene to teach for a visiting lecture series. There were just two courses, one on noise in electrical circuits and one on microwave antennas and circuits, and Gene was pleased to be asked. He not only liked Van Vleck but was pleased to be back in an academic setting and among engineers he respected. The fact that he was being asked to teach at Harvard was appealing as well. Gene coordinated his teaching days with committee work among others at MIT, so he minimized any lost time at AIL or in Washington.

Gene enjoyed the classroom experience, but ran into trouble when he tried to employ the techniques that Fermi had used. On his exams he would ask his students the same questions Fermi had asked him: "Why is the sky blue? Why is the snow white? Why is the grass green?" Not surprisingly, the students complained bitterly. They saw no relevance to the material they had been studying, and such questions seemed arbitrary and meaningless. Many went to Van Vleck and complained. When he approached Gene about it, Gene explained that he was not testing the students' acquired knowledge; they were all brilliant and highly educated, so what was the point of that? He, like Fermi, sought to determine whether they could think and reason. He told Van Vleck that to the question, "Why is the grass green?" many would simply answer that grass contains chlorophyll, which makes it appear green. The real, deeper, underlying reason that grass is green is that in the solar spectrum, the place where the density of energy is at its maximum is at green. If you want a plant to shape its color so as to get the maximum energy from the sun, it must evolve over time to be green.

Van Vleck understood, and he respected Gene's approaches. But the fact was that this way of teaching was too Socratic and by the 1950s, science education simply wasn't performed in this way. Gene finished his course load and returned to Long Island. It would be fair to say that the students were thrilled to see him go, and Gene had learned that he was not a great classroom teacher of theory. His gift was to teach others through experience, practical application, and collaboration.

At AIL, the collaborative approach was distinguishing Gene from others who were using a more command and control method of overseeing engineering departments. For example, AIL and Gene had attracted to the company a new microwave development engineer named Jesse Taub. Taub's first project was to design a strip line filter bank of 225 band-pass channels covering the 8-10.5 GHz frequency range that was required for the Air Force. After a month on the problem, Traub decided the filter bank could not meet all the specifications AIL had promised the Air Force, so he began to formulate a new approach to the design that might come closer to meeting the requirements. He took this new approach to Gene, who was appreciative of the innovation and intrigued by the ideas behind it. Gene took Traub home to Brookville on nights and weekends and together they would challenge each other and flesh out the approach. Together, they solved the problem for the Air Force. Taub went on to publish the work with another colleague at AIL and his career was enhanced not only within AIL but now in the broader academic arena. Gene got together with others at MIT to share this new approach, and together broadened the work into a general theory that would aid in the future development of high band frequencies. Without the collaborative approach Gene favored, such a development would likely not have happened. It was a boon to AIL (which was thus a boon to Gene's career and stature), and it was a boon to those who Gene took under his wing. Taub was but one of many whose careers Gene aided and who, looking back, would identify Gene as the major contributor to their success.

Russian radar continued to become more sophisticated, and with every step the Russians took forward, the Americans felt the pressure to keep pace with countermeasures and improved radar of their own. The Navy was advised through its committees and flag officers to develop a new search receiver to replace those that were rapidly becoming out of date. Requests for proposals were issued and AIL, as well as other larger companies, responded. AIL was not selected for this new program because the technology involved was untested in the field, but Gene convinced the Navy to fund continued research at AIL on its new developments in search receivers, and to continue basic research on the science underlying the ECM efforts. This effort, known as DLD-1 technology, held great promise, and Gene wanted to ensure that its future development be continued. It was a typical move by Gene: create opportunities, even in defeat, and always be looking "two chess moves ahead," as he liked to say.

In fact, as the DLD-1 program illustrated, Gene and AIL were ready for more challenges. Gene was tired of AIL being a subcontractor on components for full-systems contracts driven by the larger companies. Despite its acknowledged accomplishments, AIL was considered too small to manage a complete system development. The Armed Services as well as the less important (at that time) Pentagon procurement staff were reluctant to put large-scale deployment in the hands of a small, untested company. They would rather ask another larger contractor to be the "prime," and have it take on the risk of development and deployment by utilizing the large network of other suppliers as "sub-prime" contractors. Gene saw no reason that size should equate with the ability to be a prime contractor. He decided it was time to take on this challenge.

Over time patches and upgrades to the ALD-4 receiver, which was ubiquitous in military airborne operations, were going to be insufficient to keep pace with both recent science and the ever-evolving challenge of staying on pace with the Russians. The replacement would not be the DLD-1 receiver the Navy had previously turned down; whatever the replacement would ultimately be, it would need the technology Gene and his team had continued to work on for two years with the Air Development Center funding. As a result of the continued efforts on the base science, AIL had technology nobody else had, and it was calculated to deliver exactly what Gene had forecasted that the Navy and the Air Force would need, and what, in fact, it now did need. It was also the type of functionality that the National Security Agency was demanding for its surveillance and intelligence gathering operations. Specifically, these agencies and services were going to need fully automated airborne search and direction finding from 30 MHz to 40,000 MHz, with active operators in the loop along with onboard computer analysis and ground analysis. The integrated system would be a massive undertaking combining the needs of mechanical, electronic, and digital computing technologies. It was to be one of the first and largest integrated ECM systems ever developed and deployed.

The conventional approach to prime and sub-prime contractors left no room for Gene and AIL to provide all the elements of such a system and function, effectively, as the prime contractor. If Gene was to position AIL as the prime contractor, he would have to challenge the thinking that size was essential to playing the key integrator role. He knew that AIL could sub-contract the elements it couldn't handle, and he planned to simply sub these elements to those that were used to being the prime contracts. After all, AIL had the core technology.

Complicating the picture, however, was the fact that technological prowess was not the only consideration for the Services and the Defense Departments. The financial health and size of a contractor was just as important as its technical abilities. The Armed Services wanted to be sure companies with which they worked were able to take on the financial risk and provide needed working capital for their programs. This would certainly be an issue on the receivers contract. This had already been an issue with other contracts at AIL; the company was still quite small and had limited financial resources; therefore, it also had limited ability to bear financial risks. Indeed, the replacement of the ALD-4 was going to be at least a $40 million project, and while AIL was growing faster every year, it still had only a total contract volume of under $10 million a year. Not coincidentally, Hector Randolph Skifter had already begun looking for a larger company to take on AIL. The hope had been that a larger company would acquire AIL and let it remain as an independent, autonomous division that would have the larger corporate balance sheet as a security blanket for its government clients.

The request for proposals for the replacement receivers was issued. It contained the requirements that almost exactly fit the template for what Gene and his section now called their replacement receiver, the USD-7. Gene now faced the daunting task of convincing a consortium of other, much larger companies to come alongside AIL to jointly bid on the program. He held two critical trump cards. First, the AIL technology was "spot on" in its ability to meet the contract requirements. The second was Gene himself. No one knew more about the topic than he.

Gene contacted the companies whose capabilities he needed. Aerojet-General, Raytheon, Sperry, Sylvania, Ling Temco, and Filtron were all on the list. Representatives from these companies likely assumed that Gene and AIL would be taking their usual role of sub-contractor. Gene had other ideas. Slowly, methodically, he presented his vision of the project and the RFP they would need to present to get the contract. He did not specify roles for the companies, but rather outlined a scenario where the prime contractor was not necessarily the one with the greatest implementation strength, which traditionally would have been the natural lead. No, Gene suggested that the lead should be the one with the best technology—a seemingly intuitive approach, but one that was quite out of the ordinary at the time. He did not say which company this would be. Indeed, he did not assign even proposed roles for any of the companies. He simply presented the rational, even undeniable, idea that the RFP would be strongest, and the project completed to its best and fullest, if the company with the most expertise, the best thinking, and the deepest understanding of the work stood out front and called the shots.

Now, everyone involved in the project knew who Gene Fubini was. By this time, Gene had been in the field long enough to have worked with a great many of these men, and certainly to be familiar even to those with whom he had not worked. They all respected Gene's work as an engineer, and the more he talked (and talked and talked) the more it began to seem to them that he was right: Technological expertise would carry the day, and should be at the center of the project. And the more he talked, the more the same idea burst into each of their brains: AIL was the one with the best technology, and Gene Fubini himself was the man most familiar with it. Gene had led them perfectly to the conclusion that AIL should take the lead without ever having explicitly suggested it. Because it seemed to be their idea, it was naturally more palatable to them.

Bolstering the case for AIL was that fact that the other companies knew Gene had the ear of the Air Force. He understood their needs and concerns, he understood their culture and how best to deal with them. He was, in short, connected.

While all this talking and cajoling and convincing was going on, Cutler-Hammer, an electric equipment manufacturer in Milwaukee, agreed to Skifter's plan to buy AIL and keep it as a separate division. And this sealed the deal. Cutler-Hammer's more robust and substantial balance sheet would be more than enough to quell any misgivings the Air Force might have about AIL's size. The larger companies agreed to present AIL as the prime contractor. To no one's surprise, AIL won the job.

Then, in the fall of 1957, something happened which would reorder the priorities and realities of the entire defense industry: the Russians launched the Sputnik orbital satellite. It was a shock to the U.S. intelligence community, and to the world. The Russians were thought to be years behind the U.S. in the ability to put any sort of payload into orbit, and so the U.S. had been taking its time with space. After the war, the German rocket scientist Wernher von Braun and many of his colleagues had sought out the Americans and surrendered to them. They'd since become the heart of the American rocket effort and had given the U.S. the sense that all the expertise was theirs. Unbeknownst to the Americans, however, the Russians had captured most of von Braun's production group at Peenemüde and started its own rocket program with the same focus as the U.S., which was ultimately to develop weapons using orbital science. And the Russians, unlike the Americans, had made it a high priority.

For the public and the press, catching the Russians was suddenly an urgent matter of pride, but for those in government generally, and the defense industry specifically, it was much more serious than that; it was a matter of the utmost urgency to national security. The use of space for surveillance and weapon delivery was going to be critical to the future security of the country.

At AIL, Gene quickly formalized an initiative that came to be called Space Technology and Research (STAR). His section had done considerable work in the area of space-based efforts, and now it would have to reach across the company and embed these ideas into all other AIL programs. AIL would need to develop satellite electronics for every aspect of its flight control, communications control, and reconnaissance programs. It would all mean many more committees, many more study groups, more conferences, more time in Washington—much more work. It would also mean even less time for his family.

11

The Defense Department and Potomac

$\mathcal{S}$usan arrived in March 1957, and after six children in eleven years Betty finally said, "No more." Now with a family of eight, horses, dogs, and other pets, the Brookville home was a constant hub of activity. Morning chaos, after-school activities, horses, church, and an endless stream of playdates with friends all made for a wonderful mix of activities, family gatherings, and, as one daughter remembered it, "genial chaos."

Two Christmas cards of the era seemed to capture the spirit of the family at the time.

The 1956 Christmas card was a black and white picture of Betty with two-year-old David on her lap and the four older girls around her. The picture was taken in the summer under the tree in the front yard at Brookville. The card was plain and straightforward, with "Merry Christmas" written over everyone's heads. On the back of this particular card, one of the girls had printed in her uneven hand, "The Fubini family—only their father is not there." Beneath that, another of the girls had written forgivingly, "And all but Susan, our little sister, is not there either."

Proof of photo for Christmas card with Betty, the four older girls, and David.

In 1960, instead of a family portrait, Betty took a picture of just the children. It was taken in the fall with the leaves down and everybody sitting on the split rail fence in front of the barn. The two horses, which were hams for the camera, stood with their heads over the fence among the bigger girls. Baby Susan was balanced between David and Laurie. Everyone looked happy. Betty had her family, she had her horses, she had Brookville, and everyone was healthy and happy. She was content.

Gene was now often out of town, traveling almost constantly. When he was in town, he usually got home after Betty had put the children to bed, the two of them ate dinner, and then he worked more in his home office, went to bed, and got up at five in the morning to go back to the office. On the weekends, if he needed to clear his mind, he drove his tractor. The noise kept everyone away, and sometimes he cut the fields two or three weekends in a row. He did, as he'd told Betty he would, put the children into his schedule. For the school-age kids, he worked through their week's homework with them. He made what could only be called appointments with them, and saw to it that they were being challenged by their schoolwork and were responding appropriately. Amid the homework sessions with the children and the time on the tractor, he also brought people home to walk and talk, people like Taub or more senior people like Dyer. In the winter, when he couldn't get on the mower and couldn't get people to walk in the snow, he got on a bus and went skiing for a day with Dick Close.

1960 Christmas card with all the Fubini children (and horses) in Brookville, New York.

Betty Fubini in the 1960s in Brookville, Long Island back yard.

Every summer, they all drove up for two weeks to Cape Cod at Betty's family's cottage in Wellfleet. Gene enjoyed that time. They kept a small Sunfish Gene could take out, though, being an unskilled sailor and easily distracted, he could not be trusted to sail far from shore. Most days they picnicked on the beach, and home movies from the time show him lounging on the sand and taking the children into the water on his shoulders. When Betty's sister Kay was there with her husband and their children, Gene realized how well Betty did with her own children. Kay was competent, but Betty had a gift. She knew them instinctively, as if they were a part of her, and always seemed to be one step ahead of their needs, their worries, and their small obsessions. She knew them better than he could ever imagine knowing them. There was, he saw, an ease between Betty and the children, a naturalness he couldn't fathom. But if he couldn't understand it, he at least could bask in it. For two weeks out of the year, Betty managed to get Gene to be a typical father, relaxing in the middle of his happy family.

Gene Fubini with Sylvia on Cape Cod (Summer 1946).

In 1959 and into 1960 Gene continued to develop and sell his STAR program, working to get AIL electronics into the developing space programs. His committee work increased. The USD-7 project flourished, with companies as sub-contractors that were five and ten times the size of even the Cutler-Hammer-backed version of AIL. Gene set up a project management organization that was all but separate from the rest of AIL. He interviewed throughout AIL for his staff and then used the rest of AIL as if it were another one of the team, like Raytheon and the others. Dick Close was his project manager and Mel Saslow became the business manager. Saslow was representative of others like Dick Close, whom Gene had spotted early on and drawn into his circle of collaborators, colleagues, and friends.

In both business and the military, Gene would become an adept talent evaluator. When he saw individuals whose intellect, drive, and orientation to succeed were up to his standards, he made it a point to get to know them, stay in communication with them, and, if the circumstances were right, hire them. He would introduce them to others in the network, give them counsel and stay connected with them. His network was growing and was now both extensive and substantive.

Gene's reputation as a mentor and assessor of programs was also becoming widely known. Paul Heller recalls that he was a very junior mechanical engineer in 1959, working on STAR with Gene's group. Six months after joining the group, Gene assigned him the task of defending an Ampex on-board flight tape recorder in a design review. The recorder was housed in a box of about one cubic foot, a hermetically sealed package. Although it was a brilliant design, it had some troublesome problems that AIL was helping Ampex resolve.

Gene held several dry runs to prepare everybody for the design review. He did so, Heller remembers, never having seen the actual device or the box itself. Gene, nonetheless, began to grill Heller with the kind of questions that would make you think he had been studying the thing for years. He asked one killer question after another, all exactly on the mark, and of course given Gene's reputation, Heller was terrified. But whenever Gene asked a tough question Heller couldn't answer, Gene would say, "Ah, they are not smart enough to ask that, so don't worry."

With the issues clearly defined, Heller went back and prepared answers for all the tough questions Gene had asked. Again, Gene was right, as the customer never asked those tough questions. Eventually, Heller and his team resolved all the problems on the recorder, but they were difficult design problems and required intense efforts to resolve the issues. Every day as they tackled the design, Heller reminded himself how amazing it was that Gene had grasped the intricacies of a very complicated device without ever having seen it before.

Gene, and everyone in his AIL management group, made it a point to know the mindset as well as the corporate and personal psychologies of their counterparts in the other companies of the USD-7 consortium. Despite the differences in size between AIL and these companies, Gene encouraged his AIL group members to be mindful of the differences between the sub-contractors and to make their work together seamless. He also always behaved as if AIL was the equal of the other companies in scale and capability. To Gene, there was no reason to behave deferentially.

Gene also kept close watch on what the project was producing. It might have been in the interest of some companies to build a component that was a lot more advanced (and, correspondingly, more expensive) than the project required; in such a circumstance, that new equipment could be a stand-alone product that might belong to another company outside the USD-7 project. Gene exercised absolute control over the work being done, confronting other members of the consortium, when it was necessary, to keep the project focused and on target.

He and his group met in person with the representatives of the other companies to discuss every decision of any significance, and they traveled to each company at least once a month for updates and to walk through the relevant work areas and see what was physically happening. That was how Frederick Terman had done it at RRL, keeping a finger on the pulse and cutting through the waves of paperwork that flooded back and forth. When the companies headed toward conflicts with one another, Gene tried to get in front of the problems. Rather than impose his own packaging specifications on all the companies, each of which had their own proprietary packaging standards, he got the packaging men from each company together and let them decide if they thought there ought to be a uniform standard for the project. When he learned the Air Force was facing a budget cut, he broke down the effect of several possible cuts that might be inflicted on the USD-7 project, so that as soon as the actual figures came in, he was ready to assign cuts to each of the participating companies and was also ready to work with them to nevertheless maintain the project's momentum. Conversations took a different shape with each company. All of this orchestration was, in truth, only a small part of the effort. Gene spent 80 percent of his time actually coordinating between the project and the Air Force.

In 1959, Hector Skifter, the founding president of AIL, accepted the position as the principal deputy to Herb York, then Director of Defense Research and Engineering at the Pentagon. When Skifter decided to leave Washington in 1961, he recommended Gene as his replacement. It was a great opportunity for Gene, but nonetheless it gave him pause. The work at AIL was still exciting and challenging, but he saw that accepting the open position would put him squarely in the company's management. While this was good for his paycheck, it would mean less hands-on work, and hands-on work was where his passion laid. He felt good about his time with AIL to that point, and with good reason: Thanks to his leadership and contributions, the company was on stable ground, as he and others had helped it to diversify and survive to become a terrific contributor to defense electronics; the organization was among the leaders as a system integrator and a prime contractor with his USD-7 and STAR programs; AIL's size had doubled thanks to the USD-7 program, and the company was now on a sound footing. He was busy surveying these accomplishments and thinking that he was ready for a new challenge when York called.

York's offer was to come to Washington and to join the team working under Defense Secretary Robert McNamara and President John F. Kennedy. Gene didn't know York personally but he knew that York had studied at UC Berkeley under the Nobel-winning physicist Emilio Segré, and that meant that York would value the intellectual thinking Gene would be able to bring to the role. York had also gone on to become the first director of Livermore Nuclear Weapons Lab, and from there, he'd come to Washington to start the Defense Department's Advanced Research Projects Agency (DARPA), which he had run for a year-and-a-half before being named Director of Defense Research and Engineering. Those were credentials Gene respected. He also saw potential in the position, ways he could move the Defense Department to a new level of sophistication, better able to harness the power of exciting new technologies which were rapidly coming available. He had made a huge difference at AIL; now he saw an opportunity to make a huge difference on a larger, more national scale. He accepted the position.

There were, however, considerable concerns about how the move would affect his family. The salary of the new position was $18,000, a sharp drop from previous positions. With six children and a gaggle of horses, this mattered. Furthermore, Betty was worried about the how the older girls would respond to a change in schools at such difficult ages: Sylvia was in high school at Friends Academy where she had just begun and was struggling to find her place. Sandy and Carol were on the cusp of going to high school and they had liked their school experience in Brookville. For the younger ones, the challenge was not as great. For herself, Betty loved the Brookville house. It wasn't losing the Brookville community itself, and it wasn't that the move would force them to downsize, given the realties of Gene's salary. It was that she loved the Brookville house as if it were a part of her, perhaps because it felt so much like the house she'd grown up in—large, rambling, unpretentious, warm, and full of laughter and children. It was the house in which Betty wanted to live the rest of her life, and she knew houses like that didn't come along often. Leaving the house in Brookville would be a wrenching experience.

As was her way, however, she was determined to look on the bright side. First, she was sure Gene wanted the job and would be happy at the Pentagon. Second, if they were all in Washington, and he didn't always have to go there for committee work, Gene might (she reasoned) be able to again spend a more significant amount of time with the family. Gene's workload and his complete commitment to whatever professional endeavors he undertook, had long ago rendered him something of a ghost in their family, appearing infrequently enough—the occasional weekend, the Cape Cod vacation—that he was something of a novelty to his children. The arrangement hadn't done much for his closeness to Betty, either.

Almost immediately after Gene's arrival, York had a heart attack and his illness forced him to leave the Defense Department. President Kennedy and McNamara then named Harold Brown to take over as DDR&E. That made Gene a political orphan and put him at risk of losing his new position almost before he had begun his work. When York left, Gene wanted to be sure that he kept his appointment and that he would be able to be effective under Harold Brown, who he had not known. Gene called Brown right away.

The Brookville, Long Island house—Betty's favorite.

Gene had met Harold Brown once before, at a small dinner party for an Italian physicist in New York not long after the war. At the time, Brown was still at Columbia University. Gene didn't remember Brown, but Brown, like everyone else, only needed to meet Gene Fubini once to remember him. Characteristically, Brown's recollection from that party was that Gene had been in the middle of everything, holding forth on every topic raised, and drawing people to him magnetically. He was, in Brown's initial opinion, surprisingly likeable.

Gene's call to Brown clearly made sense if he was going to be one of Brown's deputies. Brown, who had taken over the Livermore labs in California, could not start in on the Pentagon job immediately, but suggested some days when he and Gene might get together in Washington over the coming weeks. Gene, not to be deterred, said they should meet right away and that he would come to California for the weekend. Harold saw immediately that Gene's performance at the dinner party was representative: Gene was highly energetic, curious, quirky, and a bit lovable.

Gene wanted to be sure they would get along, and get along they did. Brown immediately felt as though he was being interviewed by a superior. He was also impressed with Gene's technical skills and insights. He was far from the typical Department of Defense appointment, a huge positive for Brown. Gene spoke about how important his family was to him, and he made an immediate connection with Brown's children. The children were still small enough that Gene could throw them up in the air, which had them laughing and squealing for more.

At the time of Gene's visit to California, Brown was only thirty-four and Gene, who would work for Brown, was fifteen years older. Brown had graduated from the Bronx High School of Science and had subsequently studied and received three degrees from Columbia University. Like Gene, he had received a Ph.D. in physics at twenty-one. After a short period of teaching and postdoctoral research, Brown had become a research scientist at the Radiation Laboratory that was connected to the University of California at Berkeley. In 1952, he had joined the staff at Lawrence Radiation Laboratory located at Livermore, California, becoming its director in 1960. Also like Gene, Harold had been the member of numerous committees and advisory groups in the 1950s and had been the senior science adviser at the 1958-59 Conference on the Discontinuance of Nuclear Tests. Despite their differences in age, Harold and Gene were great intellectual mates, and they soon became close personal friends. Their bond would last for the rest of Gene's life. Gene called their friendship perhaps the most fulfilling in his life.

Meanwhile, Betty searched for a home in Washington that could house all six kids, allow horses to be kept, ensure that the family could find adequate schools for the children, and be at least somewhat affordable. Betty did all the house hunting. Gene was by now too busy for such tasks and willingly delegated all this to Betty. It proved to be a difficult search, but Betty finally found a small house in a suburb outside of Washington, in Potomac, Maryland. The house lay just off River Road, a main route into D.C., on Bronson Drive. Thankfully, the home had enough land and a small barn in the back so that the horses could be kept on the property. The house itself was small for a family of eight, with just four bedrooms—which meant that the three older girls had to share a bedroom. The other children were distributed around, with Carol and David eventually each taking a turn being housed in a poorly heated, above-the-garage bedroom. But the house did provide a comfortable study for Gene off a screened-in porch, and there was a small back yard dominated by a huge weeping willow. Gene had a driver (one of the few perks in his new position), so Betty was worried less about his ten- to fifteen-mile commute to the Pentagon.

Potomac House—Fubini family home during the Pentagon years.

Gene had trouble understanding why the older girls were so upset about leaving their school and lives on Long Island. After all, weren't they keeping their horses? Wasn't Washington a fascinating city, and the Sidwell Friends School, where they were to be enrolled, a far better school than the one they'd come from? The crying and emotions from the older children were dismissed as "nonsense." Gene never seemed to have thought much about the effect that the move was having on the family.

Sylvia was already fifteen, Sandy nearly fourteen, and Carol a bit younger still. The transition was difficult for all of them and made easier only for Sandy and Carol by the ability to have horses, which was not only a pleasure in itself, but would provide an opportunity to bond socially, as horseback riding was popular in the Potomac area. None of the girls were particularly happy with Sidwell Friends School. Not only was it a considerable drive to reach the school, but it was a private school, and came with the usual private school cliques and pretentiousness. And of course, there was the matter of the many friends they had left behind.

Gene, now at the age of fifty, jumped into the Pentagon job with excitement, enthusiasm, and the passion of a much younger man. He was anxious to use the new position to effect substantial and meaningful change in short order. His first piece of business was to come to know Brown and McNamara, understand their agenda, and determine how best to be supportive of their aspirations.

Harold Brown was brilliant, although not in the academic way of Fermi. Still, Gene would often say later that Fermi was the only person he'd ever met whose intellect exceeded Brown's. Only in his thirties, Brown not only had the technical ability, but also a confident and pre-determined understanding of what he needed in a demanding job. McNamara was personable, urbane, accomplished, and also very intelligent. The Department of Defense—which had previously been know as the War Department—had become an organizational monster, growing in size and complexity beyond anything anybody could have imagined at the end of the war. McNamara had quickly sized up the issues with the department and had devised a plan to bring it under control. Part of his plan was to shift the focus away from the individual services, bringing it more firmly under the control of the defense secretary. He knew that efforts in this direction would create a battle within the department, including enormous resistance from the uniformed officers who did not wish to yield influence to politicians and nonmilitary men. Nor were they going to like the men, including Gene, who would have to implement this new approach. During the war, Gene had been a rogue individual among military men, and he had always been working for them in ways they could appreciate. Now he would be working for McNamara in ways the uniformed services would find threatening.

Brown and McNamara quickly recognized the breadth of Gene's ability and his responsibilities rapidly increased. His portfolio included reviewing all current defense weapons programs as well as vetting the appropriateness of new programs desired by the various services. To do this, much of his day-to-day activities involved listening to proposals on weapons systems from the various services. Major after major would come in with thick books of diagrams, graphs, and equations to explain ideas and proposals for needed budgets and investments. Some of these proposals were well thought-out, concise, and backed by fundamental scientific principle. All too often, though, the military was suffering from being on too steep a learning curve and was not yet able to demonstrate competence in its proposals. Much of the science of digital communications, electronics, and space/satellite technologies was too new, and too few of the men who came to see Gene were able to incorporate the science into their proposals. The result was often naivety of thinking, poor designs, and simply bad engineering.

Gene's understanding of system complexity was greater than anyone else who came before him to brief him. He was quick, insightful, and often ruthless in his comments, reactions, and conclusions. It was said that when he was at his most challenging he would wait for the large contingent of the military service members to file into the room, and wait for a presenter to set up an easel while he flipped through the first pages of their briefing books. Gene would then suddenly stand up, give back the book and say something as cruel and blunt as, "Go away," before walking out. He explained that at this time, with so much to be done, there was just no time or energy for mediocrity, and those who were not prepared did not deserve kindness. Gene quickly became feared throughout the Pentagon by those who had to present to him. His reputation for savaging presenters and expelling people from his office for weak or poorly planned proposals was legendary in only a few months. However cruel it may have seemed, it was undeniably a force for change.

Not all proposals, of course, were treated in this manner. Some were even accepted. Many included sound ideas and bold plans for ECM, communications, field systems, or satellite-enabled activity. For those with good ideas, Gene's questioning was intense and the dialogue often heated. This intensity of discussion made the proposals better, and the results were better for it as well. Gene made some enemies, he made nearly everyone uncomfortable, but he made the research better. For Gene, it was a fair trade.

The knowledge and passion for excellence that Gene possessed didn't take long to disseminate into the leadership of the services. Lt. Colonel John Marks at Strategic Air Command Headquarters in Washington got to know Gene in those early days, and he quickly realized that nobody with any power in the Department of Defense had ever been truly knowledgeable about electronic warfare. Now there was Gene. If McNamara needed to know anything about intelligence or electronic warfare, he went to Gene, and this fact gave Gene enormous prominence in electronic warfare community. Gene was always punishingly well briefed. He was also the most dynamic individual Marks would say he had ever encountered in all his years in the military.

Jack Ruina was representative of some who had a decidedly more mixed view of Gene. During a leave of absence from MIT, Jack served from 1959–1960 as the deputy for research to the assistant secretary of research and engineering, U.S. Air Force. He also served as Assistant Director, Defense Research and Engineering, Office of the Secretary of Defense, for a year and then, in 1961, he became Director of the Advanced Research Projects Agency. From Ruina's perspective, Gene always seemed highly erratic. He had all that energy. Nobody had ever seen anyone like that around national security or in the Defense Department. He wasn't just loud and outspoken; he was always moving, all different parts of his body going all the time. It made Ruina nervous. Anyone could tell Gene was smart, but Ruina thought he tried to be too smart for his own good. Gene, he felt, always had to have the ideas that came from the least likely direction—even if they weren't necessarily the ideas that worked the best.

Gene was everywhere inside the halls of the Pentagon. He would talk to as many different people in as many different disciplines as he could. As he had done at the RRL Lab and again at AIL, he knew that engineering value often came from the ability to integrate across systems and disciplines. To do this he had to be aware of what others were doing and be able to integrate this thinking into the combined programs that were not just technically sound but workable in a broader context. Gene also continued his outreach to others outside the Pentagon. When he was not traveling to installations out of the country, he was out frequently to California, across the river to the NRL in Maryland, and down to the rocketry operations in Huntsville and Redstone. He seemed to talk to everyone and no program or operation was too unimportant for his review. He asked to be briefed at every stop and seemingly about issues and programs well outside his assigned areas of responsibilities. But Gene saw the tremendous value in an omnivorous approach to knowledge and information.

At MIT, within its Lincoln Labs, he had come across J.C. Licklider's behavioral work and insights about interactive computing, natural language, time-sharing, and networking—the beginning of the thinking that would lead to what we now know as the Internet. Licklider was a true visionary, and Gene recognized that his ideas could be revolutionary. Gene saw that the applications of Licklider's ideas could revolutionize communications for not only the battlefield but for the whole of the Defense Department and beyond. Gene championed Licklider's work and promoted his activities to multiple audiences. Jack Ruina, who by now had taken over the Advanced Research Projects Agency, needed someone to drive a project on developing new methods for command and control. Gene traveled to Cambridge and persuaded Licklider to take the lead for the project. In comparison to the massive focus around nuclear delivery and the ancillary weaponry effects, this program was tiny. Yet Gene knew that it was just these kinds of seed projects, done under the auspices of the Defense Department's research arm, which could break open opportunities far more quickly than any commercial enterprise could manage. Gene sold Licklider on the opportunity, and he agreed to lead the project.

The work that Licklider and others were undertaking was representative of the broad-based research that Gene was advocating. President Kennedy rejected nuclear first strike capability programs and, at first, McNamara came out for a flexible, limited response strategy. But before long, the forces at work within the larger government were pushing for a strategic defense policy that prepared for unconditional nuclear warfare. Both Gene and Brown were constitutionally incapable of this sort of monomania, no matter how great the Russian threat must have seemed. Their answer wasn't to deter the pro-nuclear feelings of the government—to the contrary, they saw nuclear armament as crucial. But concurrent development of new and more effective conventional weapons systems with vastly improved command and control would, to their way of thinking, provide a vital second option.

Gene and Brown's insistence on a fallback of conventional weapons kept a wide variety of systems proposals flooding in. Most of them met untimely deaths at Gene's hands. His expedient approach may have cost him a few interesting projects but, he reasoned, he was more than capable enough to spot the great ones and most of the good ones. By this time of his life and career, Gene knew that his mind operated most efficiently and most effectively when it was operating at its fastest, and he naturally supposed that it made more sense for those around him to speed up than for him to slow himself down. When he saw a proposal that was anything but clear, concise, well-conceived, bold, and confident, he didn't hesitate to wave off the officer presenting with a curt, "I understand your argument and can state it to you and for you." When he began to respond to a presentation by saying, "Let me explain," officers knew they were in trouble and their proposal was either dead or in need of serious restructuring. Gene was who he was: impatient and abrupt, disdainful of carelessness and stupidity, and never afraid to give his unvarnished opinion. He knew he had made enemies, hurt feelings, and stepped on toes, but he didn't waste time worrying about it. There were far too many other things to be done, far too many genuinely talented minds to foster and encourage.

Reviewing proposals, setting strategy and priorities, dealing with the majors who tried to sell the proposals, discovering talent—it was all work that needed to be done, and it quickly became routine for Gene. Inevitably, most of the best proposals came in through side channels and less from the chain of command in the services; it was another example of the value of Gene's external network of close confidants and advisors he knew from industry. Today, of course, this kind of relationship between government decision-makers and the private industry seeking to sell their technology to the government would never be allowed. But at the height of the Cold War, it was all quite the norm. For example, Bert Fowler, still at AIL, was one of a number of people interested in developing and deploying moving target indicator (MTI) radar for the Army. Gene would champion these projects, working closely with Fowler and AIL, despite the fact that his having come from AIL might have placed his objectivity in question. For Gene and others, the science and the results were all that mattered.

Robert McNamara had so many challenges when he first arrived at the Defense Department that he could not recall his initial meeting with Gene. He had left staffing to Harold Brown and was confident of Brown's ability to find good people. Inevitably, McNamara became aware of Gene and his abilities, and realized the value of a man who could explain the technicalities of science quickly and succinctly. McNamara noticed that Gene always seemed to be making the rounds of various offices, he was aware of all the various technological issues being addressed in the building, and his insights and knowledge were consistently invaluable across a variety of areas. One of Gene's real talents was his willingness to take an aggressive, active role in questioning conventional wisdom and suggesting alternatives. These were qualities McNamara valued immensely.

He pushed the science to new levels, of course; this was his area. But his intellect and confidence made him unafraid of expressing his opinion, loudly, in areas outside his expertise. In the coming years, McNamara would rely often on Gene's fearlessness and sense of objectivity.

Gene was, in fact, willing to confront anybody (including Harold Brown himself, or any of his other close associates) if he saw flawed reasoning or thinking. Gene's boldness was indiscriminate; indeed, for Gene, superior military rank, pay grade, or managerial position was negated by lack of intellectual rigor. He was more than happy to point out the errors, miscalculations, and missteps of senior uniformed officers, CEOs, or important experts in virtually any field. He would loudly call attention to the mistakes, and then begin his lecture with the familiar, "Let me explain." To Gene, it was his duty to make these corrections, and if he did so in what often seemed an unnecessarily blunt or brutal way, he did it without personal cruelty. His purpose in life was, quite simply, to correct errors and misperceptions. Those who were left hurt, embarrassed, or even publicly humiliated by the encounters would be, Gene supposed, more careful next time.

What was most amazing was how, despite frequently playing role of adversary to the uniformed military, Gene established and maintained warm relations with many officers, even beyond those in technology positions. He walked around the Pentagon like he owned it, but even in that competitive, pressurized atmosphere he had outstanding relationships with people of all ranks and backgrounds, especially on an individual basis. Certainly, it was because they respected his intelligence, but it wasn't intelligence alone; there were plenty of smart people in the building. What distinguished Gene was that, even as he could be cruel and dismissive of others' feelings, he liked people. He was curious about people. This made him unusual not just in government, but in life. He would genuinely engage with those he met, and this genuine attention made most people feel flattered, even when what was coming out of Gene's mouth may have been challenging and potentially unkind. He wanted to help others get their work done, even if he had nothing to do with their work. If Gene thought he could help in their lives, he offered to help and, most importantly, delivered on those promises.

The truth was that once colleagues met Gene's standards, he could be among the best allies and mentors around. For instance, in 1963, Harold Brown asked Dan Fink to come down and interview for DD&R Deputy position in charge of strategic suppliers. Despite a great career outside of government, Fink knew he was right for the job and knew he would take it, if and when it was offered. He and his wife, Toby, liked Massachusetts, and he was in a comfortable private industry; he had no compelling reason to be seeking a new job. Nonetheless, there were a handful of interesting components to the situation. To start with, Fink felt that if one was asked to serve their country, one served. The position was also a rare chance to be among incredible minds with nearly limitless budgets. And, not least of all, the word "strategic" was in the job title, and in the defense world that meant nuclear. To say he was enticed is an understatement.

Fink went to Washington and met with Brown, McNamara, and everybody else on the senior staff—except Gene. Gene, Fink recalls, was too busy to meet. How could it be that Deputy Director Brown had time, Secretary of Defense McNamara had time, but Gene could only hurry past in a cocky, run-walk that you didn't want to get in the way of? During the visit, Brown officially offered Fink the job, and Fink accepted, assuming he'd meet Gene at some later date. But as he was headed to the exit, he heard Gene yell down the hall to him. Here was Gene running down the hall toward him, saying, "We need to talk. Fly to LaGuardia with me tonight. We'll talk on the plane." It was not a request.

Fink, like many who'd had only short interactions with Gene, was prepared to dislike him. But during the trip, which involved changing at La Guardia for another plane to Boston, their conversation covered a wide range of topics and subjects. Gene was particularly interested in Fink's perspective on those he had met. Fink remembers saying that they were impressive, but all of them could all use a little humility. Gene laughed like hell about that. They were fast friends by the time they landed, and remained friends for years to come.

Everett Greinke was another example. He was still a young and inexperienced engineer with the Navy when he went in to present a weapons system modification to Gene. He knew Gene's reputation, and he went in prepared. Greinke remembers that he had hardly begun talking before Gene shocked him by saying, "That's not true! I know what you're talking about, and I know you're wrong. Actually, I think you have been lied to or you are lying to me. Don't continue, this briefing is over," and storming out of the room. Even by Gene's standards it was remarkable brief and unpleasant.

The experience was like a "drive-by shooting," Greinke recalled. He never knew what hit him, and then he was bleeding on the floor. When you're in the Navy (or any other branch of the military), you don't take a swing at Department of Defense big shots, but the thought crossed his mind that day. Who did this little scientist think he was to accuse, insult, and yell, and then rudely dismiss a team that had prepared so diligently for this briefing? In the military, you take the putdown from someone senior, and Greinke took it. But that didn't assuage his anger, which would have been great enough simply based on Gene's manner; it was even worse because Gene had been dead wrong.

Then something even more shocking happened: Two days later, Gene telephoned to say just that: he'd been wrong. He urged Greinke to return to present his ideas as soon as possible. Greinke hardly knew what to do, so he simply began to gather his materials again. Members of the Secretary's office never admit they are wrong, and they never follow up on an item like his. They just move on to the next topic; introspection and course-correction are not typically on the agenda, and neither are admissions of wrong-headedness. When Greinke went back the next day he was on his guard, but immediately Gene repeated his apology and said that the fault lay with him. This time, Gene listened thoughtfully to the proposal. In fact, it was a good proposal, and Gene said so, and they talked it out and went forward with it. Greinke was both stunned and impressed by the entire experience: apologies, acceptance of responsibility, and contrition were all qualities seldom seen in the Pentagon. Greinke wouldn't have thought it possible, but two days after their original meeting he and Gene became good friends, and again the friendship endured.

During a Marine landing exercise, in the early 1960s, on the beach at Camp Pendleton in California, Gene met Norm Augustine under the table—literally. Augustine was an aeronautical engineer and businessman who was becoming very active on armed forces committees. This demonstration was a simulated water assault out on the beach, and tables and chairs had been set up for invited observers, guests and dignitaries. As the simulation proceeded, the pre-planted explosives in the sand (meant to indicate the incoming Navy-supported bombardment) began to explode all around. The charges were either too large or the observation stands set too close, but either way the beach suddenly exploded around the observers showering them with sand and small beach debris. Everyone dove under the tables seeking cover. Here is where Gene met Augustine, under a table seeking shared cover. Augustine had heard of Gene, and knew who he was immediately: there were only so many small scientists with big reputations walking around shouting in thick Italian accents. Augustine was to become one of the leading figures in the defense industry, and would later plot the growth of Lockheed Martin into an industry powerhouse. Gene and Augustine would become colleagues for many years to come, always striking a clear contrast: the short, slightly dumpy Gene and the tall, aristocratic Augustine.

In 1960, Alain Enthoven moved from the RAND Corporation to the Department of Defense, where he held several positions before being appointed, by then-President Johnson, to the position of assistant secretary of defense for systems analysis. In 1965, a young chemist named John Deutch, who worked with Enthoven, said in an unguarded moment amongst several DOD executives that the conflict between the analysts and the military was a case of arrogance versus ignorance. While others might have taken offense, Gene loved it and sought Deutch out. He welcomed the debate with Deutch and, rather than take up what might have been adversarial positions, they became friends. At times, each thought the other was a bit ignorant and too smart for his own good, but their friendship endured and evolved over the years. Deutch went from Defense to the Department of Energy and eventually to the CIA. Gene was also close to Johnny Foster, who'd been an RRL advisor to the Fifteenth Air Force in Italy and since then had come up through the Lawrence Lab and been on advisory committees with the Air Force, the Army, and now ARPA. Brown, Ruina, Fink, Garwin, Deutch, Foster, Gene himself, and others like Augustine and Fowler, all were accomplished engineers and scientists. Perhaps part of the reason Gene was able to make so many friends despite his manner was that all these men had at least some background in science. Just as many had foreseen, by the 1960s the defense industry was filled with scientists and technologists who had real authority in the national security affairs of a powerful nation. And Gene was squarely at the core of this group.

12

The Defense Department and Intramural Conflicts

*I*n October 1962, U-2 surveillance flights over the western part of Cuba photographed missile bases being constructed—bases that belonged to the Soviets. With Soviet nuclear missiles positioned so closely to the U.S., the country was sent into a panic. The Cuban Missile Crisis was born. Gene simply disappeared from his Potomac home in the dead of night, and was not heard from for more than ten days. Communications were minimal between Gene and the family, and Betty just told the kids there were important matters that their father had to attend to. It is telling that none of the children found it strange that their father would leave for ten days without notice or explanation; it was not out of the ordinary.

Gene worked twenty hours a day to be sure McNamara and Kennedy were kept abreast of Soviet movements and intentions. He personally oversaw much of the defense intelligence flowing to McNamara from the Pentagon. He also worked as part of the team that ensured that American military movements, in response to the crisis, were revealed to the Russians only in the way and to the degree that American tactics required. As soon as it became apparent that missile-launching sites were going up at night, and later that missiles were being transported at night, night reconnaissance became essential. The only plane available to perform that reconnaissance had to fly at altitudes well within range of Russian SA-2 anti-aircraft batteries. The problem was that these planes had no countermeasures equipment. Gene, working with Alex Flax and George Steeg at Sanders, jury-rigged the planes with pods and jammers by cobbling together the equipment in functional configuration and installing it immediately.

In less then two weeks, the crisis was over. The strategy discussions with Dan Fink and the debates over intelligence gathering with the CIA went on just as they had before the interruption. But something important had shifted as a result of the crisis: the doctrine of no nuclear assault on cities slipped away, and the idea of mutually assured destruction—as a military tactic—gained support. Production of Minuteman and Polaris missiles accelerated, and development toward multiple independently targeted re-entry vehicles progressed rapidly. The renewed nuclear threat became the new pulse beneath the reassertions of routine. Strategic nuclear determent continued to consume more and more of the time and budgets; the more conventional command and control, as well as ECM measure, remained important, but began to lose their status as anything like a centerpiece of defense. Space and communications via satellite became increasingly important, and Gene adapted as best he could to the new priorities.

Gene re-engaged in the cycle of Pentagon life. Change, as always, was to be expected. In 1960, Cyrus Vance, a forty-three-year-old Wall Street lawyer, joined the Pentagon as the General Counsel for the Defense Department. Two years later he became the secretary of the Army. Gene and Vance quickly became close confidants and colleagues, because so much of what Gene did in terms of program direction was to the benefit of the Army. The Army was a major source of investment, particularly around command and control systems, integrated field operations in particular theaters, and new communications techniques. Vance was aristocratic, smart, and unassuming. Once again the contrast between Vance and Gene was striking, but the relationship developed and the friendship grew. Even upon his initial arrival into the department it was clear to Gene that Vance was going to be a powerful force. As was standard practice, Gene reached out to him early on, and remained close to him throughout his time at the Pentagon.

The influx of proposals resumed its steady stream, and as worthwhile proposals surfaced, and as many advanced toward at least initial development, Gene had to select which proposals should now be carried to full implementation. In making selections, Gene tried to honor the disciplined analysis template that McNamara's systems analysis approach called for. These decision templates attempted to organize all the various aspects of a given decision into specific, definable tradeoffs and ensure that all the relevant aspects were weighed to maximize impact and minimize risks. In this same spirit, Gene would later say that he developed his own selection template, which argued: "The very best proposal, even if feasible, will not stay feasible. The second best will cost too much, take too long, and require too much logistics support. Take the third best; it will work and keep working."

In truth, Gene admired the departmental reorganization McNamara had accomplished in so short a time. Although it is unclear whether he bought fully into McNamara's belief that civilians could generally analyze military matters more effectively than the military, he did believe the services lacked objectivity and were far too parochial in their interests. There was no way that the services could have the technological know-how of the scientists and engineers who came from a civilian background, and they could never have the integrated perspective so critical to McNamara's vision. McNamara's views, while necessary in light of the escalating costs of weapons and the technology explosion that was refining future defenses, were not calculated to please the military. The main source of conflict was related to inefficiency and the cost associated with it. The military believed that overlaps between programs with narrow applications were inevitable. This inefficiency led to greater expense of both money and manpower; no one disputed that. But the military saw those costs as justifiable, given the defense needs of the country. McNamara believed otherwise. He employed a bevy of systems analysts, most notably Enthoven and Smith, who calculated to the penny the cost-versus-performance of every project, and used this data to prioritize the selection of programs. To most career military officers, this was the worst kind of bean-counting bureaucratic idiocy; to the McNamarians, it was a maximization of resources, resulting in the best defense system possible. A culture of conflict and debate was therefore inevitable in the overall management of the department.

While Gene and others embraced McNamara's vision, it didn't necessarily make things easier for any on the senior staff. Tensions with the services were very high. Gene sympathized with the military, but with space-based systems becoming a priority second only to nuclear weapons, cost-benefit equations were unavoidable. Gene was seeing $18 million contracts balloon to $150 million or $200 million, and while the original contract might open avenues of research that justified soaring costs, there was still a point at which somebody had to say, "No."

Gene grew to be a bit more of a politician, as well, which was probably inevitable given the environment. Gene did not want to risk his own authority in the wrong arena and overstep his area of direct control. However, he had to be wary of being too dogmatic, and softened his program review stance as he tried to put together consortiums of services, external defense contractors, and Defense Department research staff to bring needed programs forward.

For example, he chose to avoid the entire debate around the need for anti-ballistic missiles. This was a battle not easily won on the merits of the science or the engineering alone. This was to be a dispute based on emotion (not Gene's area of expertise) and politics (not his area of interest), and it had a growing public profile. Dan Fink was going to advocate the need for such missiles, and McNamara was always going to be against it, objecting on grounds of cost, logistics, and other higher priorities of the department. All sorts of politicians and popular activists were weighing in. Gene recognized a dispute in which his voice would have no effect except to make enemies of people on one side or the other.

Gene was never one to shy away from a fight, however, and he, Brown, and others were involved in some of the most contentious weapons decisions of their time. For example, Gene and Brown had a number of major showdowns with the difficult, sometimes-brilliant General Curtis LeMay. In 1957, LeMay was named Vice Chief of Staff of the SAC, and when Thomas White retired in 1961, he was elevated to the position of Chief. The new management philosophy of Secretary McNamara contrasted harshly with the more varied and expansive views of the joint chiefs of staff under then-Chairman General Maxwell D. Taylor. LeMay, trying to implement the Air Force's varied approach to delivery of nuclear and convention weapons, found himself at constant odds with the technology leaders at the Pentagon. In his four years as chief, LeMay argued strenuously for new air weapons such as the Skybolt missile and B70 bomber, and against the swing-wing fighter plane, the TFX. He lost all these battles, and the major reason was Gene Fubini, working quietly but effectively in the shadows.

The B-70 had begun with research and development studies in 1955, and was to be the Air Force's long awaited large, long-range strategic bomber. Using new technology in materials and engines, it was going to be designed to fly at Mach-3 and carry nuclear as well as conventional weapons. At the time, the B-70 was thought to be a natural successor to the B-52. It was designed to be nearly 200 feet in length and have a height, at the tail, of more than thirty feet. It would weigh more than 520,000 pounds, and require a minimum crew of four: pilot, copilot, bombardier, and defensive systems operator. It utilized a large delta wing and six, G.E.-designed turbojet engines in a large pod underneath the fuselage. The wing was swept at about sixty-five degrees and the wing tips were folded down hydraulically to improve stability at the aircraft's supersonic speeds. A large canard near the front of the fuselage with a span of over twenty-eight feet was required for stability. In addition to its sharply swept delta wings, the B-70 had two large vertical tails. The aircraft was to be fabricated using advanced materials like titanium and brazed stainless steel. The airframe would be manufactured in a "honeycomb" fashion, which would withstand the external fuselage heating that would accompany sustained high Mach number portions of the flights.

But the B-70 proved to have limited maneuverability at high altitudes, making it easy to track and for an enemy to intercept. The weight and drag of the plane also limited its range. The airframe had a radar signature that was easy to detect, which also made it vulnerable to land-based surface-to-air (SAC) missiles. Indeed, as the Federation of American Scientists concluded in its summary of the program: "The B-70 was an aircraft which fulfilled the criteria it was designed to meet, but whose mission had been eliminated by defensive threat technology."

In 1961, the Defense Department shut down the B-70 program. President Kennedy announced that the program was to be reduced to research only, citing high costs (more than $700 million per prototype) and the vulnerability of the plane to more modern countermeasures. In a classic case of the dominance of the tradeoff analysis McNamara thought was so valuable, the Defense Department (not the Air Force) had determined that ICBMs were more cost effective method of delivering a nuclear payload because they were less vulnerable and were cheaper operationally. Gene was at the center of this analysis, and he among others killed the B-70.

The Strategic Air Command wanted the B-52 to carry an air-launched nuclear ballistic missile. Development for such a missile, named the Skybolt, had been initiated in the late 1950s. Studies at that time showed that it was feasible to air-launch ballistic missiles from high-flying strategic bombers. The Air Force awarded development contracts to Nortronics (guidance system), Aerojet General (propulsion), and General Electric (re-entry vehicle). Full-scale development was approved in January 1961, and the first drop tests of non-powered Skybolts occurred later that year. Powered and flight tests began in April 1962. Unfortunately for the program, the first five tests were all failures.

Despite considerable lobbying by the SAC, General LeMay and the many large and important defense contractors involved, Gene was highly skeptical about the program. The missile had substantial technical difficulties and it was well behind schedule; indeed the merits of the project thus far made its elimination a no-brainer. Only the intensity of the lobbying in its favor made the decision over its future a controversial one. Ultimately, Gene came to feel strongly that the program should be eliminated. Despite the military's fondness for it, the program was shut down on the very day of the first successful deployment trial of the new missile.

Weapon development was always a difficult and politically charged process. The need to embrace McNamara's cost/benefit vision with the conflicting and politically driven requirements of the services, while also ensuring appropriate use of rapidly evolving technology, created formidable design tasks. Gene became highly skilled at navigating these waters.

The Tactical Fighter Experimental (TFX/F-111) program was one of the most controversial and difficult programs of the early 1960s. McNamara wanted to commit the Navy and Air Force to a single development program that held out the prospect of saving in excess of $1 billion in design costs in an effort to build a multipurpose tactical fighter/bomber capable of supersonic speeds. The Navy and Air Force were committed, much against their will, to this Defense Department/ civilian-inspired program that called for developing a single aircraft to fulfill multiple missions. The F-111 was going to have to give the Navy a fleet-defense interceptor while the Air Force wanted it to be a supersonic strike aircraft. Brown and Gene were charged with the process of melding these often conflicting objectives into a common design process. It was a messy development process and ultimately the requirements of one military branch—in this case the Air Force—came to dominate the design requirements. The plane eventually got developed and deployed.

Despite the controversy surrounding its creation, the F-111

achieved one of the safest and longest operational records of any aircraft in Air Force history. The F-111 saw action in different forms, in a widely varied number of locations, and was a stalwart of Air Force defense for many years. In retrospect, the joint requirements were nearly impossible to satisfy. The Air Force became dominant in the development and then the Navy was left to try and retrofit the program in a way that would allow carrier-based naval operations. The naval aircraft version was never placed in production. The Air Force program was produced in a variety of models and the plane endured, in various forms, until the mid-1990s.

Gene influenced these programs and others like them by keeping his focus on issues within the Defense Department and outside the public view. He found he operated most successfully when he influenced events below politically observable levels. He preferred the behind-the-scenes role where he could make change happen out of the glare of public debate, away from the necessity for spin. Gene never sought, nor really wanted, the public recognition for his efforts. His goals were their own reward: the creation of effective, efficient programs and systems that made his country safer and more secure; and the respect of his peers and colleagues within the network of scientist and technologists. In the value Gene placed on this group's approval and admiration, in his devotion to their principles, and in the emotional relevance they held for him, they were—perhaps even more than Betty and the children—his family.

As McNamara cut the budget, or cut its growth to make available more funds for the competing interests of the nuclear determent efforts as well as the increasing conflict in Vietnam, Gene had to manage even more effectively. Gene's cost-cutting aphorisms became the core principles of how to manage Pentagon technology programs: "People innovate; product development processes don't." "Always insist on fixed prices, incentives, big penalties, and corrections of deficiencies." "Remember that a worried contractor is a better contractor." "There is an American syndrome that says one should initiate a program even if others say it cannot be done, and even if it costs too much. Avoid such programs at all costs."

Kennedy nominated Gene to Assistant Secretary of Defense for Intelligence and Research & Development in June 1963, stepping in for John Rubel. Now, two years after joining the Defense Department and only eighteen years after becoming a naturalized citizen, Gene was to go before the Senate to be confirmed as one of the most central players in U.S. Defense efforts.

Gene's confirmation hearings before the Senate Armed Service Committee in late June 1963 were dominated by then-Chairman Senator Strom Thurmond. It was a raucous affair. Thurmond asked about Gene's membership in an Italian student fascist group, obtusely implying that a Jew who had fled from fascism, fought for the Americans, and now served in the Defense Department with highest security clearance, was in reality a former Nazi and maybe a communist. Gene calmly stated that he had indeed joined such a student fascist society, because his failure to do so would have put him risk of not only social and academic ostracization, but also imprisonment. Gene told Thurmond such membership "was almost compulsory" if one wanted to study. This further infuriated Thurmond, who seemed aghast that Gene was not more contrite about his affiliation with the group. Thurmond asked in great detail how it was that someone so newly arrived in the U.S. was on the front lines in the Allied war effort providing radar countermeasures, acting with free reign with high security clearances. Thurmond implied that Gene was not to be trusted and was possibly an agent for the Italians or the Germans.

Gene, ever the realist, just let the facts speak for themselves. Thurmond went further to ask about the circumstances of Gene's immigration to the U.S., how much money he had upon arrival, and his means of travel. Gene again answered factually, without emotion, but later would say that Thurmond's questioning was an invasion of privacy, hurtful, and mean-spirited. Gene also later said that the confirmation experience was one of the reasons he was always so careful about conflict of interest and never desired any future public office. Despite his cool handling of the process, he came away from it determined never to repeat the experience.

The Senate panel confirmed Gene, although Thurmond remained steadfastly opposed to his appointment. He was the only senator to vote against Gene.

Gene receiving Department of Defense citation in Pentagon with Susan, Betty, and Carol (1963).

Four months after Gene's confirmation as assistant secretary of defense, President Kennedy was assassinated in Dallas. The shock to the nation was profound, and the shock to the defense world and to Gene may have been even greater. The changes in the defense world and within the Pentagon were immediate.

Among the changes that followed the assassination was the addition of new personnel to the Pentagon. President Lyndon B. Johnson appointed Cyrus Vance, then-Secretary of the Army, to the post of Deputy Secretary of Defense. Gene had befriended Vance when he first arrived as counsel to the department, and had continued a warm working relationship with him. Vance found this association helpful, as he was not technically oriented. There were many subjects on which the two of them would naturally converse. Vance, like many in the Defense Department, often had to grapple with the very difficult and complex issues that new technologies introduced. Gene could naturally help with this.

Gene and President Lyndon Johnson (1963).

Vance vividly recalls just such an occasion. As he related to others later, he said it summarized much about Gene, his desire to educate, his willingness to confront nearly anyone, and his unique personality. Gene had been asked to Vance's conference room to help Vance and several very senior admirals and generals understand a specific military space program. Gene decided that as a group they first needed a basic understanding of the principles of astrophysics. Just as Gene began with his, "Let me explain," Vance got a phone call he had to take, and he told the rest of them to continue and left the room.

When he returned, he found Gene standing on the conference table and directing the admirals and generals, who were walking attentively in circles around the room. One highly decorated general told Vance with grave seriousness, "We are satellites revolving around the earth. Fubini's teaching us how a satellite can remain stationary over a rotating body."

Soon McNamara's attention, and much of everyone else's, went to Vietnam. Yet, an underlying issue, both with Vietnam and more fundamentally in terms of overall defense policy, was the Russians' nuclear capabilities. It followed that intelligence and the ability to monitor Russian activity was at the core of U.S. defenses. And the importance of this component set up one of the great debates of U.S. national security: Who should be responsible for the oversight of reconnaissance?

Land-based electronic-enabled intelligence sites around the world gave increasingly comprehensive understanding of Soviet radar, radar-controlled weapons systems, and missile control systems. The CIA had enabled many of these monitoring sites to be put in place and had supplemented this activity with "human assets"—agents on the ground. However, technological improvements had made overhead reconnaissance from satellites extremely effective and satellite imagery had become increasingly critical. The need for such satellite reconnaissance was particularly acute because the government has lost the ability to use U-2s in Russian airspace. McNamara wanted satellite production and satellite intelligence management transferred from CIA to the DOD's National Reconnaissance Office. The CIA disagreed and felt that their responsibility extended to oversight of all satellite reconnaissance.

John McCone, then-Director of the CIA, had an independently powerful constituency, and the CIA had not only developed the U-2 but also (with Advanced Research Projects Agency, under York) the Corona satellite program. McCone reasoned that because the CIA was going to have responsibility for deciding where to target reconnaissance, and because they claimed first call on interpreting the resultant intelligence, the CIA ought to be in charge of developing future satellites. McNamara, who didn't want to get the middle of the issue, was prepared to serve CIA intelligence gathering needs but insisted that the Defense Department develop the hardware and that all strategic intelligence flow through a single coordinating filter at the department in the National Reconnaissance Office (NRO). There was logic to both sides, but logic doesn't necessarily prevail in Washington. Gene was going to have to advocate McNamara's position.

Joe Charyk, then-Under Secretary of the Air Force, tried to set up a governance agreement defining the role of the NRO, and neither the Air Force nor the CIA were happy with the proposed arrangements. Complicating the issue was the fact that the Air Force had its own launch vehicles and burgeoning satellite program, and it wanted in on the debate, too. The CIA was trying, without success, to advance the Corona program to a next stage. The situation was muddled at best, and needed clarification for the good of the country. Gene, regardless of whether he could argue the relevant science, initially lacked authority to get real attention from either McCone or the Air Force. But when he became the principal deputy as well as an assistant secretary, he was anointed as Brown's right-hand man and therefore had greater access to McNamara. Now, Gene had more authority, and when Charyk left for the private sector, Gene became central to the debate.

It was a Byzantine conflict. The science arguments were numerous and were being used by all sides in the debate over who had responsibility. Everyone involved could see that it would be an ongoing source of major program activity for years to come. It wasn't always clear what the sides were or even, after a time, how many sides there were. On top of that were the personalities of those involved. Gene consistently ran up against John McCone's second-in-command, Marshall Carter. He seemed to dislike Gene, and the feeling was mutual. Fortunately, Carter, while important, was secondary to McCone, with whom Gene got along well. The debate was contentious, personal, and often ugly, but in 1965 Gene, McCone, Wheelon, and Vance finally crafted an agreement that everyone could live with.

Gene was also trying to bring discipline and oversight to the National Security Agency (NSA), where he wished to consolidate control of electronic intelligence. As Assistant Defense Secretary, he was the new civilian head of NSA and it was his job to get better results from the efforts of the agency. This time Gene's perspective on the oversight of NSA did not prevail. It was a rare defeat for Gene, who became used to getting his way where the NSA was concerned. For example, the Strategic Air Command wanted to hold onto its Ferret aircraft, and Lt. Colonel Marks of the SAC gave frequent briefings that argued for the SAC's needs over Gene's desire to control the Ferrets. Colonel Marks's briefings were good, but Gene contended that the NSA, from all its sources, could define the enemy command and control structure, and that there was no way the SAC could do that by itself. Knowledge of an enemy's command and control system was the most important intelligence you could garner. With the knowledge of the command mechanism it was far easier to find ways to interfere with the enemy and to hit the prime node rather than a less important sub-system. Marks fought long and hard, but by the end he was ready to admit that the country was better off having one agency in control of Signals Intelligence (SIGINT). It was a position he never thought he would or could be forced to adopt. Few, in Marks's opinion, could outthink or out-argue Fubini. Over time, he just wore you down.

While fighting the political battles behind the scenes, Gene also had to face the rising tensions and failures in his own home. Sylvia, as the oldest, was the first to emerge from childhood and, with an increasingly adult perspective, be forced to confront her father's unique personality and methods. She had few friends at Sidwell Friends School in Washington and, despite the fact that she hadn't been particularly fond of Friends Academy on Long Island, she resented that she'd been forced to move in the middle of her high school years. Gene was a taskmaster when it came to schoolwork, and now most of her interactions with her father were around schoolwork, college, and her plans for future study. At the Pentagon, forcing efficiency, discarding distractions, and focusing entirely on results had made him one of the most successful men in government; when he brought the same approach to his parenting, however, the approach was nothing less than destructive. He had a clear view of the ways his children needed to perform and behave to achieve specific practical goals: good grades, admission to good colleges, professional excellence. Emotions, human relations, and the very specific and powerful challenges of adolescence were, in Gene's eyes, distractions from these goals.

Upon graduation from Sidwell Friends, Sylvia applied to a number of women-only colleges, and like her mother chose Smith College. The other older girls, Sandra and Carol, were at Sidwell Friends School, as was Susan. Laurie and David were at the Maret School in D.C. In Laurie's case, there was simply no room at the overbooked Sidwell; David had been rejected because of developmental and learning issues.

Sylvia both loved and feared her father—feelings all the children would come to experience. Sylvia understood and admired his intelligence, and she understood the importance of the positions he held. She could trace the change in her relationship with him—indeed, in the entire family's relationship with him—to the move. On Long Island he'd been accessible and present, even if he was usually surrounded by AIL colleagues. In Washington, things were different. His work schedule meant that the children only saw him occasionally, as he normally returned home well after bedtimes. Their only real time with him was during their scheduled homework reviews, which hardly constituted bonding. These sessions, in fact, were a primary venue for Gene's volcanic anger. It bubbled up whenever he was frustrated, or when something slipped out his control. His sly, impish sense of humor, which once had been readily seen, now made few appearances, and his patience with the older girls had become minimal. The girls learned not to "poke the lion"; his roar was both powerful and painful. Though his anger was never expressed physically, his verbal assaults could be vicious and cruel.

Fortunately for the children, there was Betty. She readily and ably filled the vacuum created by Gene's absence, raising them, in effect, single-handedly. And she was always ready to soothe hurt feelings and mitigate Gene's outbursts.

Sylvia, as the oldest, saw more, heard more, and understood more about the tensions developing in the relationship between Betty and Gene. She knew that her mother was not a socially oriented woman, was painfully shy, and lacked confidence in herself. Betty was increasingly overwhelmed and stifled not only by Gene's innate intelligence, but his need to dominate all circumstances both within the home, in social settings, and in their married life. Gene's willingness to flirt with other women—and their obvious responsiveness to him—exacerbated Betty's insecurities. On occasion, Betty traveled with Gene on official trips when wives were expected to join their husbands, but these trips were worse than being home, alone, with Gene off to who-knew-where. She had no real friends among the other wives, did not enjoy shopping and gossiping with them, and hated travel generally. And, needless to say, the trips never afforded any time with Gene, as he was always involved with work. Traveling under these circumstances had, effectively, all the usual drawbacks of being at home without any of the comforts.

Gene's boorish behavior in restaurants and social gatherings alarmed Betty, but it was not her tendency to confront him. Amelioration was her preference and her strong suit, and she often found herself explaining away his behavior and apologizing to those he had insulted or offended. The children, too, learned to adapt to, rather than attempt to change, their father's behavior. When he stormed into a restaurant kitchen to confront the chef when food took too long, or when he made cruel, demeaning comments to their friends, they simply adjusted, apologizing if necessary, changing the subject if possible. They understood, even if only unconsciously, that their father's needs were dominant.

During this time Gene was traveling to bases overseas or to development labs around the country. Betty wasn't sure where he was or why he was going, or for that matter what he was actually doing. Like her children, Betty knew few, if any, of the particulars of what Gene was working on. Even when he was at AIL, whether it was outside committee work or work ten minutes from where they had lived, most of what Gene did was secret. Naturally, nearly everything Gene worked on was highly classified, so sharing particulars with his wife was never really an option. Nonetheless, the culture of secrecy bled into every aspect of their marriage, limiting the degree and depth to which husband and wife could be open with one another, and further cementing the dominance of Gene and his needs throughout their marriage. Starting with his work in Cambridge and the Radio Research Laboratory, Gene had never been able to come home and share what was happening at the heart of his work. Instead of discussing things and rejoicing in them or griping about them and then letting them go in the pleasure of conversation with her, he came home with nothing ordinary to talk about. Gene usually came home with an agenda, and his life with the children began to seem like a second job. His role was to challenge the children to do more, faster; study harder; and excel more quickly. Failure was not to be tolerated, and time for fatherly reflection and caring, comforting support, was not on the agenda, nor deemed necessary.

13

IBM and Connecticut

$\mathcal{T}$he Advanced Research Projects Agency (ARPA) was a place of singular pleasure for Gene. It was part of his oversight responsibilities when he became assistant secretary, and in the breadth and uninhibited scope of its research, the agency was an eye of genius looking out into the world in every direction with no preconceptions. It was the largest defense research lab in the world; its scope was unparalleled, its resources considerable. Spending time around ARPA was of Gene's greatest joys. It kept him intellectually sharp and allowed him the means to know where the leading edge of thinking was and how one might harness some of the world's most exciting technologies. These projects would soon encompass digital and satellite communications, space surveillance, the Internet, laser-guided munitions, stealth, and a bevy of other techniques and applications. ARPA was the counterpoint for Gene for the time he had to spend racing through program reviews and issues of short-term execution. ARPA was a connection to the best of his own scientific self.

At that other, far duller end of the creative spectrum, Gene contributed, as required, to McNamara's Planning-Programming-Budgeting-System with each year's Five Year Defense Plan and the several-times-a-year Draft Presidential Memorandum. Gene, like all other assistant secretaries, had to submit paperwork on readiness, information, and control tables, and development concept papers. The process was, in Gene's view, tiresome.

The Gulf of Tonkin conflict in August 1964 brought the Pentagon's already singular emphasis on Vietnam into even sharper focus. Johnson wanted a decisive victory in Vietnam and McNamara supported his president. However, there was, even at this early stage, a feeling in the government that the war (which was not even yet being called a war) was escalating and, effectively, not winnable. This was the view held by McCone and the CIA, and Gene—and, privately, perhaps even McNamara—suspected they were right. Gene began to think about his options, and whether the Defense Department was the best of them. As resources for things unrelated to Vietnam became more limited, the process of budgeting and planning became more stringent and, thus, more time-consuming for Gene. Reviewing his portfolio, Gene saw that the ARPA efforts around pure science and development were his first love, and he wondered if he might not secure a position in the private sector that would allow him that same focus on research. And then there was the issue of money, which had weighed on the Fubini family since the move to Washington. With six children (three already were near to entering college and the three more to educate and support) Gene and Betty had to build up greater family resources. To date, they had lived largely on savings accumulated at AIL, an unsustainable approach.

He pushed hard on a land- and satellite-based collection of communications and signals intelligence around the world, as well as photographic and radar imagery, and monitoring the Soviets for conventional and nuclear activity alike. He oriented and implemented activities in support of the Limited Nuclear Test Ban Treaty. He also watched for Chinese nuclear testing and provided support for intervention in the Dominican Republic. He brought every available intelligence resource to bear on Vietnam, including the moving target indicator (MTI) equipment that Bert Fowler was encouraging and that people like Jack Ruina had turned into a Side Looking Airborne Radar attached to a Grumman Mohawk. The Mohawk could fly at a safe distance and send out a lateral beam to trace vehicle movement on Vietnamese roads, a vast improvement over previous technology.

The Soviet Union retained overwhelming conventional troop superiority up and down the western edge of the NATO countries, but Gene believed some movement to remedy that, without nuclear confrontation, was taking place in Vietnam with the active theatre implementation of command, control, communications, and intelligence efforts. To build on that effort, Gene pushed hard to follow up Licklider's vision of accessible interactive computing so that field officers would get the full and immediate benefit of available intelligence and communications.

Aside from any other factors, a limited tenure in his current Defense Department position was an inevitable outcome of the manner in which Gene operated and the way that McNamara, Brown, and Vance used him in the Pentagon. He was a change agent, and as such he drove people hard, made tough decisions, and inevitably made enemies. In Gene's July 1965 *The New York Times* interview, which marked his departure from his position, the *Times* characterized Gene as "in many ways the driving force, if volatile, mainspring of the Pentagon's $7 billion a year research and development program."

Gene was also the front man for the debate on how best to get value from the huge research investments that the military was sponsoring.

The New York Times article pointed out that there was, not surprisingly, controversy over the way forward. As reporter John Finney stated, "Within the military and more recently in the Congress there was criticism that [Gene's] office was attempting to exercise excessive control over the research program, and was misguided by the mistaken assumption that a plateau had been reached in weapons development."

Gene countered with the view, stated to Finney, that "much of the criticism springs from the mistaken assumption that we are still fighting a war of strategy." Finney wrote that Gene believed "that weapons progress must not be gauged on whether a new strategic weapon, such as the Polaris or Minutemen, is developed."

Gene was prepared to leave the Defense Department, secure in the belief, as Finney states, "that development of new weapons is limited chiefly by man's imagination."

Gene was also a believer in simplification and efficiency in weapons, and resisted the temptation of investing in technologies as pure showcases of new technologies. Wrote Finney: "Part of the disagreement between Dr. Fubini and the military also arose, in his opinion, from different concepts over how to capitalize on new technology. New weapons, [Fubini] believes, should be made as simple and cheaply as possible to do the job and not necessarily as complicated as technology will permit."

If Gene's views were not controversial enough already, Gene closed the interview with a parting shot at military contractors by stating, "They do not always face up to their responsibilities in deciding upon the feasibility of technical proposals in their desire to obtain research contracts." Although Gene had never been one to sugarcoat his opinions, speaking so bluntly in *The New York Times*, of all places, was perhaps an indication of his eagerness to move on from the Defense Department.

In late spring of 1965, Gene began to consider alternatives to the department.

Southern Methodist University wanted him to be the Dean of its Engineering School. Gene was intrigued, as it was a chance to return to his academic roots and help build a powerhouse of engineering talent. Betty and the children, however, were not excited by the prospect of Dallas. Leaving her native New England had been one thing, but Betty loathed the idea of leaving the East Coast altogether. And nothing about the climate of Texas, meteorological or social, appealed to the older children.

Gene was also tempted by an offer of a tenured professorship at California Tech in Pasadena, California. However, it was just a professorship, and for Betty California sounded even worse than Texas. Not unsurprisingly, Gene got a number of lucrative offers from any number of defense contractors, but in all his public statements he made it clear why he would steadfastly refuse this direction: he would not work in an industry that answered to the government because he didn't want any appearance of conflict. On the other hand, not everything about returning to academia excited him. The disaster of his Harvard experience was front-of-mind. Moreover, he had always felt strongly connected to development and technology, and wanted to remain in contact with that world. He was being constrained by his own personal rules of what was acceptable from those who left the government. He was also leaving a lot of money on the table by refusing to consider the offers from defense contractors at a time he needed to rebuild the family's equity. He was stuck.

Then Tom Watson, the CEO and founder of IBM, came to Gene and said that he could make a huge difference at IBM. IBM was one of the country's largest and most successful corporations, and it was becoming involved with advanced technologies about which Gene knew an enormous amount. Many of these developments dealt with advancements in digital as well as circuit design, communications, and satellites. These were arenas where Gene had deep knowledge and substantial experience both with the basic research and with the applications. IBM was spending large amounts of capital and had staked its corporate reputation, and Watson's, on the idea of innovation. The well-known corporate mission of the company at the time was communicated to all employees by the simple mantra of "Think." IBM was at the forefront of computing technologies and it had begun to help revolutionize the way businesses, government, and to some degree individuals, managed their lives. IBM was also already a large and growing presence in contracting work with the government through their Federal Systems Division. Through the FSD, Gene would have a conduit back to the government through which he could remain connected to his existing network of colleagues.

Watson was offering a historic opportunity to Gene, and, like most big opportunities, it was fraught with risk; in this case, there was plenty for both Gene and Watson. IBM had prided itself on its ability to promote from within and was largely, if not exclusively, a place where executives spent their entire careers. This policy of mining internal resources did not allow for the inclusion of outsiders, so Gene's hiring would fly in the face of espoused corporate philosophy. It was also a very conservative, uniquely American, operating culture. This was the era of the white shirt, blue suit, dark tie, professional man at IBM. Everything from the dress code, to the manner of collaboration, to the method of presentations, was performed in a uniform way prescribed personally by Tom Watson and/or his brother Dick, the COO. The success of IBM's demanding and singularly unique conformist culture was heralded in the public press and was the subject of much academic study. Gene, with his compulsion to dissent and his habit of breaking rules in which he did not personally see value, was the very antithesis of this culture.

In Watson's opinion, IBM needed Gene, and he created a position of chief scientist specifically for Gene. Gene was intrigued with the idea of doing much of what he had done within the Pentagon within one of the largest and most respected corporations in the world. He agreed to Watson's offer. *The New York Times* and other papers ran prominent articles about Gene's leaving the Pentagon and going to IBM as its chief scientist, citing how unusual it was for such a high-ranking executive to come from outside IBM.

The family prepared to move to the New York area so Gene could be near the headquarters in Armonk where he would be working. While Gene certainly did not choose IBM for the money, he was to be very well paid, which must have been an enormous relief. This new income would allow the family to have a different standard of living than that they'd had in Potomac. Betty looked at many houses and was a bit shocked both by the size and prices of the homes in the area. She also had to be concerned about schools, because although Sylvia was now at Smith, and Sandra was at Michigan State, where she would be studying veterinary medicine, the others were still in primary schools. Carol was in her high school years at Sidwell Friends, Laurie was in middle school, and David, who had just gotten into Sidwell for his fifth-grade year, were now being uprooted again. Susan was already showing signs of being very bright, had skipped second grade, and needed to find a good school to foster her continued growth. Betty finally settled on Connecticut, and bought a large house at 57 Pepper Lane, in New Canaan. Truthfully, Betty didn't like the house, which she felt was too large, or the lot itself, which she felt was too small. The horses that had been a staple of their time in Potomac could no longer be housed on the property. This new house was more of a showcase home, with lots of entertaining space and little exterior land. Nonetheless, there were good public schools for Carol, Laurie, David, and Susan, and Gene's commute (no longer conducted by a driver, but by the impatient, distractible Gene himself) would only be thirty to forty minutes a day.

New Canaan House—Fubini family home during the IBM Years—Betty's least favorite home.

Though he did not say so at the time, another possible reason for Gene to leave the Pentagon was the death of his brother, Gino, in May 1965, of a heart attack. While Gene had already decided to leave the Pentagon, he did not submit his formal resignation until late June 1965, a month after the death of Gino. Gino had died at the age of 54, and as a lifelong chain smoker, he had never taken care to moderate his habit or his lifestyle; his heart problems were not surprising. Nonetheless, he was still a young man, and Gene had to recognize the parallels between his own lifestyle—too much work, too many cigarettes, not enough relaxation, little or no exercise—and Gino's. He immediately gave up smoking, much to the quiet relief of Betty, who had hated it passionately. Also, Gino's death must have reinforced the need to ensure some measure of financial security for the children. Gene and Gaby had been named co-executors of the estate, and Gino's four daughters were now Gene's financial responsibility. There was sufficient income from Gino's properties to serve the family's needs near-term, and of course longer term there would be a good deal of money from his mother Anna's estate when she passed, but as Gino's death had illustrated, life is unpredictable, and being prepared is key.

Anna Fubini, Gene's mother (circa 1965).

The emotional toll on Gene was hard to gauge. He and Gino had always had a complicated relationship. From birth, Anna had favored Gene to the near exclusion of Gino, and though their ages suggested that they should have been close, they never were. Certainly, Gene had loved Gino, but with Gene's hyperactive intelligence and need to be stimulated, he'd never found Gino terribly interesting. Gino's post-academic career was spent building homes on Long Island in the sort of repetitive manner that Gene could neither understand nor appreciate. Gino and Gaby lived a simpler life than he did, and he always seemed perplexed by Gino's willingness to be (in Gene's view) complacent and unmotivated. This view might have been challenged a bit when, at the time of his death, his obituary detailed the 1,000-plus homes and several Manhattan office buildings that Gino had built; but if so, it was a private revelation for Gene.

The prospect of the work ahead at IBM now held great promise for Gene. Four years in the Pentagon seemed enough for Gene and the wisdom of his decision seemed to be affirmed when Harold Brown chose to leave his deputy post in late September 1965, moving on to become the Secretary of the Air Force. IBM was an opportunity to be involved with the best of American companies as it developed a different order of scientific and technological momentum. Manny Piore, whom Gene knew from the Office of Naval Research, had been brought in to drive an institutional research effort, and the company had recently built several spectacular laboratories in Yorktown, New York, naming the labs for Watson himself. IBM had recently introduced its impressive and revolutionary line of IBM 360 computers. In a synergistic way, the 360 line of computers emulated the same degree of interchangeability and interactivity that Gene had been promoting with the military among command and control equipment and weapons. The 360 allowed peripherals to interact in a seamless manner with the mainframes, which provided a huge function change in IBM's efforts to remake computing as it was practiced to date. The 360 further distinguished IBM from its less innovative competitors and set the stage for even larger investments in technology in the future. IBM management was also beginning to recognize that it was going to go through a massive shift in strategy. Watson foresaw that IBM was going to have to evolve from a static design-assembly-marketing operation into a global marketing organization, anchored by innovative engineering and research. Gene was going to be one of the key, if not the key, leaders in this effort to remake IBM for the future.

With his departure from the Pentagon and arrival at IBM, Gene got considerable press in the public and even more in the technical press. He was invited to speak at more, and more varied, forums than he had addressed while at the Pentagon. In talks and interviews, he outlined in broad strokes the role of technology in history and his sense of what lay ahead. He was able to suggest a vision of a technology-enabled future that seemed to capture the interest of many, both inside and outside of IBM. He came up to speed quickly at IBM, and began to implement new research approaches while connecting through Piore to the numerous research activities at Yorktown. The transition at first seemed faster and easier than many had predicated.

The Pentagon was now physically farther away, but Gene was in Washington at least once a week and his access and influence in the Pentagon continued even though he no longer held a formal role there. Gene was quickly asked back onto numerous advisory committees and participated on a large number of industry panels. When not in meetings, he knocked on doors around the E-ring, including that of the new director of defense research and engineering, Johnny Foster, who had succeeded Harold Brown. In fact, it was Foster who asked Gene to persuade Bert Fowler to take over Gene's old job as deputy director research and engineering as Foster's deputy for tactical programs. When out of town on committee or IBM work, Gene kept up with other colleagues and connections, and cultivated new ones among both promising officers or civilian scientists and technologists. He saw McNamara occasionally and gave a fair amount of attention to McNamara's concept for an electronic surveillance border through the Vietnam demilitarized zone (DMZ). IBM was the beneficiary of Gene's connections, and a whole new beachhead of opportunity was now available to the Federal Systems Division (FSD) under the leadership of Bo Evans. The FSD began to grow at a rapid pace as a result. Gene's influence in the military world continued, his role merely shifted to a consultative one.

After he left the Pentagon in 1965, Harold Brown, in his new role as the Secretary of the Air Force, quickly reached out to Gene and put him back on the Air Force Science Advisory Board. Gene also signed on as chairman of the Science Advisory Committee of the Defense Science Board, after which Johnny Foster named him to the Defense Science Board itself in 1968. This appointment gave Gene formal access to know, once again, all that was happening within the defense community. He used the access to redouble his efforts to become familiar with all that was of importance in the various services, the National Security Agency (NSA), as well as the Defense Advanced Research Projects Agency (the renamed ARPA). Gene seemed most happy when he was back in Washington or out on Pentagon business.

One such advisory trip was to Vietnam in 1965. As he was returning from the carrier Independence, which was cruising seventy miles off the

South Vietnam coast, the plane, a twin engine Grumman C-1a Trader, developed an oil leak. Unable to return safely to the carrier, the pilot and crew diverted to the nearer air base in Danang. The plane limped to within a quarter mile of the base when the engine seized up, and the plane was forced to crash land in an urban area near the base. Gene and the crew, along with James Reston of the *New York Times*, and several other officials of the Navy Ordinance Office and the assistant chief of information for the Army, sustained only minor injuries. Gene was not worried about the crash, though it did strain his back, which would never fully recover. He even got a laugh out of William Holcomb, whose pet RA-5 Vigilante aircraft Gene had turned into a reconnaissance plane a few years before. "I can see the headlines," Gene told Holcomb. "Navy plot to kill Fubini succeeds." When the *Saigon Times* reported him as an electronic *wel*fare, rather than warfare, expert, Gene was only more delighted.

Gene's plane in Vietnam after 1965 crash.

In less than two years, Gene was promoted to an IBM Group Vice President, one of the six most senior positions in the company. He had been rewarded for his persistence at instilling a new way of thinking in IBM research, and for his ability to open the government market to IBM. He still was his old self—demanding, vocal, challenging—but the effect was more modest and not as directly fulfilling. Unlike the labs at AIL, or the Defense Department (despite the many layers at the Pentagon), at IBM there were multiple layers of people between the simplest thought and the most obvious action. Gene's ability to directly influence the outcome of his decisions and see the impact in the form of specific products was greatly reduced. Impact was slow in coming and while the process of new thinking was taking hold, in Gene's view the results seemed to lag horribly. Even more significant for Gene, the reality was that IBM's main goal had to be to meet sales targets, beat GE and Honeywell, and reward shareholders. New technology was useful and important, but the real driving force to everything they did was on the sales force and the manufacturing force. Gene increasingly felt he was a sideshow to the real action.

Not surprisingly, therefore, after having had so much authority and influence in an organization as large and political as the Defense Department, Gene felt increasingly uneasy at IBM. He had more political skills than most men, and those skills had served him well in the Pentagon. However, corporate politics were another game altogether, requiring patience and an understanding that sometimes the best ideas didn't necessarily carry the day. Gene did not feel comfortable with the rules of this new game, nor did he feel that it was an environment where, ultimately, he could flourish. He had been active in management while at AIL, but the smaller scale and start-up nature of those activities hardly prepared him for the much more complex and constrained atmosphere at IBM. Gene had liked being a unique personality in the Pentagon and had made it work to his advantage. Despite his responsibilities, he had been able to use his staff to remain an individual operator. There was little room for an individual operator at IBM. Despite Tom Watson's considerable support and active backing, Gene was tiring of the effort required to make change happen. Among the blue-suits, white-shirt culture of a corporate icon, Gene was fighting a losing battle. Further complicating the matter was the fact that the perception of Gene as an interloper had never really been overcome. Many executives were suspicious and resentful of Gene's having been brought in with such fanfare and so much power so quickly. What must have been frustrating and disappointing to Gene was that these other executives allowed their suspicions to create resistance to his new ideas. Gene could understand politics; allowing those politics to stand in the way of progress was, for him, unfathomable.

Gene had been led to understand that he was hired to use research and the considerable resources of the IBM to be a force for change and accelerate IBM's innovation efforts. Given free rein, he might have been able to accomplish this lofty goal. Since the war, research affiliates and companies like Lincoln Labs, and Missile Test and Readiness Equipment (MITRE) had grown out of the war effort and been at the forefront of new research for the Defense Department. But much of that work had, or could have, civilian application, and could or should have been controlled by interactive computing. The IBM 360 was a commercial breakthrough, but it was the tip of the iceberg and it hardly represented new science. Defense technologies were being released from security restrictions, and more would soon be released, and that meant enormous opportunities to change the way people lived. IBM was positioned perfectly, and Gene was positioned perfectly, to help that happen. Licklider envisioned a networked world and that was where IBM needed to be going: Individuals ought to have their own computers that could communicate with other computers.

How much imagination did that require?

Unfortunately for Gene and Licklider, these ideas were too revolutionary for their time. It would take another two decades of development and the work of younger, more entrepreneurial thinkers like Microsoft's Bill Gates and Apple's Steve Jobs to realize the potential of these radical ideas.

Possibly in reaction to the IBM corporate culture, and as a means of differentiating himself, Gene took to wearing clothes that were even more rumpled than usual. Gene favored comfortable shoes and soon could not be found wearing the more traditional shoes and suits which were the norm at IBM. He bought a red German Opel station wagon and proudly parked it in his executive parking space next to all the Cadillacs and Buicks of the other senior IBM executives. Everyone knew who owned the ugly, red Opel. Gene avoided the sales trips and other celebratory events at which IBM lavished praise on its sales people. For better or worse, Gene had distinguished himself yet again.

Gene tried to get Mel Saslow, his former AIL business manager from the USD-7 program, to come in and be his assistant, but IBM policy prevented the hire. Gene felt that other group executives feared he would develop a large research operation by hiring from the outside and would create an independent fiefdom. This fear, of course, was well founded, as it had been Gene's exact plan. He was told very directly that his hiring was the exception to the rule, not the beginning of any relaxation of the rule. He was to build from within. Undeterred, Gene called Herb York to suggest that York come in as IBM's chief scientist after Dr. Piore retired. However, York was a professor at Berkeley and was soon to accept the role of Chancellor of the University of California, San Diego, so his interest was limited.

Thwarted in his external hiring, Gene began to feel truly isolated. His one lifeline was Bob "Bo" Evans, the head of the Federal Systems Division, with whom he'd become good friends. Bo was, for the most part, Gene's only real friend during his time at IBM.

Evans had begun working at IBM in 1951 as a junior engineer after earning a bachelor's degree in electrical engineering from Iowa State University. In the 1960s, Evans had led the team that developed the System/360, or S/360, which allowed different applications to be run simultaneously. IBM invested $5 billion (more than $40 billion in current dollars) in the project at a time when the company's annual revenue came to $3.2 billion. Bo led what was in essence a "bet the company" move for IBM. It was at the time the largest, single private investment project ever undertaken by a public company.

"Prior to the S/360, each computer was a unique system. They were made to an individual customer's order, and there was no continuity from design to design," Colette Martin, the director of Z Series products for IBM, told CNET News.com before the mainframe's fortieth anniversary. "Prior to the S/360, they were single-application systems." Essentially the 360 allowed for a standard platform to be adapted to particular customer needs, including the addition of printers, keyboard, and monitors that were compatible with the mainframe. The product would revolutionize computing and the use of digital technologies. It also shifted IBM from a sales-only company to a more technology-driven, innovation-oriented enterprise. It required that the company move away from producing made-to-order, heavily tailored systems to a company with more continuous operations and more standardized manufacturing.

Following the success of the 360, Bo Evans was made president of IBM's Federal Systems Division (FSD). FSD interfaced with and sold to the government, principally the Defense Department. In his new position, Evans would have loved to have access to Gene when he was in the Defense Department. By then Gene had an international reputation for brilliance across a wide range of weapons and reconnaissance systems; he had a powerful influence within the Pentagon's decision-making circles, and he had acquired a voice in many areas of policy. Gene could have made things very much easier for Evans, but Gene was a guy, as his reputation also advertised, who had little time for sales calls from defense contractors. Bo had to wait.

Now Gene was in IBM and he and Bo became fast friends. Gene took to the taller, heavier man. The two, so different in size, yet so compatible in intellect and orientation, would spend hours and weeks together planning new forays for FSD and comparing notes on what was happening in the defense establishment. Bo had a photographic memory and Gene was simply brilliant. Together they formed a unique partnership that resulted in the doubling of the size of FSD, and a lifelong friendship.

Bo Evans would later describe his relationship with Gene in a memorial tribute for the national academy of engineering. He said:

"In my fifty-one years of professional life, from the vantage point of being an IBM general management executive, a venture capitalist, an executive in a high technology consulting firm, president of a Taiwan semiconductor company, president of an advanced electronics company and chairman of a leading software technology company, I have met some of the world's greatest scientists, engineers, government and corporate executives, heads of state, educators, and working people. Of all those met in my lengthy business life, the most remarkable is Dr. Eugene Fubini.

This brilliant and amazing man, perhaps five feet tall in his shoes, was a bundle of vibrant energy with infinite curiosity, compassion, warmth, and knowledge far beyond his training as a physicist. He had an abiding love for his adopted country and made significant contributions to hundreds of projects from his early days as a young engineer at Columbia Broadcasting System. He began to hit his stride as a research associate during World War II at the famed Harvard Radio Research Laboratory, where he led advances in electronic countermeasures and reconnaissance equipment.

After the war, Dr. Fubini spent sixteen productive years at the Airborne Instruments Laboratory Company, where he continued to innovate in the field of reconnaissance electronics. He produced numerous patents in electromagnetics and microwave applications.

In March 1961, his opportunity for contributions enlarged significantly as he joined the Department of Defense (DOD) as director of research in the Office of Director, Defense Research and Engineering. He had great influence on DOD research and engineering, and his reputation rapidly became international. In two short years he was promoted to assistant secretary of defense for research and engineering, and was a key part of a famed team of DOD executives.

In 1965 I became president of IBM's Federal Systems Division and longed to have access to such an important leader. However,

Dr. Fubini tended to DOD business and tried to avoid sales calls by all-too-anxious defense contractors. In 1966 Dr. Fubini joined IBM as a vice president responsible for research and other advanced development operations. Because the Federal Systems Division's activities were close to Dr. Fubini's heart, I had the great fortune of becoming a close and admiring friend. Because of his reputation for brilliance, Dr. Fubini was in great demand by the aerospace community and, occasionally, agreed to review a project. I recall vividly one instance where a major corporation had invested two years of effort on an advanced system and they anxiously wanted Fubini's overview. Dr. Fubini agreed to review the project and invited me to observe. After the company's well-prepared presentation, Dr. Fubini not only showed them why their concept was fatally flawed, but he did it in such a way that they accepted his critique and the project was terminated, probably saving the company millions of dollars and, possibly the federal government hundreds of millions of dollars!

Many a night have I spent at the Fubini's home or he at mine. The invigorating discussions still influence me. I watched as his adoring wife, Betty, brought tea and cookies to our late-night discussions. I have watched him tell each of his six loving children good night and seen the warmth in his eyes for all of his family.

Gene Fubini was remarkable as he positively influenced all the people who were in contact with him and steered technologies to high purpose. His brilliance wisely guided the Defense Department as well as many aerospace companies. The world lost a great professional when Gene Fubini passed away—yet his legacy continues."

Gene was never one to contemplate his age, and it likely never crossed his mind that one day his abilities might wane. He was certainly too busy to consider slowing down. Nonetheless, it certainly didn't escape him that his father had died a young man, and his brother Gino had died a younger man still. Gene knew he had to balance what he was doing against the inevitability that he wouldn't be able to sustain his pace forever. Against this backdrop it was becoming increasingly clear that IBM was not an ideal place for him. He was a Group Vice President, one of the four or five most powerful members of the company, and he was making a great income. He was, however, deeply unhappy and unfulfilled.

Gene believed in excellence. He also believed in not only finishing what you started, but doing so in a way that made your excellence obvious. IBM would challenge that notion. Gene had enough pride (some would call it arrogance) that he didn't want to be like the other IBM executives. Their aspirations had no value to Gene. The number of direct reports, the size of one's corporate domain, the amount of money you earned, were not motivators for Gene, and this was another way in which he did not fit in the corporate world. These were not standards against which he wanted to be measured. Among those at IBM, his respect was reserved for those doing great research, and for Tom Watson himself. Even Dick Watson was, in Gene's view, little more than a polished salesman, and the vast array of other IBM executives, too, were of questionable value. As far as Gene could tell, they did little to advance the company besides selling existing computing equipment in ever-increasing amounts. This to Gene was necessary but not noteworthy.

Of all the correspondence that occurred at that time it is unusual that there are only three memos in Gene's files from IBM. All were personal letters between Tom Watson and Gene. This exchange of letters and notes is indicative of the trouble Gene was having after less than two years with IBM.

Clearly, Gene was in the final stages of questioning the value of his efforts when this series of letters occurred.

The first letter is from Gene to Tom Watson and begins:

> Memorandum
> May 29, 1967
> Personal and Confidential
> To: Mr. T.J. Watson Jr.
>
> Dear Tom:
> I have just left you and I want to reconfirm the statement I made to you verbally that I need your help and understanding in my discussions with you. I had firmly decided in advance to not interrupt under any circumstances but, as you saw, my very best intentions failed. But I do want to maintain my direct relations with you, otherwise it would be better that I leave IBM.

The letter goes on to discuss the appointment for the position of Chief Scientist, and then concludes with:

> The reason for writing you is to show how much difficulty I have in communicating and how much help I need: Could I ask, as a favor, that you let me have a general discussion on our relations for another half hour sometime before the end of the summer. It really is necessary that I have your friendship, and not only your respect, as an essential condition for me to work satisfactorily.

Attached to this letter is an undated, handwritten note from Watson to Gene, presumably in response to the above note. It reads:

Dear Gene,

Most of the persons I respect and admire in IBM have gone through a painful process in getting to know me. I wish it were not so but must face the fact that it is. You are doing fine and I'm sure you interrupt no more than I.

Let's just consider the fact that we're pleased and proud to have you a member of the top team, to be the main controlling point. Everyone is different and everyone needs to make some compensation for his associates. You have my admiration and my promise of help whenever I can. The general discussion you mention can be undertaken anytime.

Sincerely,

Tom

A few months later, this final memo shows up in Gene's IBM correspondence file, presumably after the discussion Gene had requested:

Thomas J. Watson Jr.
Old Orchard Road, Armonk, New York 10504
PERSONAL
August 21, 1967

Dear Gene,

Apropos of our conversation the other day about your place in IBM, there was an instance which occurred recently that illustrates your tremendous value to the company. I have been ruminating about our conversations while up in Maine, and the more I think of you and your position in IBM, the more I realize your importance to our future.

The instance to which I refer is the perfectly magnificent presentation of Gardiner Tucker's which I missed but which has been described to me by a number of people. I know you had a profound effect on the preparation and content of Gardiner's review, and I want you to know I learned of this and was impressed by all I heard.

Early in September, I would like to sit down and talk more about organizational inter-relationships and anything in that area that might inhibit your operation.

Have a good Labor Day!

Sincerely yours,

Tom

Richard Garwin was a brilliant physicist who had studied under Fermi and was considered one of Fermi's brightest students in Chicago. After three years on the faculty of the University of Chicago, Garwin had joined IBM in 1952, and remained an IBM fellow at the Thomas J. Watson Research Center for the next forty years. he had worked with Gene on numerous committees for years, and was around Yorktown, as a Watson Fellow, doing independent research. While Gene and Garwin had never had the closest of personal relationships, Gene could see that Garwin was using IBM as it ought to be used. Garwin was having substantial impact and generating change by bringing the outsider's perspective to the corporation without trying to overturn everything about the existing culture. He was consulting to IBM and leveraging its resources, but not trying to change it wholesale from the inside. The culture at IBM was no secret. Gene was not going to be able to stem the wave of cultural bias that met any effort to change IBM. The organization was not going to feel comfortable listening to five new ideas a day—and even if they did listen, nothing was going to happen easily, quickly, or without a political battle over turf and budgets. Gene thought Watson had made unrealistic promises about what Gene was going to be able to do at IBM, but Gene had not paid close enough attention. He was not going to shift this behemoth. Maybe Garwin had the right idea. Possibly, he could have more impact outside as a counselor than he could inside, as an executive change agent.

Working for IBM wasn't all a grim struggle, though. For example, while visiting Stowe, Vermont (as guests of the Watson's), Gene and the younger children spent a day skiing with then-Senator Bobby Kennedy. Gene had first gotten to know Kennedy during the long hours of the Cuban Missile Crisis, and after that they had had ongoing reasons to intersect. Now Kennedy was running for president, and he talked with Gene on the chairlift about national security issues. Kennedy had his own people, but none of them were as knowledgeable as Gene about the technical issues of national security. He asked that Gene continue to brief him. Gene believed Kennedy could win, and if he did win there would be a place for Gene back in Washington. Regardless of whether Gene accepted a position, Kennedy was a very bright light next to the disheartening possibility of continuing at IBM. But it was not to be. In June 1968, Bobby Kennedy was assassinated in Los Angeles. Gene, like most other Americans, was stunned by the loss, just as he had been stunned by JFK's assassination years before, and by the murder of Martin Luther King just months prior.

It was a dark time for Gene, and it was a dark time for the country. Life demanded intelligence and hard work and luck. And at fifty-five, Gene began to become conscious of how much courage it demanded. In many ways, Gene was in his prime now—he had the brilliance he'd always possessed, but now it was tempered by his maturity; he still had his fire and spark of inventiveness but now he balanced it against the practical knowledge of how things really got done; he was still the phenom, the whirlwind, but now he had built up a network of colleagues and a resume of real effectiveness. He was, in short, a marketable and sought-after resource in his field. He understood the importance of making the most of this time in his life. He sounded out Bo Evans about independent consulting work with the Federal Systems Division. He was determined, whether or not he left IBM, to work harder, as he had the drive to accomplish more.

At home, Gene had become even more difficult to deal with. He was more demanding of Betty and the children, more stubborn, and his anger more pronounced. Betty was having to become ever more adept at controlling him but even she, at times, would have to step back and let his eruptions of anger pass rather than try and affect them. Gene's mood swings and anger were now more volatile than ever. He could be verbally vicious towards the children. Betty spent a good deal of her time and attention watching for the warning signs. She also kept him away from the children as much as possible, without making that strategy obvious. As much as Gene was callous towards the children's feelings, she was attuned to them, and seeing him brutalize them verbally was often more than she could bear.

Sylvia graduated from Smith College in 1964, though Gene,

setting a pattern for most family celebrations, was too busy to attend the ceremony. Shortly after gradation, Sylvia signed up for the Peace Corps and went to Korea for two years working in a remote health clinic. She loved it. It was difficult work and a wonderful life experience. She came home with renewed personal confidence and a greater sense of purpose. However, her relationship with her father remained problematic. She announced shortly after her return that she opposed the Vietnam War. Gene took this as a personal challenge to persuade her otherwise, and he was unrelenting in his efforts. Of course, there was no arguing with him; he was simply too knowledgeable. Moreover, it was clear that he did not want to engage in an actual conversation or debate about the subject. For Gene it was, again, just another opportunity to be right. For all anybody knew, he was against the war himself, but that was hardly the point. There was something personal in the way he attacked Sylvia, until the whole situation began to take on the quality of a mugging. The children had all been around him long enough to understand the futility of even defending oneself. Walking away, or avoiding Gene to begin with, was simply the only option.

In the late 1960s Sandra was at Michigan State studying veterinary medicine. She had always loved animals, and she was pleased to throw herself fully into school. She met Gary Willwerth while at Michigan State, and they were married in February 1969, shortly after they both graduated. Carol was at New Canaan High School, where she was popular, and was the most liberal of the older girls. She, too, was headed to Smith. Laurie was and always had been the in-between daughter—not old enough to have had the Brookville bonding experience. After her came David, who had a special place as the only boy, and then Susan, the youngest.

Laurie wasn't invisible but she always seemed to be most comfortable in the background. She excelled at school but, like most of the younger Fubini children, was not particularly social. Susan was bright and already showing signs that she would excel at school. The older girls still teased David constantly when they were home. Though they could agree on little amongst themselves, they could put aside their differences to terrorize David. And, in truth, he was an easy target. He was (of all things in Gene Fubini's house) an underachiever, watching too much TV and complacently coasting along at school with terrible grades. He was unmotivated and, in the collective opinion of the family, a bit of a dullard. Gene's mother, Anna, who was never one to coddle even a deserving child, was vicious and unguarded in her opinions of David, and never missed an opportunity to remind Betty (and David) about David's lack of progress relative to Gene at a similar age. To Anna, the best way to motivate an underperforming child was through humiliation, and she demanded that he be tested for learning deficiencies to discover his faults. To this, Betty had no response. There were too many other children who needed tending to, and anyway, she had all she could manage just managing Gene.

Susan was rapidly becoming a very accomplished equestrian rider and her talent and love of horses was becoming a compelling part of her life. After Potomac and the move to Connecticut (as Gene went to IBM) the ponies and horses moved from the back yard to a stable in Weston, Connecticut, a small town near New Canaan. The stable soon became an after-school playground for Susan and before long she, as well as David, were spending considerable amounts of time there. The stable, initially run by a low-key trainer who'd created a casual atmosphere of riding for fun, had passed on to new ownership and become a world-class, high-profile, Olympic-caliber institution with a national reputation. The shift intensified as the casual riders left for other barns, and new, more driven riders arrived. Susan was squarely among the latter group.

Susan was a natural, and her skills progressed at a rapid rate. David, so disinterested in so many other things, enjoyed riding and found a passion for the role of Susan's groom, driver, and later her banker. Nimrod Farm, as the stable was now called, had become a second home and a summer camp for Susan and David. Every day there were ponies and horses to be trained and lessons for Susan. David cared for the horses and managed Susan's show schedule. At first, Betty hid the expense of all this from Gene, but in reality, he really didn't want to know. Gene had never understood why they had horses in the first place, and he certainly didn't understand why the children were spending so much time at the stables. In particular, he could not understand David's interest, as he was an unremarkable rider and hardly even competed. What never occurred to him was that David was filling for Susan the role Gene himself—had he been a much, much different person—might have fulfilled.

Gene might have put a stop to the riding but for the fact that their involvement made his and Betty's lives easier. Gene, of course, never came to any of the horse shows, and as soon as David could drive the horses and a trailer, Betty stopped going, too. The shows were too numerous and too far away to be worth the effort, as they saw it. Susan soon became one of the leading junior equestrian riders in the country, and was often in the top ten in national competitions. Unlike other families, where such success was the product of an extended household commitment to the overall effort, Susan achieved this success on the basis of the hard work she and David alone contributed. Her success was a triumph of the collaboration of brother and sister at a time when they were competing against much larger, more financially able, and more committed families. David was a constant presence, helping to provide support, comfort, guidance, and financial support via the money earned around the stables. In a way, the energy and dedication they brought to it was a life-saving refuge: After all, it gave them somewhere to go and something to think about other than their tumultuous home life. The horse show community provided a protected place where Susan could excel, and where she and David could retreat without the constant scrutiny of their father. It was a place of joy, fun, and community spirit—the opposite of what home with their father felt like.

The only real time the family had fun together was in Vermont, skiing. In truth, the skiing itself was not fun. Gene insisted that they be at the slopes the moment the lifts opened and ski to the very last moment before the lifts closed. Lunch was carefully scheduled for after the lunch surge and before the early afternoon departing crowd would flood into the lodges. If the children were hungry before or after that, well, it was simply too bad. Weather never played a part in the decision to ski. If it was below freezing, they were simply advised to wear more clothes.

Gene also forced the children to keep a running calculation of the cost per run as they rode up the chair lifts, just to make sure their simple math skills were being tested. Yet, the family was still somehow happiest in Vermont. Gene relaxed more, relieved of even the possibility of walks in the woods with work colleagues, and fewer phone calls were made. After the skiing the whole family would sit together and have hot chocolate, enjoy a fire, and play board games. When they were on holiday, the explosive anger seemed to be on holiday, as well. The children and Betty did not have to keep a constant lookout for the telltale signs of a pending blowup. Even today, it is those times that Susan and David remember as the best times with the whole family, but especially with Gene.

Dealing with Gene and schoolwork was a constant dilemma for David. He was well aware that he was a disappointment to his father. He struggled in all his academic pursuits. He was not a natural student. He had long ago learned that no amount of achievement was ever enough for his father, and this realization had robbed him of any natural drive to succeed. Having a genius in the home was not a benefit to his school efforts.

There was no subject about which Gene didn't know more, and have more experience and more insight, than the teachers. Gene's knowledge trumped everyone else's, and it was daunting to ever consider asking even a simple question. If David did want help on an issue or a math problem, it was complicated. The answer was sure to be forthcoming, but the cost of asking a question was significant. If he asked Gene a question, for example, about algebra, Gene would first explain the underlying theory that the question or equation was testing, then he would help answer the question, and then he would hand David five more similar problems to be completed just to ensure that the concepts were fully understood. The whole process could take an hour. David, along with his sisters, quickly learned to ask for help only when he absolutely had to have it. Gene's approach had good intentions, but its real effect was to reinforce, at every turn, how inadequate his children were and how slow their progress was. The approach was never tempered by anything approaching positive reinforcement, and no reward was ever given for the bravery that it took to simply ask for help. Rather, the emphasis was always on what they didn't yet know, what they needed to know, and why they were so slow for not having mastered a given concept.

Gene finally announced he was leaving IBM in February 1969. It really wasn't a difficult decision for him as he was failing in the corporate environment and longed to get back to the defense establishment, where he felt he could do the most good. However, from a historical IBM perspective, his leaving was a bombshell. Never had such a senior executive resigned from such a paternalistic organization as IBM. Just as his arrival had broken most of the rules of the corporation's internal culture, so was his departure was unheard of in the history of IBM. Gene would later say that he simply walked into Tom Watson's office in Armonk and said, "This is as far as this short, Italian scientist can take this role. Thank you for the opportunity but I have to move on." With that Gene moved to the next and final chapter of his professional life.

14

Vienna, Consulting, and Network-Building

Gene began the 1970s by plunging back into the defense industry with his own consulting business, he being the sole practitioner. The project had the same appeal for Gene that self-employment has for most people: unquestioned authority, complete decision-making power, and the ability to choose when, where, and how he worked. His advisory role would vary across different situations, and his value would take different forms for different organizations. For some, he would be retained for the brilliance of his program review skills, and his ability to identify the flaws in proposals and anticipate both the technical and practical questions the proposals would encounter as they went forward to the government. Others would value Gene's long-term perspective on the future of alternative defense technologies. Companies would use Gene's knowledge to set priorities among alternative risks of potential investments and to understand how best to allocate limited capital. For many, it would be the simple comfort of having on call someone with wisdom and judgment who could play a wide variety of roles. Gene wanted total control of his time and refused to be beholden to anyone else. He also had no desire to create a larger consulting firm; he would bill his time and his time alone.

Gene briefly tried to work out of the house in New Canaan, but his style of work required that he be in the middle of the action. No matter how deeply he'd embedded himself in the Secretary's office at the Defense Department, no matter how closely he'd associated himself with the services, including the combat commanders at CINCPAC and NATO, no matter how current he'd kept with what was coming out of ARPA and what R&D was going forward in industry, there was no substitute for being in the Pentagon a couple of times a week. Over the years, his method of interaction with his co-workers, connection to the ebb and flow of the industry, and gathering of information were all based on wandering the halls, meeting with people, hearing and, of course, getting himself heard. That was impossible working from Connecticut. Indeed, the more he and Betty talked about it, the more it seemed that a move back to the D.C. area made sense. Had IBM and the move to Connecticut been a mistake? It was a question Gene never asked himself. As always, he was focused on the future, and gave the past little thought. It was, as he liked to say, like Italian driving: "What is behind you is of no concern."

In fact, Betty was thrilled at the notion of leaving the socially rarified atmosphere of New Canaan. The opulence of the homes and the stratification of the local society were things to which she had never adjusted. She disliked her neighbors and never, despite having multiple children involved on a daily basis, made many friends in and around the schools. The only place she actually seemed comfortable was in the midst of a group of older women that gathered together to sew and knit. A return to the northern Virginia area would be a great balm to her. They might, she thought, find a home with land, room for the horses, and a less ostentatious lifestyle.

In speeches and interviews given when leaving IBM, and in several newspaper opinion pieces he wrote, Gene described his vision of technology and implicitly advertised the scope of his own place in that vision. These works were in essence calling cards, advertising the expansive view that Gene took, and calling upon companies and executives that wanted to be a part of that world to reach out to him for help.

For example in *The New York Times* on January 12, 1970 he wrote:

> Too many scientists and engineers are not paying attention to the results of their discoveries and intentions.
>
> Scientists and engineers have underestimated social and moral consequences.
>
> Science and technology are becoming one and entering public consciousness as political issues.
>
> It is easier to have a politician learn the technological aspects of an issue than to have a good technician learn the political issues.
>
> When Eli Whitney invented the cotton gin, he was setting the seed for slavery and the Civil War. The internal combustion engine brought about the suburb and the supermarket. Progress in agricultural technology displaced the same population that the cotton gin had attracted. Who had the responsibility to anticipate these second order effects? What are the ethics of technology?
>
> It could be the beginning of a genetic engineering revolution whose consequences may exceed electromagnetic waves or the atomic structure of matter.
>
> What will be the second-order and third-order effects of the discoveries in genetics, the introduction of the video-phone, the substitution of artificial body organs, cable television, the fantastic

progress in information processing devices, the introduction of giant airliners, the possibility of television broadcasting to entire hemispheres from a satellite, the great reduction in cost of communication, the possibility of digging canals and harbors by means of nuclear explosives?

For the first time in history, finding solutions is easy; to anticipate the problems is difficult.

When communications satellites make it possible for headquarters in Washington to listen in on the conversations of a company commander with his division commander, or a destroyer commander with his squadron commander, what effect will this have on the lines of command which have traditionally followed the lines of communication?

Gene jumped fully and completely into the effort to create a consulting platform for himself. The logistics of moving the household, relocating the children and the horses, finding schools, and dealing with everyone's emotions were matters for Betty. Gene was now spending all his time in Washington and at the Pentagon; for the children, the shift from IBM to consulting was not initially noticeable. It wasn't until the announcement of the impending move that the change in Gene's employment became truly apparent.

Betty found a small split-level home in the suburb of Vienna, Virginia, at 2300 Hunter Mill Road. The house itself was modest, but it came with an extra few acres of land and was directly across the road from two riding rings and a large number of riding trails that were maintained by a local riding association, Hunter Valley Riding Club. It was about half-hour drive into D.C., where the children would go to school and where Gene would travel to a new office he would establish just across Key Bridge. The rural feel of the place and the ability to have a bit of land with the horses was too appealing for Betty to pass up. They bought the house and began to make moving plans.

For Laurie, the impact of the move would be limited, as she was finishing at New Canaan High School and preparing to apply to colleges. She eventually chose Tufts University in Medford, Massachusetts. For David, it would mean yet another school move. He was already in his second high school after beginning in the New Canaan High School (with Laurie), and then moving on to Fairfield College Preparatory School because of poor grades. Now, David would return to Sidwell Friends School in Washington, D.C. for his junior and senior years. Susan was finishing junior high school and would begin at Sidwell as a freshman.

Gene settled immediately into the Vienna home and began to work as hard as ever. He was in and out of the Pentagon several times a day refreshing his network and establishing a more updated knowledge of what was under way in the various services and with key procurement programs. Betty converted the garage into a home office for Gene so he could work at home when it made sense. The Saturday walks resumed in earnest. Soon, Sunday walks got scheduled and a long list of military and civilian defense officials lined up to join him.

Now Gene's major concern was not about compensation as much as reestablishing his position as an essential keeper of knowledge and expertise in defense. By this time, the family finances were much more stable, thanks to his substantial salary at IBM and family money from Italy that was well invested and growing steadily. His income as a consultant would, as is the nature of independent contracting, be irregular and uncertain, at least at first. But Gene believed that if he focused on returning to a position of influence in the Defense Department and making a real difference in national security, the income would follow in due time.

Clients who thought Gene could be hired to provide influence for their commercial gain soon learned not to call. Gene carefully chose those with whom he worked, and always made sure his clients shared his focus: improved science for improved national security.

Gene was now comfortable in a way that he'd never been at IBM. The best scientists reached the peak of their powers as young men, but Gene was not that kind of scientist, and he believed that his most productive years still lay ahead of him. He had never been a drinker, he had never smoked seriously, and had long since quit entirely. Gene watched his weight, and he remained active. He walked hard every weekend on the horse trails and off the horse trails in the woods behind the house. As usual, he thought little of his age.

Harold Brown, now president of Cal Tech, invited Gene to lecture at the university. With the kids all either grown, off at college or able to tend to themselves, Gene and Betty were able to visit Palo Alto for three months, to Gene's great enjoyment. Gene also lectured for Bill Rambo's engineering department at Stanford and joined the department's advisory board. Texas Instruments was soon to become an important part of his new foundation, as well. Gene and the Chairman of the company were the only two engineers on the Board of Directors and Gene played a key role as a result. Gene joined a science and technology advisory committee for the space and missiles division of Thompson Ramo Wooldridge, Inc. (TRW), where he became very close to the actual research and development work being done in this new and critical arena. Joining him on the committee were Harold Brown, and eventually Johnny Foster as well as John Deutch, all of who were who now frequent walking partners in Vienna on the weekends.

Gene saw no reason for a lull between his departure from IBM and the establishment of his consulting business; he wanted things up to speed (and high speed) quickly. With his usual inexhaustible energy, he made the rounds, worked the phones, and soon had more leads than he actually had time for. Kathy Kennedy, his longtime assistant, was told to schedule him to the minute, and she did. The office was always full of people. Some of them got four minutes, some got half an hour, and some had to be told to leave if Gene was running behind, which happened often. Gene, after all, was a talker, so discussions often became intense and simply too interesting or contentious to be abandoned. At other times, political protocol had to be observed, and a Deputy DDR&E, for instance, might call and want to stop by for a chat. This would bump back appointments with lesser status.

Among Kathy's many other duties was the maintenance of an extra set of ties for Gene. After lunch, coffee, a snack or, in truth, any interaction with food or drink of any kind, Gene always needed a fresh one. Personal appearance was something Gene never cared much about, but Kathy conspired with Betty to, at a minimum, keep Gene from appearing before generals with food on his tie. Kathy was also in charge of the details Gene could never manage on his own: she reminded him of the endless appointments, made him find time for meals, scheduled travel, made sure the right papers were in the right briefcase for the right trip, and, above all, made sure he was fully prepared for any driving trip to anywhere other than his home or the Pentagon (his driving had by now deteriorated from unacceptable to dangerous). The phone never stopped ringing.

Kathy began scheduling his meetings on the actual flights, or in airports along the way. Off he would go to Loral, TRW, Gould, and Hoover; to Dallas for Texas Instruments Board meetings; sometimes just to New York and back for AIL and other firms such as Warburg Pincus, Wolfensohn & Associates, and Grumman. Sometimes he would travel to the Far East for the Pentagon, sometimes to Italy for Electronica, and then to NATO bases, talking to somebody different from Rome to Paris, and Paris to Frankfurt, as well as Frankfurt to Brussels. He always asked for more people to meet with, more brains to pick, more opportunities to learn something he hadn't known. The only time he ever got angry with Kathy, she recalled, was when, after she'd had him around the world with at least a dozen stopovers, he had a layover in Los Angeles for an hour with no one to meet.

While Gene was reveling in his new freedom and enjoying the demands and positive reinforcement from companies, committees, advisory groups, and individuals, the situation at home was worsening. Gene was oblivious to it, but serious fissures were developing.

Most of them had resulted from the move back to Virginia. Moves like this had been easier and simpler, of course, when the children were younger. But for Susan, who had put down deep roots at Nimrod Farms, and David, who had invested so much of his time and life in Susan's equestrian career, the move was devastating. The ability to keep the horses on their property was a huge plus for Betty, but for Susan and David it was a crippling blow. Gone was Susan's trainer, Roni Mutch, gone was round-the-clock care for the world-class show horses, gone were the indoor riding facilities, the specialized blacksmiths, the video teaching methods, and (perhaps most importantly) the active horse show circuit of Connecticut. And gone with those things, they both feared, was Susan's riding career. The environment in the area of their new home simply didn't support serious riding.

Susan's success had been a huge—and much-needed—boost to her and David's self-esteem and senses of identity and accomplishment, and that's what made the move so unbearable. It was another reminder that the children's needs were nothing beside Gene's, that the things they valued and cherished would never be even a minor consideration, that even when they could find a small place in the suffocating atmosphere of Gene's home to create something special, it could be taken away if it was any inconvenience to Gene. The move permanently harmed whatever relationship existed between Gene and Susan.

For David the move was less catastrophic, but certainly exacerbated his ongoing issues. Struggling to establish some beginnings of academic confidence, he was forced to move to his tenth different school in the twelve years of his elementary and secondary school education. Whatever friends he might have reconnected with from his previous time at Sidwell would be of little use to him: Nearly all his classmates lived in the immediate Washington, D.C. area, but Vienna, Virginia was in the far-distant suburbs, a 90-minute round-trip drive that David and Susan made themselves every day. Off-hours socializing with any of his classmates became a logistical tangle. He enjoyed many in-school friendships, and played on the varsity soccer team, but without out-of-school activities, he couldn't bolster these relationships in any substantive way.

Gene was now away more than ever. When he was home on the weekends he had a line of men over to walk with him every Saturday and, increasingly, on Sunday. It was left to David to do much of the work around the Vienna home, which included mowing the fields, caring for the horses, repairing and painting fences, and general maintenance. It wasn't much fun for a teenager, but he grimly reminded himself that at least he wasn't breaking any social engagements to get his endless list of chores completed.

After the first summer of trying to make the riding work in and around Virginia with a lousy local trainer, David and Susan hatched a plan to improve the situation: they proposed that they might return to Connecticut and Nimrod Farm over the summers. David did much of the planning. He identified a place for them to stay with friends of a family they knew in Wilton, Connecticut. Because David had already worked at the Nimrod Farm stables as a groom, he knew he would be able to get full-time work there for the summer. He didn't love the work, which was hard, but the pay was good, and the tips from wealthy owners were even better. Susan would work braiding manes and tails before shows when she wasn't riding, which was equally lucrative, and together they would make ends meet. When she wasn't working, Susan would ride her horses and help train others. They presented the plan to their parents.

Betty approved it. No objections came from Gene, who, in fact, may not have even been consulted. In retrospect, it is astonishing that such an audacious plan was even considered viable. David, just seventeen and Susan, thirteen, were to travel alone in a station wagon towing one or more horses in a two-horse trailer, to go live apart from the family in a different region of the country. They would leave in late May, travel the eight hours to Weston, Connecticut, live with other families, ride with a clan of people their parents did not know, and return three-and-a-half months later just as school resumed in September. David would work with the farm and arrange the care of the horses, be responsible for Susan, watch over their living arrangements, tend to the finances, and help plan the logistics of the travel to and from Virginia and to the shows.

For the next three summers they made the trip to Connecticut. The second summer Susan lived with another local family and David lived in a house trailer on the Nimrod property. David drove the horse trailer to the shows or arranged for others to do so when he was called upon to drive the larger, six-horse, Nimrod truck. He worked with the trainer to plan the schedule for Susan, figuring out the shows and judges with whom she'd do best. (Such considerations were normal at her level of competition as the judging was highly subjective and the art of scheduling to maximize exposure with certain judges was a well-accepted means of furthering one's reputation and prospects for future success.) The whole campaign, of course, was very expensive, and both David and Susan were mindful of how the bills would be received back home. David applied as much of his wages and tips as possible to defer expenses, and Susan got up early, often as early as four in the morning, before show days to braid other people's horses.

Expensive and bold as the whole venture was, it proved to be well worth the cost. Nimrod gave David the set of friends and colleagues he so lacked everywhere else in his life, and provided a sense of accomplishment and identity. Susan was an outstanding talent and, with her primary horse, Eloise, remained one of the top ten junior riders in the country for several years in a row. Given the wealth and resources others brought to the sport, the Fubini shoe-string effort was a singularly remarkable achievement. It was perhaps no coincidence that it had all happened not only away from their father's house, but hundreds of miles away.

In general, things for the Fubinis had improved. Betty was now happy being able to lead a simpler life that no longer required entertaining and traveling to IBM affairs and meetings. She loved looking out at the horses in the back yard, and had a large wooden porch built so she and Gene could sit outside on nice days. She enjoyed some additional land they'd been able to purchase and secretly wished for a larger farm now that they had the means to afford one. Gene was happier and the tensions between them had eased. On nearly every Saturday and Sunday Gene had men out for walks and Betty would greet them all, and offer coffee and snacks after their return to the house. Betty also learned to keep a supply of extra clothes and boots, as many of the newer walkers came unprepared for the rigors of the walks with Gene. The rookies would often return covered in mud with ruined dress shoes, as they often underestimated the pace of Gene's walk and the ruggedness of the terrain. Many walkers were left to wait while Betty quickly laundered muddied pants or soiled coats. Gene reveled in the resumption of the friendships he had been missing in Connecticut, and he was clearly back in his element.

As for his children, Gene, as usual, worried about them much as one would young protégés, and saw them more as individuals to give direction to than as children who needed warmth, love, encouragement, and understanding. He was not raised with such warmth and support and it was not something he felt comfortable giving as a parent. So he didn't. His concerns centered more on early career decisions and judgments about the serious boyfriends and potential husbands.

Sylvia, after her return from the Peace Corps and work on a master's degree in public heath in Boston, was off to Ohio State for yet another degree, this time a Ph.D. in economics. She had begun a serious relationship with a man named John Moore, who she'd met while she was studying for the master's and he was finishing his doctoral work in Natural Resource Economics, and marriage soon followed. Sandra, having graduated from Michigan State, had relocated to Manassas, Virginia with her husband to open a small animal clinic and begin a family. Betty was pleased to have Sandy so close and, before long, welcomed the first of what would be many grandchildren. It was a sign of things to come. Between what would eventually be four children, a thriving veterinary business, and involvement in the raising of racehorses, Sandy's time was stretched thin, and Betty would ultimately pick up much of the slack.

Carol, the liberal of the family, returned from a stint in California helping the George McGovern presidential campaign, and then headed to Boston to attend Suffolk University Law School. She would later work for the Office of the Attorney General of Massachusetts in its Trusts Division. Laurie, meanwhile, was off at Tufts University, where she met Robert Jacobs, a Philadelphia native. Laurie would later finish Tufts, join G.E. working in its Space Division, and move to Philadelphia to marry Robert.

Susan continued to ride with help from David, but it was becoming logistically more difficult. David was now at the University of Massachusetts Amherst and would come down on weekends to help with the indoor fall shows. After the first three summers of David's direct support of her activities through his work at Nimrod Farm, Gene had finally intervened and insisted that David get what Gene called a "real" summer job. Gene helped arrange for David to work first at IBM and then at the technology company PerkinElmer in Connecticut. Both were in the Fairfield County area near Nimrod, so for the fourth and fifth years of Susan's campaigning as a junior equestrian, David could stay close and help.

After David finished college in 1972, Susan tried to continue her riding from Washington, but with David now beginning work at Johnson & Johnson in Philadelphia, it was more difficult. After Susan turned eighteen and was no longer a junior, Gene insisted that she start doing something "sensible" with her life, and in truth it was a natural turning point for Susan, anyway. To ride in the senior circuit was a different kind of commitment from what she was used to. The real competition in the senior circuit was in Jumper classes where one was judged on the heights of the jumps, and this made the quality of the horse quite critical to one's success and safety. Susan's horse had been adequate for her riding to this point, but wasn't appropriate for Grand Prix jumping, so a redirection of interest was needed.

Susan soon started working with a local Connecticut veterinary office to gain experience and see what life might be like as a vet. Sandra was now running a successful clinic for small animals and had effectively paved the way for Susan, who soon decided she wanted to be a large animal vet. She went after this goal with a laser-like focus. Having already skipped one grade in elementary school, she now applied to Tufts University after her junior year of high school because it had announced intentions to start a vet school later the following year. The plan was for her to finish her high school degree after completing one year of college. When Tuft's plans fell through for lack of funding, Susan immediately transferred to Virginia Military Institute, which had a contract with the University of Georgia to admit seven Virginia vet school students based on merit every year. (In this way Virginia could say it offered a vet school education without building a school themselves.) Susan applied and was accepted; off to Georgia she went. Her future was now clearer than ever before.

Betty was making plans. She could see that Gene was never going to slow down, and that the drive to the Pentagon was going to continue for the long term. That meant a move into Washington at some point in the future would make sense—it was only about fifteen miles, but every inch counted with Gene's driving. She looked around and bought a small home in Arlington near his Key Bridge office. They didn't move in right away, though the house was fully furnished. Betty knew that should the demand arise, they were prepared.

The early 1970s saw several important changes for Gene. Despite his busy professional life, he made several trips to Turin to visit his sick mother, Anna. She'd been spending half of every year in her native city since shortly after the war, and on one such visit had taken ill with what was diagnosed as a bleeding ulcer, but was more likely stomach cancer. Confined to a hospital for a long stay, she was later moved to something akin to a hospice care facility. There, numerous family members—including Gene, her niece, Joyce, and her grandson, David—visited her. The family discussed moving her to America, where the care was likely better, but soon it became clear that her illness was severe. She died in March 1973, and was buried in Turin beside her husband, Guido.

The whole Fubini family, May 1975. Top row, from left: David, Betty, Gene, Sylvia. Bottom row, from left: Carol, Susan, Laurie, Sandra.

The changes in politics were just as relevant for Gene as his mother's death. Richard Nixon had resigned the White House in 1974, and by the late 1970s the political scene had shifted dramatically. As Jimmy Carter came into office in 1977, having defeating Gerald Ford in the 1976 presidential election, he reached out to and appointed Harold Brown as his Secretary of Defense. Gene began to work as a "minister without portfolio"—a government official unconnected to any specific role or responsibility. He worked behind the scenes to support Brown as he prepared to take over the Secretary role. The two met almost daily and laid plans for many of the technology and development priorities of the Carter Administration. Cyrus Vance, Gene's old colleague from the Kennedy/Johnson Administration, was tapped to be Secretary of State, so suddenly Gene's network and relationships, which had always been extensive, were without parallel.

Brown, who was living in California at the time, was without housing. Gene quickly offered the vacant and fully furnished Arlington home that Betty had bought. Brown accepted the offer and moved in while he and his wife sought more permanent accommodations. Gene and Brown hunkered down in the Arlington house and went to work planning the transition to a new Brown-led Defense Department.

One of the most critical decisions Brown had to make was who would be the head of DDR&E. Gene and Brown had reviewed many lists for many positions and this was one of their most critical selections. Bill Perry, a Stanford-educated mathematician with a Ph.D. from Pennsylvania State, had been a director of Electronic Defense Laboratories of Sylvania/GTE and president of ESL, an electronics firm that he helped found. He was also first on Gene's list of candidates for the DDR&E job. Brown called Perry, but he politely declined. Several of the next people on Gene's list also declined.

The truth was that in the wake of Watergate, such positions were no longer as attractive as they had once been. The pride and swagger that had blossomed throughout American government after World War II was gone, replaced by paranoia and apprehension. Where filling these government posts once was a matter of pride and honor, candidates were now faced with the reality that they would be regarded with suspicion and laid open to boundless public scrutiny. As Brown and Gene looked further down the list and didn't see anyone Gene wanted, Gene told Brown that he would talk to Perry directly.

ESL employed a thousand people and was growing rapidly. It was clear to Perry that ESL was going to be a major company and he had hopes of being another Dave Packard. He and his family were happily settled in Los Altos down the bay from San Francisco and a short drive from his work. So when Harold Brown called and asked him to come to Washington and be Director of Defense Research and Engineering, Perry didn't give it a thought; it would be one thing to be asked to uproot his family and leave a good job; being asked to do so to leave a company he had founded was unimaginable. Further, if he did leave, he'd be forced to give up his founder's stock, which was going to increase in value by a factor of five or even ten when ESL went public, which it would soon. He was not in a position to walk away from that. Indeed, few people ever are.

Then, Gene called and asked if it was true that Perry had turned down the DDR&E appointment. Perry said it was so, and Gene said, "That's the wrong answer. At least come to Washington and talk about it with me. Will you do that?"

Perry had gotten to know Gene in the mid- to late-1960s when they worked together at Sylvania's electronic defense lab on a government advisory panel. They worked together again during the CIA's Rhyolite project: a series of satellites that would be launched to create an operating set of geosynchronous satellites (an early GPS system). Gene had thought the project would never work, but this assessment was based more on his feelings for the project's chief advocate, Bud Wheelon of the CIA, than it was on objective analysis. (Gene and Wheelon had a years-long contentious relationship, including one notable occasion in which a relentlessly hectored Wheelon turned to Gene and screamed, "If you'd just shut up and listen, maybe you would fucking understand!") Ultimately, the project went through and was a great success, thanks in large part to Perry's intelligent and diligent handling of the matter. It left Gene with considerable admiration of the man, even if it had resulted in the creation of a project Gene opposed.

Knowing Gene, it wasn't surprising that Perry agreed to talk to him about the open position. But neither was it surprising that Perry braced himself; he knew full well Gene's powers of persuasion, especially one-on-one. They met at the Pentagon, and Gene took Perry into what had once been Gene's office, and would be Perry's office should he accept the job. There Gene told him, "I'm not going to say anything. I'm just going to listen. You tell me why you turned down the job." This was about the last tactic Perry had expected Gene to take, but he began his explanation, making his points at considerable length, and outlining his goals for his company, his finances, and his life.

Gene sat still for all of Perry's points, carefully listening, before giving his own perspective in an emphatic and almost fatherly manner.

Perry, remembering the meeting years later, recalled Gene saying, "All good points. But weigh that against the job itself, what it will mean to you. I don't think you understand that aspect. Let me explain. It's like being the chief defense technologist and senior design engineer of the entire defense community of the entire country. All the technology and the most gifted scientists in the world will be available to you, and you'll have the power to set the agenda for their work, you alone can shift the focus of their efforts, you can add where you see opportunity, you can subtract when you sense failure. You can take the effort where your best judgment says it needs to go. It will be the most interesting job in the world and one in which you will excel."

Gene drove this theme home again and again and went on to describe the potential impact and the value of the position, to the country and to Perry personally. He was passionate, he was challenging, and he was thoughtful, all the time punctuating his points with lots of arm waving. Then he summarized by saying, "When you take this job, it will enlarge your mind so greatly you will be a different person. It will forever change your life." Gene also appealed to Perry's patriotism, which as a grateful, successful, self-sacrificing immigrant, Gene could do better than anyone. Finally, Gene said, "You're going to take this job, and you likely fear that you don't have any experience working the Pentagon. I do. I'll be here and I'll help you succeed." There was no denying Gene's passion and Perry knew that Gene would be true to his word.

Bill Perry was a successful, accomplished executive on the verge of an IPO and certain success both financially and personally. Yet somehow, after the meeting with Gene, having subsequent conversations with Brown, and taking a long period for private reflection, he realized that what Gene said was right. Perry signed on to the job and his career changed forever.

15

The Harold Brown Era and the Defense Science Board

*H*arold Brown's Defense Administration gave Gene a whole new opportunity for influence both within and outside of the Defense Department. Gene was a constant force throughout the technical areas of the Pentagon and the military. In ways both overt and covert, he pinpointed problem areas, learned of people and departments that needed his help and expertise, and connected the right people to make the departments function better internally and between themselves. As currency and leverage to enter these dialogues, Gene employed his access to Brown and Perry, his well-honed skills as a program reviewer, his extensive external network, his innate sense of future technology, and his desire to help (without regard to public recognition). His was an unusual mindset in Washington and within the Pentagon, where a hunger for publicity was more the norm, where politics was sport, and where appearances often meant as much as results. For Gene, appearances were of no concern. Results were all that mattered.

Pope John Paul II and Gene.

Gene receiving the Navy Distinguished Service Medal from
Admiral Jim Hayward, Chief of Naval Operations.

Increasingly, Gene realized he had something else to offer beyond the immediacy of the programs and the technology reviews. He had traveled many of the career paths that executives could follow into and out of government, the Defense Department, and national security work. With the RRL he'd been close to active duty military; he been in industry; and he'd been among both military and civilian men in government with the Defense Department; he'd gone out to the corporate sector with an industry-leading company; he'd come back as an individual to consult for industry and the services within the gravitational pull of the Pentagon. From his own experience he knew the demands of the different career paths, and he knew the dynamics of transition from one path to another. When men needed guidance in these matters (and there were plenty who did), Gene had become somebody who could help. Counseling others in these matters became one of the most satisfying roles he would ever play.

Gene worked his ever-changing, constantly growing network of associates, friends, and colleagues who flowed into and out of varying jobs, committees, and academic positions. He was at the core of many other peoples' networks, and he became a critical figure for many others considering any major transition. Those in industry looking for those who were departing the government, and those in government seeking people with industry experience, both sought his advice. He became for many a critical "transition point" on the way into and out of the Defense Department. His weekend walks became a ritual, and invitations were coveted. The result of all this counseling was many placements that were not only good for the individual, but good for the country.

So the network wheel turned and Gene continued to help move people around and champion complex technologies that others, whose view was too shortsighted, chose to ignore. He connected individuals with other individuals and made the processes work—all serving the same ultimate goal: a stronger, more defensible United States.

The enormous potential of this advice and counsel could be seen for example at the Defense Advanced Research Projects Agency (DARPA), where careers of great scientists and bold concepts were conceived, tested, and brought to life.

J.C. Licklider, who Gene had brought down to the DARPA from MIT, in turn brought a very smart young fellow named Craig Fields to DARPA from Rockefeller Research Foundation. Gene would go on to champion the work of Fields, who would later have his own brilliant career and eventually chair the Defense Science Board in the mid 1990s. Licklider himself was not going to stick around at the DARPA any longer, because George Heilmeier was coming in as the DARPA's director, and Heilmeier would want timely delivery on specific research objectives clearly identifiable with best interests of the Defense Department. For Licklider, who was brilliant but undisciplined, this would be an obvious conflict, and he wanted to avoid it. It was clear he would lose the free rein that Jack Ruina had first given him. Licklider had had a terrific run at DARPA. Unknown at the time, Licklider's work on networks and communications had laid the cornerstone for the future of the Internet and for important advances in interactive command and control systems. These were developments that led to wholesale changes in defense and as well as societal communications.

Gene, trying to not let personalities get in the way of continuing influence opportunities, stayed in touch with Licklider, but also remained as an active counselor to George Heilmeier. Heilmeier had been a White House fellow working under Johnny Foster for a year and then had stayed on as a deputy to Foster. Gene had begun to work with Heilmeier while he was with Foster and tutored him on the specifics of the defense systems business and Pentagon process. Now Gene dropped in on Heilmeier regularly to keep up with DARPA's ongoing command and control work, their exploration of ocean acoustic transparency, and, most especially, the stealth concept—the ability to hide aircraft and regain the possibility of surprise in the face of airborne radar.

Stealth was just a concept in the mid-1970s, and it was one that Gene had championed for some time both in concept and now in application. It called for a radical rethinking of airplane design. Instead of designing planes for aerodynamic capability, the DARPA project was designing for the lowest possible radar cross-section (or "signature," as it would be later be called) and accepting whatever aerodynamics resulted. The theory being that the resultant design could be made aerodynamic once the stealth signature was minimized. It was a totally new mindset for airplane design. Gene was very excited about the prospects for stealth aircraft, and he made a point of getting other people in the Pentagon excited as well. Under Heilmeier, DARPA built and flew the first prototypes out of the Lockheed skunk works by late 1977, and the planes had the radar cross-section of a small bird. Following this huge success, Heilmeier was ready to move on, and Gene connected him with Texas Instruments, which needed a chief scientist. George would go on to great success at TI as well as later at Bellcorp.

Many leading lights of this era of defense could track their career routes, at least in part, back to Gene.

Norm Augustine had served on many panels and committees with Gene. Augustine was an aeronautical engineer when he had first met Gene under a table on that sandy beach during a military demonstration gone awry. The two became close colleagues and Augustine would go on to become a senior executive at Martin Marietta, CEO of Lockeed Martin, and leader of the Defense Science Board.

On an Army as well as National Security Agency Science Board, Gene began to work with Joe Braddock, a physicist, who was the nephew of the famous prizefighter James Braddock, and who had started a defense consulting group, BDM, which was already enjoying great success. In this case, Braddock and Gene worked together closely to champion the work of BDM and the results that it could help produce. Gene brought technical and political skills that Braddock could use on specific Defense Department projects where BDM had distinct and unique capabilities. Together, Braddock and Gene partnered on many European projects, taking advantage of Gene's European knowledge and strengthening Gene's global network. An example was a series of efforts with the Italian government strengthening electronic, counter-terrorist surveillance.

Over a period of many years, Gene helped George Steeg, (who'd been so responsive during the Cuban crisis) move successfully from Sanders to NSA and on into the DDR&E, then eventually back out to AIL.

Gene, while acting as a consultant to the National Reconnaissance Office, asked to be briefed on the advanced, high-security research and development work at the Space Systems Command in El Segundo, California. This was a major effort that required a huge investment by the government, and Gene was dispatched to assess the merits of the efforts to date. Major Paul Kaminsky handled the briefing and later recalled that he started off the briefing with a few minutes of context and overview of the work of the Space Systems and explaining how pleased he was to be in front of Gene. Paul recalled vividly how taken aback he was when Gene said, "Okay, Paul. Knock off that bullshit. I'd like to understand what's going on, and I'd like to hear it straight. So let's cut the crap on the nice stuff and save that for the Pentagon Brass that care… I don't, just tell me the details." Kaminsky thought that was terrific and proceeded to give Gene a detailed briefing. Afterwards, whenever Gene came out for the Air Force on some aspect of National Reconnaissance Office activities, he asked to work with Kaminsky. They developed a great friendship, and because Gene was so much older, he (who almost never spoke of his youth in Turin) did so to Kaminsky. In turn, Kaminsky confided to Gene that he worried about the number of years he had to put in before advancing from colonel to brigadier. Gene encouraged Kaminsky to stick with it as he thought it was too soon for him to think about getting out of the Air Force. It would prove to be useful counsel.

Meanwhile, Harold Brown thought the Defense Science Board (DSB) had become an organization of too many academics, too interested in collecting research projects for their schools, and not having the impact that such an assemblage of talent should be able to produce. The DSB was supposed to be the key industry advisory board to the Defense Department, and Brown thought it could play that role a lot more usefully if it had more experienced and effective people and a broader, more aggressive agenda. Both Brown and Bill Perry saw the solution. They would unleash Gene on the Board as its chairman, and give him the mandate and the access to them both that would be essential in turning the group around.

Brown knew he could not possibly bring Gene back inside the Defense Department itself. For one thing, Gene would soon be sixty-five. He was too old and too controversial to be confirmed for any official role. Also, his greatest value was behind the scenes. In this role he wielded greater power and was a more positive force for change than if he had had a formal role. More importantly, he had connections to so many people in so many ways that his enemies, of which there were more than a few, would block any attempt at an appointment by pointing to all kinds of conflicts of interest. Nonetheless, Brown wanted to have Gene nearby for his technical acuity, for his political connections, and for his resolve in using both. Brown also knew that Gene had paid his dues; he deserved to be involved. The DSB role would be a perfect forum for Gene.

Soon the DSB became a singular passion for Gene. Later, he would be remembered as the individual who, more than any before him or after him, was the driver and principal architect of a more modern DSB. This new version of the DSB would soon have enormous influence over the development of defense technology priorities and the deployment strategies for next forty years.

The DSB was a consultative group that few outside of the defense world would know. It was composed of former defense officials, executives, and academics who helped shape defense policy at the highest levels of the government. The DSB was chartered as a consultative arm of the Defense Department, originally during the Eisenhower Administration, and its charter has been revised several times since. Yet, its mission remains fundamentally unchanged: to be the single most powerful consultative voice of the civilian community to the priorities and strategies of the Defense Department.

As both Harold Brown and Bill Perry wanted, Gene became the Chairman of the DSB in late-1977 and went on to serve as its Chairman or Vice Chairman for the next ten years. Through his leadership, a wide variety of studies were undertaken that reshaped the U.S. defense strategies from the 1970s through the 1990s. It was also a principal means by which Gene would stay current with all the major developments in the defense world and build, maintain, and enhance a huge network of relationships with a wide variety and number of Defense Department members, executives, military leaders, and even politicians. He was, as many DSM members recalled, the "father of the modern DSB."

On Bill Perry's first day at the Pentagon, there, as promised, was Gene in Perry's office to welcome him. Gene told him, "You'll do a great job, but you don't know anything about the Pentagon. I'm going to help you with that. Let's get started."

One of the first orders of business was securing a military assistant. Gene suggested that the primary criterion was to find someone you thought ought be smarter than you are. In that vein, Gene had recommended Paul Kaminsky. Perry dutifully tried to secure him, but Kaminsky's superior officer refused to release him. The following week Gene came by the office and asked, "Where is Kaminsky?" Perry explained about the superior officer's refusal to make him available. Perry was well aware that, despite his seniority in the Defense Department, he had no direct authority over officers of the Air Force or any other military branch, and he, a civilian, didn't want to begin his tenure by stepping on the military's toes. Gene jumped up and down and waved his arms shouting, "No, you don't understand! It doesn't work that way. You have all the leverage here! When the Air Force wants a weapon system approved, they have to come through you. The last thing the command staff will want to do is piss you off. Trust me, they want to make you happy, not make you beg for someone." With that, Gene picked up the phone and called the Air Force chief of staff. The next morning Kaminsky reported for work as Perry's assistant. The ways of the Pentagon soon became clearer to Perry, and Gene continued to help show him the way.

Gene came in almost every Saturday morning after his Vienna walks to confer with Perry. He always came with an agenda. He would keep an ear to the ground during the week and learn what was going wrong in the department and he always had ideas on what needed to be done. But work within the Pentagon wasn't his only area of expertise. If something needed attention in industry, he seemed equally informed about that topic. After seeing Perry, Gene would wander down the hall into Brown's office with a similar, but broader agenda. He was "ubiquitous" and worked the halls of the Pentagon "as if they were his," Perry recalls.

Five months after Perry sold his participation in ESL, the company was bought out by Thompson Ramo Wooldridge, Inc. (TRW) at a stock price five times higher than what Perry had sold for. But by then he was firmly ensconced at the Pentagon and beginning to understand the rare opportunity that job represented. Gene had been right about the life-changing job he'd chosen in Washington, and Perry would have no regrets.

Gene loved the role of the gray eminence, in part because he was so effective in it. He evolved quickly to be one of the most influential advisors to both Perry and Brown and had more impact over what happened in the Defense Department on the science and technology side than almost anyone in the building or in the Congress. He was integral to Brown and Perry's effort to focus technology against the evolving Soviet threat. Together they got a critical new generation of tactical missiles built and deployed to face the overwhelming numerical superiority of Soviet forces. To avoid the danger of using the missiles, they developed what Brown and Gene called their "offset strategy" of achieving a technical superiority in smart weapons that would be sufficient to offset the Soviet's numerical advantage in troops.

One of Perry's greatest contributions to this effort would be what history may show as the biggest single accomplishment of the era, the Stealth F-117. Stealth was a small R&D project at DARPA, and Gene had championed it and followed it through the success of a prototype just before the start of the Carter administration. Gene brought the stealth project before Perry, who immediately realized its importance and put it into deep cover with Ben Rich at the Lockheed skunk works. The budgets were enormous and the risks, both political and strategic, were outlandishly high. But against high odds and despite expenses that ate up 10 percent of the Air Force budget, Perry persevered. It took all of Perry's personal and institutional resources to make it happen. Key to applying those resources were Paul Kaminsky's ability as a supervisor of high-technology line management, and Gene's ability to open the right doors at the right time, and to grease the appropriate wheels. In 1981, the Stealth F-117—now known as the First Night Hawk—was introduced. It would be a vital part of the Air Force arsenal for twenty-five years and redefine air superiority.

"This is a strategic weapon that really reshaped how the Air Force looked at strategic warfare," said Lt. Col. Chris Knehans, commander of the Seventh Fighter Squadron, twenty-five years later. "It doesn't matter what defenses you put up, how deep you try to hide or how much you surround yourself with collateral defenses, this airplane will come and get you."

This fact has made the Nighthawk a vital part of the Air Force's various campaigns since the aircraft's introduction. It has seen service in Panama, Iraq, Afghanistan, and Bosnia as part of such campaigns as Operations Desert Storm, Allied Force, Just Cause, and Enduring Freedom.

Retired Gen. Lloyd "Fig' Newton, one of the first F-117 pilots, said at the twenty-fifth anniversary of the plane's introduction that "Whenever its nation called, the F-117 answered, providing capabilities that had never been known before. If we needed the door kicked in, the stealth was the one to do it. Modern technology may have caught up with the F-117, and new aircraft may be set to take its place on the tarmac, but none will ever be able to replace it."

Stealth was a fine example of how the trio of Brown, Perry, and Fubini worked seamlessly at all levels to achieve a much-needed upgrade in the defenses of America. Using all their technological know-how and their tactical and political skills, they formed an alliance that was formidable. Gene played the role of both technical visionary and detail man in realizing the vision. Gene knew he was more feared than liked by much of the military, but all knew of his influence and knew they crossed him at their peril. It was this leverage Gene used to help get things done.

What John Deutch, the future director of the CIA and former Deputy Director of Defense, recalled most vividly about the Gene Fubini era was primarily the challenge of trying to manage Gene himself. When Gene took over as Chairman of the Defense Science Board, Deutch became his Vice Chairman. It was widely recognized that Gene was not a skilled manager, because organizational detail was neither his strength nor his concern. Deutch got to watch a great mind at work while retrieving the schedules and proposals that such a mind left scattered in its wake. As he recalled it later, this was a role that was more fun than it sounded.

The DSB met quarterly, and in addition met every summer in a secure location (often San Diego) for a two-week summer study session. The summer sessions were used to convene around work done during the year by various study groups, which Gene and Deutch organized and guided. Eight-to-ten studies or task forces ran throughout the year, and sometimes beyond one year into the next, and their findings and recommendations were reported back to the secretary of defense.

The DSB took on the pace and culture of Gene's seemingly limitless energy, and its agenda and study ambitions reflected this newfound energy and scope. Much of the DSB's effectiveness in this new era was due to Gene's access to Brown and Perry, and to the military's understanding that the DSB was now a powerful and, to some extent, undeniable voice. Ignoring it altogether tended to be bad for one's career. Gene's defining genius, in Deutch's view, was that he made the Board understand how to give technical advice in a way that was useful and relevant to policy makers. Gene was unique in his ability to give advice within the bureaucratic reality of the ever more complex defense community. The ability to communicate the way Gene did came to be a hallmark of DSB procedure. Gene's "Let me explain" technique was sometimes an amusement to those who knew him, but, in fact, he did explain, and he explained so anyone and everyone could understand. For good measure he threw in the management assumptions contingent upon his explanation, as well as the follow-up assumptions. He was brilliant at these communications.

Gene also knew his weaknesses. Deutch saw this self-awareness as a great strength. Gene knew he made enemies everywhere, but most of the time it was a conscious choice, a difficult tradeoff to push through a project he believed in. He was also lousy in purely political forums. When there was Congressional testimony to be given, Gene always asked Deutch to fill in. Deutch was viewed as more of an academic (as he was now a key player at MIT), and was more articulate in public, more polite and more measured in political forums. Deutch was also a willing listener when a congressman talked, a skill Gene had never cultivated in himself.

Gene's willingness to be blunt and outspoken wasn't confined to the defense world. At a Texas Instruments Board meeting held in Rome at a Marriott Hotel on the hills overlooking the city, speaker after speaker spoke of the beauty of Rome, this experience of Italy's rich heritage, and the awesome history that had taken place all around them. Gene knew that the Board had scarcely left the confines of the Marriott for so much as a visit to a tourist attraction (let alone any more authentic interaction with actual, native Romans), and was happy to point out this hypocrisy. Indeed, as was his way, he stood up on a chair at a formal black tie dinner to do so in his less-than-subtle, directly challenging way. Those who knew Gene from the Board smiled with amusement, as Gene's ways were well known to them. Others, including the spouses, were dumfounded at the gall. Gene, in truth, knew exactly what he was doing on such occasions, and found his iconoclastic reputation not only useful but enjoyable.

The warmth Gene was able, in his unique way, to engender in colleagues was still not evident in his family life. He continued to be harsh and often uncaring in his treatment of his children, in particular.

The University of Massachusetts was a turning point for David. It was the first time in his life he'd been in the same school for more than two years and he soon found that he was able to excel. He realized that when judged against a more normal standard than that of his family (especially his father), he was actually a bright kid. His father had always pushed him toward science, but he'd never taken to it. Away from his father's oppressive presence, he found he had a passion and knack for business. He worked hard at school, made friends, was President of a large part of the student government, and graduated first in his business school class with a 3.98 GPA. The hard work paid off, and only a few years after being considered by everyone (including himself) unremarkable intellectually, he was accepted to Harvard Business School on a deferred acceptance, which guaranteed entry after two years of work experience. To David, it was an unmitigated triumph, and he called to tell his parents the news. After so many years of academic struggle, he'd managed to go from high school failure to one of the most prestigious institutions of higher learning in the world. He'd finally found himself. His father didn't see it that way. To him, it was just more bad planning and poor judgment. There were no congratulations, and there was no acknowledgement of achievement. "So, what are you going to do for two years?" Gene demanded. "You need a job. Have you not planned for this contingency? Why not? Where are you going to get a job? What is your plan?"

David graduated from UMass in spring 1976 at the top of his class, summa cum laude. Betty came, but Gene was too busy to attend the ceremony. Four years later when David successfully graduated from Harvard Business School, with distinction, Gene, again, was too busy to attend.

When Sylvia wanted to quit her job, and go out on her own as a health care consultant, Gene quizzed her about how many clients she had and how she thought she was going to make it. He didn't just ask, of course, he bullied her about it. He told her he had had more than a dozen clients already lined up when he went out on his own after IBM, never acknowledging the possibility that any other approach might be valid. He demanded to know why Sylvia hadn't done the same. All Sylvia wanted was some encouragement, but it felt more like a competition. Gene had to be dominant in this, as in everything.

Gene even challenged Laurie on her decision to marry Bob. They wanted to be married soon after they both graduated from Tufts, but Gene was adamant that they were too young. Their lack of planning for the future, he said, was indicative of their lack of maturity, and he demanded they wait. Taking it a step further, he set forth strict guidelines that had to be met before he would honor their desire to marry. Sandra, who was spending enormous amounts of time with Betty, was also getting all kinds of criticism from Gene for her plans to expand her interests from veterinary medicine into horse breeding. However, Sandra simply ignored her father's advice and used Betty as a buffer. She, more than any other sibling, had found a way to deflect Gene's overbearing and demanding personality.

Sylvia's husband, John, had no such buffer and faced unyielding pressure from Gene to do more and be more aggressive in his work. John had the misfortune of working in the congressional budget office as a staff economist on the Energy Desk of the Congressional Research Office. Gene knew just enough about the job to be relentless with his opinions about what John should be doing to get ahead. At every interaction, Gene would ask of John what he wanted to do, what kind of work he was good at, and where it might lead. Every time they met, John recalled, Gene would ask (with the appearance of concern), "Have you thought of this? Have you talked to this person? Have you looked into this topic? He looked for any weakness and just went for it until he broke you."

During this time Gene's temper got, if possible, worse than it had ever been. He was never physically violent, but the verbal abuse could be even worse. His angry outbursts were unpredictable and uncontrollable, seemingly even for him. Something would set him off, and he would erupt, crazed and screaming for minutes at a time. Then, just as suddenly, the anger would dissipate and he would calmly retreat to his study.

Through it all Betty would placate him, remove the children or herself, let the rage blow itself out, and then act as if nothing had happened. It was an atmosphere of pure dysfunction, and left the children questioning their own perceptions.

Nobody got very far telling Gene to slow down, and Betty was no exception. With Harold Brown and Bill Perry in the Defense Department, Gene was even more manic than was the norm. He was irrepressible and in more of hurry than ever. He was now over sixty-five, and he prided himself on not feeling his age. Before long, his earlier smoking habit, his high-stress life, and the genes that had killed his father and brother all began to show themselves. After he failed several stress tests, his physicians recommended bypass surgery.

Gene had the surgery in the late spring of 1980. In this era, this procedure was relatively new and highly invasive, requiring open chest surgical procedures and three- to six-month recovery periods—torture for someone like Gene and, as it would turn out, Betty, too. It was no surprise that Gene made a terrible patient. Indeed, he was a sight to behold. He was like a caged lion roaring, raging, and unrelenting in his demands. He could not be restrained or satisfied, despite the fact that a lifetime of just such behavior had gotten him to that point. Gene, of course, came back too fast, too soon, and Betty and his doctors told him it could be to his long-term detriment if he did so. Gene ignored them. He was, in truth, torn between concealing his illness from people and bragging over his quick recovery.

In late 1980, Carter lost the presidency and with the change in administration came a new Secretary of Defense and a whole new set of deputies. Before he left office, Harold Brown had brought in Norm Augustine as Chairman of the DSB. Augustine was extremely intelligent, well-regarded by all, and acceptable to the incoming Republican administration. It was a deft move, as Augustine would ensure that the DSB maintained the quality of its work and its apolitical independence. In an unusual move, Harold Brown requested, and Augustine agreed, that Gene be kept on as Augustine's Vice Chairman, further ensuring the continuity of the efforts Gene had begun several years before. This was the first time in the twenty-four years since the DSB's inception that a former chairman was asked to stay on as a Vice Chairman during a transition between presidencies.

At this point in the DSB's history, prominent executives from the defense industry were invited onto the Board to ensure industry representation in the setting of the strategic priorities of the department. Inevitably Congress, the press, and lobbying groups were going to worry about the potential for conflict of interests, but the involvement of industry leaders ensured that a far more realistic and complete picture of what needed to be done and what could be done was delivered by the DSB.

The time would soon come when Congress and the press wouldn't tolerate a Gene Fubini with a foot in both worlds. It would be a dramatic loss not only for Gene but for others who could see both sides of the equation. As long as one had integrity necessary to live in both worlds, it would pay huge dividends to the work of the DSB. Gene was, as almost all of the others from industry were, a man of exceptional integrity and dedication. He could have made his fortune several times over if he hadn't chosen to serve his country. Without Gene's so-called conflict of interests, the Defense Department would have lost an astonishingly broad and functionally necessary range of perspective.

Augustine had not been eager to chair the Defense Science Board.

He had just been made President of Martin Marietta Aerospace in Denver, and had already put in a number of years working in the Secretary of the Army's office. He was enjoying a healthy salary and with little savings and a couple of children to educate, he had to worry about his private sector role. Unfortunately, Augustine let Gene Fubini lure him to Washington for a visit, and then out to Vienna, where Gene made him walk through the woods until he agreed to accept the position.

Augustine agreed to commute from Denver while he was Chairman of the DSB. He continued to work full-time as President of his company. He refused to give that up. The whole experience was as hard as he ever worked in his life. To be fair, Gene worked just as hard to help Augustine's tenure be a successful one.

Only occasionally did Gene's efforts to help go awry. When Augustine sat down to run his first meeting as chairman of the DSB, for example, a lens fell out of his eyeglasses. Gene, who wanted to be sure everything went smoothly, jumped up and grabbed the lens and the glasses from Augustine, said he'd get them fixed and went off with his rapid shuffling walk. Everyone made get-acquainted small-talk waiting for Gene to come back. Augustine assumed Gene had just gone down to the concourse to find an optometry shop, but after a while Gene had still not returned, so Augustine went over the agenda with the people in the meeting. Still he hadn't returned, and there was more small talk. When, after close to a half-hour had passed, there was still no Gene, Augustine went ahead and started the meeting. A short time later, Gene rejoined the meeting and handed Augustine the glasses. Gene had taken it upon himself to glue the lens back in. The frame was smeared and swollen with epoxy, and the lens had become opaque. "What you need," Gene said, "is a new pair of glasses."

In addition to his faults as a handyman, Gene was not an organizational genius. But in every other way, he and Augustine made an effective team. Gene had great credibility with the military and with the civilian R&D community, and Augustine had credibility with the Republican Party and with Secretary Caspar Weinberger. Gene was, as he had always been, full of ideas and the energy to persuade others. Perhaps most importantly, he believed that the real work started after the DSB put out its final report. Gene followed up on the reports out of the summer study and saw to it that they didn't just land on a desk and disappear.

Gene's impulse to take charge was so reflexive that it could be somewhat indiscriminate at times. In one Pentagon meeting he began, as he was wont to do, by asking questions. Before long, he was into his full "Let me explain" mode, up at the blackboard, running the meeting. When the man designated to run the meeting turned up and asked what group Gene was with, Gene looked out at the unfamiliar faces he'd been lecturing, and said with composure, "I must be in the wrong room," put down his chalk, and left.

After the changing of the guard at the presidential level, Harold Brown went back to California and joined a large number of corporate boards befitting his more public stature. Bill Perry went off to Hambrecht & Quist, a major venture capital/private investor firm in San Francisco. For Paul Kaminsky, the next move was less clear, so it was off to walks in the Vienna woods and dialogue with Gene about transitions. Kaminsky asked whether he ought to continue in the Air Force and work toward making brigadier. Gene counseled that, now, he could do more for the country and the Defense Department in the private sector. The next several weeks they met for Saturday morning walks at Gene's house and worked out how Kaminsky could best make the move. The result was that he went to work with Bill Perry at Hambrecht and Quist. Unknown to them both, Bill Perry and Paul Kaminsky would soon be returning to the Defense Department.

16

FOFA/JSTARs,
Arlington, and Slowing down

$\mathcal{B}$ruce Henderson, the founder of the Boston Consulting Group, was a legendary management consultant whose insights shaped a generation's understanding of business practice. One of Henderson's trademark activities at his consulting firm was to send out regular (and much read) internal bulletins in which he discussed consulting, management, strategic perspectives, and whatever else was on his mind.

The issue of November 17, 1982 dealt with a chance interaction between Bruce Henderson and Gene on an airplane. The discussion began after they were seated next to each other, and they were comparing their views on career management. After the flight Bruce went back to his office and penned an internal memo on the interaction for his colleagues at BCG. It appears in its entirety below. What Gene understood, and graphed, were the elements comprising success in life. Henderson presented Fubini's wisdom so that others in his firm could consider its relevance to their personal and professional lives.

I saw the little man when he walked into the airport departure lounge. He was short of stature and slight of build. Perhaps he was sixty-five years old. He walked with confidence, even a little bravado. I paid little attention, however, until he walked up to the man seated next to me and greeted him warmly.

They had obviously known each other for some time, although apparently only casually.

"And what are you doing now?" said my seat neighbor.

"I am a management consultant now!" replied the little man quite firmly and proudly.

"And is it going well?" my neighbor asked.

"Yes indeed," the little man replied. "But please excuse me. I am late for my plane." With that he headed for the boarding gate.

My neighbor seemed talkative. So we chatted for a while. He was a newspaperman who lived in Washington and had spent most of his own career there. I commented that he seemed to know the little man. He acknowledged that he knew him casually but knew of him primarily because of his career. I could not restrain my curiosity. I asked him, "Is he really a management consultant?"

As I had watched the little man talk with him before I could not help myself. I felt a little sorry for the little man. He had said he was a management consultant. He had looked cheerful. But he did not look like a management consultant. I wondered how many businessmen down on their luck called themselves consultants. Maybe this newspaperman would give me a clue.

"Yes," he replied, "he probably is a consultant if he says he is. He had an extraordinary job before he joined IBM as assistant secretary of defense, then deputy director of defense. He had an incredible reputation as a brain. You would probably recognize his name. I don't know what he is doing now."

He did tell me his name, but I didn't recognize it, although it sounded familiar. Just then the loudspeaker system announced the departure of my plane. So I made a dash for the departure gate.

When I boarded the plane I found myself seated next to the little man. It was in first class too. He couldn't be too far down on his luck. That was the beginning of a several hour conversation. I will long remember it.

Years ago, he had been a vice president—group executive of IBM making half a million dollars a year. He came to feel that the job was unsatisfying and resigned. After that he had taken up his present activity. As a management consultant he worked alone, mostly with defense contractors. He enjoys what he is doing now very much. He takes on the assignments he wants, if and when he wants to do so. His clients match their schedules to his convenience.

Now he is almost seventy. For a while he had been slowed up until he had undergone a coronary bypass operation. Now he was up to full speed again. He had researched the statistics and there was a 25 percent chance he might need to undergo another one in about ten years, otherwise he had no intention of retiring.

As interesting as this was, that is not what I will remember best. I will remember him best for the "Fubini Curve." His name is Eugene Fubini. The Fubini Curve is his philosophy about work.

According to Dr. Fubini work is one of the major pleasures of life. It is the basis of your own sense of personal worth and the perception and respect of those who know you. Success in it is the source of psychic energy. Work determines what kind of people you spend most of your life with, where you raise your children, and what kind of challenges you meet. Therefore, it is the psychic satisfaction of work that overwhelms all other factors according to Dr. Fubini.

Then he drew what he called the "Fubini Curve" for me. The value of money varies according to the law of diminishing returns. The more you have, the less a given increment is worth.

Plotted it looks like this:

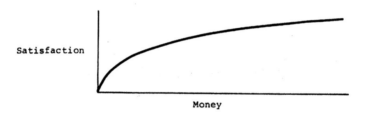

There is some money level which must be reached to achieve a normal and satisfactory life style. However, it is considerably less than most successful people achieved or can achieve.

Let that be represented by the dashed horizontal line and the dashed vertical line. Anything less than the intersection of these two is inadequate.

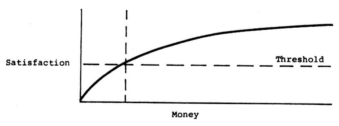

However, it is possible to offset money with psychic satisfaction. Therefore, the requested psychic satisfaction curve is the inverse of the money satisfaction curve pivoting around the threshold axis.

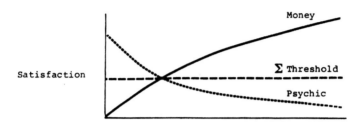

But psychic satisfaction does not have the same diminishing returns as money alone. By definition it is at least linear and it may be exponential. As a consequence, the actual trade-off between monetary and psychic satisfaction results in far greater net gains for psychic satisfaction vs. monetary satisfaction after the threshold level.

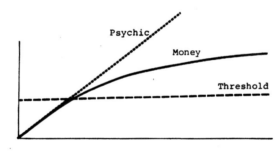

Consequently once the threshold is reached, then the tradeoff between psychic vs. monetary satisfaction continually and increasingly favors the psychic values.

So for equal satisfaction the monetary payout must go like the black line to offset the psychic satisfaction of the dotted line.

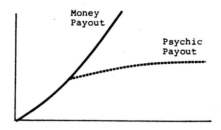

The data are soft. The mathematics are indeterminable. The curves are only symbols. But there is no question that Dr. Fubini is right. Once you have enough money and security to live well, it is the psychic satisfaction that matters.

It has been a year or so since my chance encounter with Dr. Fubini. Since then I have often thought of that discussion.

If you accept the "Fubini Principle," how would you construct and manage a firm?

Bruce, of course, sent a copy of the memo to Gene, who responded with a note:

Dr. Eugene G. Fubini
2300 Hunter Mill Road
Vienna, Virginia 22180

Dear Bruce Henderson:

I have not forgotten you and BCG are initials that I remember fondly.

I don't want to change your little story about me but you should know that you have added some embroideries that are very good and for which I deserve no credit at all.

The only objection I have to your story is that I have never defined myself as a "management consultant"—consultant, yes; never management consultant. I leave that to BCG, McKinsey, Booz Allen & Hamilton. Also my business is not doing well; it is doing very well. And in this "very well" I include both M (money) and P (psychic income). And, these days, I would say that, for me, P is equivalent to 10M. I am very satisfied and I hope that you are as content as I am.

Very sincerely
[the letter is typed, the signature scrawled.]
Gene F.

Vic Reis was a physicist in the ballistic missile defense business who worked ten years at Lincoln Labs. It was there that he first learned of Gene Fubini. Gene had been responsible for getting funding for the experimental communications satellites work under way at Lincoln Labs in the late 1960s. By the mid-1970s, when Reis first saw Gene in person on an elevator in the Pentagon, Gene was such a famous character that Reis was too shy to say hello.

When Reis came into the Reagan White House, as Assistant Secretary of National Space Security, Gene visited with Reis. It was to be the first of many conversations and Vienna walks. Gene took Reis under his wing and began the process of educating him on the ways of the national security world.

Soon Reis and Gene were discussing his continuing conflict with George Keyworth, Reagan's science advisor, over the Strategic Defense Initiative, the so-called "Star Wars" operations. Reis was ready to quit, and make noise while he quit, about the value of the proposed operations. Gene calmed him down and counseled him, rightly, not to burn bridges. Leaving was one thing, but doing so in a manner that brought short-term fulfillment but long-term damage was just foolish and shortsighted.

If, as it turned out, Reis really meant to leave the Reagan Administration, Reis learned that he was required to take the Gene Fubini "course" on how to get a new job. The course entailed, in addition to the Vienna walks, writing a to-whom-it-may-concern letter stating fully and exactly what he wanted to do and why. He had to address his life as well as his work. He had to show the letter to family and friends to see if they recognized the guy who wrote the letter. Then he had to show it to Gene. Reis and Gene came up with two choices. He could work for Joe Braddock at BDM where Gene was on the board, or go to SAIC, a defense technology firm where Gene was a consultant along with Harold Brown, Bill Perry, Melvin Laird, and Bobby Inman. Reis decided on SAIC, which worked out well for both Reis and SAIC. A friendship was born that would endure through the rest of Gene's life.

Gene was now in his seventies and while his stamina and durability were wearing down, his memory and recall about colleagues and defense issues remained sharp and vibrant. His lucidity about other life details, however, was now highly suspect. Susan remembers calling home one evening from school and talking to Betty when suddenly a breathless Gene, hearing that Susan was on the phone, interrupted on the extension in his study. He must have been looking out the back picture window as he started shouting to Susan on the phone, "What happened to the horses? The horses are gone!" Gene had failed to notice that the horses had been gone for several years.

Betty and her sister Kay Carr (1989).

During this period, David had met Bertha Rivera and they were married in 1989. In late 1989, David, Bertha, Susan and her husband Rory (who is from Australia) took Gene and Betty to Australia for a two-week visit with Rory's parents and family. It was a terrific trip and the first time anyone could remember when Gene had traveled so extensively for any reason other than work. Rory's family loved Gene. He told World War II stories, and they wouldn't let him stop. Gene only lost his composure once, when the service was slow in a restaurant. For a few tense, surprising moments, he was the old Gene again—tense and angry. Rory's parents and extended family were shocked at the unexpected display of anger and uncontrolled fury from someone who, moments before, was telling casual, humorous stories. At this point, not even Betty could control him. Only David had evolved to a point where he could handle Gene. As he did in other settings and other times, David quietly removed Gene from the restaurant and forced him to walk around the block for twenty minutes until he had regained his composure.

Back home, Gene's professional life endured. Despite the fact that Washington was dominated by Republican administrations during this period, and without the resultant direct contacts in the Defense Department he'd once had, Gene still had more than enough clients. In fact, he was one of the few consultants of his type who still commanded an actual retainer from companies. Executives paid to know they could reach out and get Gene's advice whenever the need arose. He had been forced from the Texas Instrument Board when he turned sixty-five, but he had gone straight from there onto Joe Braddock's Board at BDM. Gene still maintained a rigorous schedule, traveling to various clients and meetings. His Saturday and Sunday walks continued uninterrupted with a wide variety of colleagues.

He spent even more time now counseling people on their career choices, helping to move the network around to improve it and ensure opportunities for all. Everyone knew by now that Gene didn't make introductions without a reason, even if Gene couldn't, for reasons of confidentiality, make the reason immediately apparent. Gene was particularly adept at helping people as they came out of government or the military. His office was packed every day with men who wanted to pay for his time on specific technology and program issues. Equally important to Gene was that there were always men who wanted to talk about their future and he made time for them, either at the office or on the weekend. Some of them came by only two and three times. Some he allowed to work out of his office if they need the space. There always seemed to be four or five other men doing their own consulting work out of his office space in Arlington.

About this time, Gene gladly accepted the leadership of the Defense Science Board task force for Follow-On Forces Attack (FOFA). The concept was that NATO could withstand an initial assault from Warsaw Pact forces, but could not withstand the follow-up forces that would be brought forward from the enemy's rear and thrown into a second wave of the attack. In the past it had not been possible to track troop movement behind enemy lines well enough to target it for attack and interdiction. Now there was the technological know-how to do just this. The surveillance technology, if used properly, would dramatically raise the threshold at which nuclear weapons were thought to be employed— which had all along been the point of his and Harold Brown's off-set strategy.

The centerpiece of the effort was the Joint Surveillance and Target Attack System (JSTARS), to be developed with, and for, the Air Force and the Army. Using JSTARS, NATO and U.S. forces would safely be able to see, track, and target force movements far behind enemy lines. It was command, control, communications, computers, and intelligence at the highest level, and it made perfect sense. Yet, the Air Force did not want to divert budget from fighters to reconnaissance and surveillance. The Air Force was always reluctant in this era to dilute its fighter budgets, and the demands of the JSTARS would be such that huge sums of money would need to be diverted. This was an expensive and very far-reaching proposition. It would require dedicated aircraft, new radar, a new JTACMS missile component, extensive integrating software, and new command and control protocols supported by new communications equipment on the ground.

Gene would have to buck the Air Force resistance from all sides and he would have to fight with the General Accounting Office to prove the worth of such a huge undertaking. This project was in many ways a culmination of what Brown, Perry, and Gene had begun many years before. This program was at the core of Gene's central philosophy of using satellite surveillance, and stand-off weapons, guided by command and control, to affect a successful outcome on the battlefield. Its routine thinking now, but it was revolutionary in the mid- to late-1980s.

Bert Fowler, Gene's oldest and one of his closest friends, came in as DSB chairman in 1984 and asked Gene to stay on as vice chairman. Gene would not have been happy if he weren't asked, but in fact Gene had made the Board into what it was, and Fowler wouldn't have wanted to try and run it without Gene. So Gene continued to remain active in the leadership as he entered nearly ten years of service on the DSB. He was now seventy-two years old.

Gene had taken on the DSB's FOFA task force, knowing that it would be a long crusade. He and the DSB lacked the leverage they once had, and although the theatre commanders, the Europeans, and NATO wanted it, the Air Force leadership dragged its feet. The Air Force, as predicted, didn't want to relinquish any of its fighter acquisition budgets, so Gene was left having to persuade one staff member and one colonel at a time to adopt the JSTARS concept. What Gene had lost in leverage, he made up for in sheer persistence. He and Fowler worked hard to push the FOFA forward.

When Craig Fields took over as Director of DARPA, in April 1989, Gene insisted he come out and walk on a Saturday. Fields, an urbane New Yorker who thought "a walk" was what you did between a taxi and your apartment building, showed up in a suit and business shoes. He had to run to keep up with Gene through all kinds of brush and briars, and by the time he got back to Betty's coffee and biscotti, he had mud inside the shoes and his pants were covered with burrs. He learned a lesson that day and came more prepared in the future for the rigor of the walks. He became a regular on the Vienna walking circuit.

Gene used the walks as a means of staying informed as to what DARPA was up to and it also allowed him to comment and give advice to the new director. Gene talked fast, instantly got to the bottom of a subject, and had a wide range of interest. One week, Fields recalled, they would speak about biotechnology and bioterrorism, and the following week the subject would be supercomputers. Every conversation was a passionate one. Gene still liked to challenge figures, ask questions, and demand detailed answers. He used these occasions not to win arguments, but to gain clarity and insight. Fields was impressed that Gene didn't need to be right, and he didn't need applause. He was secure enough to know that if one didn't seek credit, one could get a lot more done. He never talked about past accomplishments. He lived in the present and into the future; he felt that every day he had to accomplish something; and, like all great people, he had no hesitation about attending to details. He helped Fields sort out large strategic issues, and yet also corrected punctuation on his response memos. Gene genuinely cared for Fields, to whom he became a valued mentor.

Old friends found out that Gene didn't always wait to be approached for advice or guidance. Sometimes, he would seek them out proactively. Everett Greinke, the engineer Gene had unjustly berated, and then befriended, in the 1960s, and his wife Claire, got back to the United States after serving in Brussels with the NATO command, and it was clear to Gene that Greinke was ready to get out of government. Gene actually went to Greinke before he had a chance to call Gene requesting help. Greinke took the Fubini "career course," and they walked on Saturday, and Gene said he had room in his office for as long as Greinke wanted. He was not offering Greinke work, merely the use of his office space and secretarial pool. Dan Fink was doing the same thing, along with another colleague, Jasper Welsh, and a couple of others. Kathy Kennedy continued to provide administrative support to them all.

Greinke took up the offer and kept going out to Vienna for the walks. He took the early shift, seven o'clock, and the two of them would talk about FOFA and JSTARS. Gene was as determined as ever about JSTARS, even in the face of long odds. Greinke, Bert Fowler, and Dave Heebner helped Gene keep the idea alive well into the late 1980s, against all odds. There were weekends when, as Greinke remembered it, Gene would be as excited as a kid, as if JSTARS was his first program. Something had happened, somebody had come around, and it would be, "JSTARS really needs this. It's the first time we've had a chance to make this go." Monday morning Gene would be back on it.

While Gene's acumen for business didn't wane, neither did his shortfalls. In fact, they became worse. His legendary lack of driving skills, for example, stopped being just a humorous side note to his personality. It was now obvious now, to Betty and David, that Gene could no longer be trusted driving from Vienna to his Arlington office, much less to the Pentagon. Every moment Gene was behind the wheel was now a life and death experience for passengers or anybody on the road or sidewalk. There were days when he returned home in a cab not remembering where he had left his car and not caring to look for it. One weekend, having conspired in advance with his mother, David appeared with a rental truck and, over the next few days, loaded up the essentials of Gene's study, Betty's kitchen, and the clothes the two would need, and moved the two of them to the Arlington house, only minutes from Gene's office. Betty and David never really consulted Gene. He was just told to start showing up at the Arlington house, and he did.

Gene was still a core member of the DSB and an active participant in the summer studies in San Diego. But Toby Fink's memories of those times together were different from her husband Dan's, who saw Gene primarily though the lens of a colleague and fellow technologist. Toby Fink saw Gene through the eyes of a mother and a wife. Her favorite memories of the summer studies were the times in San Diego when you had to go up the hill from the meeting rooms to another building for dinner. Dan Fink, having had polio, could not walk the hill and so had to catch a ride. Gene, on the other hand, with all his energy, had to walk, and somehow that left Toby to walk with Gene and keep him company. Of course, Gene could not talk about anything they were doing on their task forces. That was something the wives got used to and lived with. Security was a wall over which you never saw, and if you paid too much attention to that, you could think you were living in half a marriage, so you didn't pay attention. It was life. It was no problem at all with Gene, because Gene could talk about anything and everything. He was wonderful company.

Three generations of Fubini men: Gene, David, and grandson Michael (1991).

Dan and Toby also recalled that Gene never showed much sympathy for, or understanding of, his children. After Toby and Dan moved to Philadelphia, Gene called to say that David was in town, as he had secured a job after UMass, working for a new division of Johnson & Johnson that was introducing Tylenol to the consumer market. He said David was living in a suburb of Philadelphia, near the Finks, and seemed to be alone and rather socially inept. Gene implied that he was bit of a misfit, as Toby recalled, and asked if Toby might try and help.

Toby, feeling bad about this and wanting to help, invited David to dinner at their home with some other friends of their children. The contrast between Gene's description and the reality was somewhat startling. Where Gene had made David out to be something of a layabout, they found a young man with plans to attend Harvard Business School and a successful job at McNeil Consumer Products. Where Gene had described him as bland and socially inept, they found an engaging story- and joke-teller, and Toby even fielded a few inquiries from some of the single women in attendance. How, Toby and Dan wondered, could Gene have such inaccurate impression of his own son?

The Fubini family May 1992—the last time Gene, Betty, and Carol (who died in 2006) would be photographed together.

In 1988, Bert Fowler finished his term as chairman of the DSB, and Bob Everett came on as the new chairman. Gene finally concluded his ten-year run in a leadership position of the DSB. However, he and Bob Everett were close colleagues. Everett had known Gene for years, dating back to the days when Everett worked at Lincoln Labs and more recently when he was the head of MITRE and had been a client of Gene's. It was clear that Gene would remain on the DSB and continue to play an influential role even though he would no longer be chairman or vice chairman of the group.

Gene was now seventy-five years old and was concluding his fiftieth year in the United States. Still vibrant despite his heart condition, Gene powered on and was to have a good year as he pushed several agendas forward, and continued working with clients and traveling to various military installations. Gene's effort with regard to FOFA as a whole and with JSTARS in particular seemed to be finally showing signs of a major breakthrough. He had kept the issue front and center as world events and defense economics went through inevitable cycles of change. Gene and others had pushed and pulled the Air Force into making sizable commitments; Gene he had also fought several ugly battles with the Government Accountability Office over funding and accounting. Like any major change effort, particularly something led by Gene, these confrontations left their marks on people and relationships. There were individuals left in the wake who thought Gene had been heavy-handed, too opinionated, discourteous, and dogmatic, all of which was certainly true. Yet, as Gene also knew, this was an inevitable by-product of change.

In the spring of 1988, Betty arranged a party to celebrate Gene's seventy-fifth birthday and it seemed everyone was there. Much of the defense establishment of the past thirty years was in the room. Bob McNamara and Harold Brown attended as did much of the leadership of the DSB, old AIL colleagues, several members of the present and past Joint Chiefs, and other leaders of the more secretive "lettered agencies" (CIA, DIA, NSA). Old friends such as Dan Fink, Everett Greinke, Vic Reis, Johnny Foster, Norm Augustine, and Paul Kaminsky came by, as did Craig Fields. It was a reunion of several generations of true patriots, individuals who had given much of their careers to making the defense of America more vibrant and more technologically advanced then any country on the planet. These were the men who had made the world a far more secure one by ensuring the use of defense technologies in a manner that acted as a deterrent to the spread of nuclear weapons and helped control the advance of communist nations. It was a unique group that gathered that evening.

They had come to honor and celebrate the individual who in many ways had been their chief technologist, their mentor, and their conscience. They came to celebrate the little man with the loud voice and the undying affection for his adopted country, who had preferred to be behind the scenes to help them remake the defenses of America. They had come to celebrate Gene Fubini.

It would be the last time this group would gather and it would be the last time Gene would be healthy enough to enjoy all their company.

17

Sickness, Loss of Betty, David and Bertha

*P*erhaps it should have been better anticipated and Gene should have seen it coming. Positions on the Defense Science Board ran for four years, so every year a quarter of the membership of the board came up for re-appointment. Gene's particular "class" reached the end of its four-year term at the end of 1989. Johnny Foster was the incoming chairman, but appointments were the privilege of the Under Secretary of Defense for Acquisitions. This was John Betti, and he was coming into office and facing two boards, the Defense Science Board and the Defense Manufacturing Board. The Manufacturing Board had been established a year or two earlier and had been run in a parallel fashion to the more technology-oriented DSB. Betti decided to merge the boards and cut down on the collective numbers and recruit younger members.

As a result of this merger, Gene's term on the board had come to an end. After more than twenty years of service to the DSB, Gene was dismissed with a form letter.

In time, Johnny Foster was able to weed out the manufacturing elements and restore the integrity of the DSB, but it was too late to address Gene's appointment and role. Bert Fowler and others felt that Foster should have gone over John Betti's head to Secretary of Defense Dick Cheney and insist that Gene receive a new appointment. Gene had days when he was not at his best, but he also still had very good days, and he had earned the right. Gene was the father of the Defense Science Board. He was, in the eyes of many whose careers he had championed and whose efforts he had made possible, been treated poorly by an organization that he had made relevant and meaningful. But it was not to be. Time and politics were finally beginning to catch up with Gene.

Joe Braddock and Gene had worked together for years helping build BDM into a Washington consulting powerhouse. Over time Braddock stopped coming to see Gene for business reasons and increasingly came by to simply visit him and see how he was doing. Vic Reis did the same, and soon both were fixtures in Arlington on the weekends. When it got difficult for Gene to walk, they both would sit in Gene's office in the back of the house and talk. It wasn't idle chat but it was more a reflective type of conversation covering the overarching trends in the defense world and the geo-political scene. Joe remembered that Gene, while clearly slowing down, was still full of brilliant insights. For example, he recalled that one day they were discussing the location of U.S. military bases throughout Europe and trying to figure out the logic of the locations and how that logic might evolve. Gene pulled out a National Geographic map of the Roman Empire, and there were the Roman troop positions overlapping the U.S. positions almost exactly. Two thousand years, and the military logic had not changed. Gene and Braddock were thrilled, and when Betty came in with their coffee, Gene brought her over to look at the map and see what they had discovered. Betty, forever sanguine about such announcements, said dryly "Well, if you're so smart, tell me why our children aren't living closer to home."

But there were warning signs on the horizon. When Gene was in Florida visiting their Pelican Bay condominium in Naples (which Carol and her husband Kevin had found and purchased jointly with Gene) Gene suddenly became disoriented and had trouble with his balance. Betty, fearing he was having a stroke, called emergency services. But when they came Gene refused treatment, insisting he was fine. The next day Betty loaded Gene into their rental car, headed to the airport, and flew back to Washington D.C. She would later say it was a ghastly trip as Gene was unable to focus, disoriented, and having trouble walking.

Gene was admitted into Fairfax Hospital and diagnosed with hydrocephalus, an excess build-up of fluid in the brain. He had to undergo emergency surgery to have shunts placed in his neck to drain the fluid. Unfortunately, his prior heart problems had left him ill-equipped for the physical rigors of surgery. While on the table he suffered a small heart attack and was left in a critical state; following the procedure, he was admitted into the intensive care unit. Gene would spend nearly a week in the I.C.U., after which he slowly improved. After a long hospital stay he was able to return to Arlington where he was greatly weakened but still alert and able to generally function with aid from Betty. But he had turned a corner, and would never fully recover: his balance continued to give him trouble, stairs were a hazard, and he tired easily.

The burden of care now fell fully on Betty. She would monitor Gene's activities to make sure he wasn't overextended and that he didn't attempt to do more than was prudent. Gene now required more medical care, as the hydrocephalus and shunts caused frequent problems. The children urged Betty to bring in outside nursing help, but she refused. She hated the idea of strangers in the home, and she did not consider Gene's needs severe enough to make it absolutely necessary. Sylvia lived near, as did Sandy, so they were a great support. David visited most weekends and the others came by as often as they could.

Then in late August 1993, Sylvia arrived to visit and found Gene sitting in his study alone. He said he was worried because Betty, who had taken to sleeping on the living room sofa, was difficult to wake up. Betty had died peacefully in her sleep during the evening. How could this be, the family thought. She was so strong, so stoic. She was the backbone of the family for the children. Gene was the one who was sick, and in all the worry over him, it had never occurred to anyone that Betty might be the one to go first. Betty, they all assumed, was going to outlive him and spend her last years happily visiting with her children and playing with her grandchildren. She had a hair appointment the day she died. She couldn't be gone. Yet, she was and Gene was aware enough to know that she was gone, and he was scared. He didn't know what was going to happen to him now.

At the time, David and Bertha were in London for a short visit after a long summer of balancing the birth of their two small children; the relocation of the household to Boston, where David had moved to lead McKinsey & Company's New England office; and the constant travel not only for David's work, but for visits to help Betty with Gene. They both rushed back to Washington. David sat with Gene, and Gene asked what would happen to him now. Bertha and David had by this time talked about options, and it was clear to all the children that only David was in a position to take Gene in. Sylvia, for example, was close but, living in a small home and having recently gone through a divorce, she was not able to handle the burden. Sandra was also now divorced and dealing with her recent relocation back to Virginia (she had moved into the old family home in Vienna). Her priority was a stable household for her four children, and it was hard to imagine Gene enabling that. Carol was in Boston and raising two small children; she was not able to accommodate Gene, either. Laurie and Bob were in Philadelphia with their two girls and could, and did over the next few years, help immeasurably. Susan and Rory were in Ithaca, New York, in a smallish home and already had two young children.

David and Bertha were more financially secure and had already planned to move to a large suburban home that could be retrofitted for their father. Also, the children knew that Gene would be most comfortable with David. In truth, only he had a relationship with Gene that would allow Gene to be controlled. Chalk it up to Gene's chauvinistic attitudes, but Gene wanted to be with David. He was relieved to the point of tears to know that he had a home in the wake of the shock of losing Betty.

A funeral was held later in the week at the Good Shepard Church, just a few hundred feet down the road from the Vienna home that had been the site for the thousands of Gene's trademark walks in Vienna woods. What was expected to be a small gathering of family and close friends was soon a gathering of hundreds of neighborhood people who had heard of Betty's passing and came to pay their respects. The outpouring of friends and acquaintances surprised everyone. After all, Betty had been an intensely private person. She had lived her life largely behind the scenes caring for her children and her children's children, and of course Gene. Yet, here were all these people who had been touched by Betty. Gene was in tears, not so much for his feelings of loss, but as he said to David on that day, "I had no idea that she was so loved by so many."

The children had lost their parental compass and they dealt as best they could. Gene had never been the rock of support that their mother had been. Betty had spent her life insulating them from the harmful aspects and challenges of Gene's personality. Even now, in his compromised state, the children feared him even as they continued to try to meet his expectations of them.

David now took up the responsibility of preparing for Gene's arrival, and over the Labor Day weekend in 1993 Gene made the move from Arlington to Boston. Gene would never again see Washington, where he had spent so much of his life and career. He would never set foot in the Pentagon again.

Gene's arrival was going to put a huge strain on David. Thankfully for him, and the rest of his sisters, David had his wife Bertha. Bertha was to become a surrogate daughter to Gene and she immediately took him under her wing and cared for and protected him.

Bertha was a first-generation American. She was the fourth among eight children of parents from Monterey, Mexico who had relocated to the south side of Chicago. Bertha went to parochial school, graduated from Loyola, and received an MBA in marketing and international finance at Northwestern University in 1985. She was the first of her family to attend college and was the only one to go on to graduate school. After graduation and a stint at Johnson & Johnson, Bertha moved to New York to work for American Express. Coming from an immigrant family with limited means and an insular culture, she had thoroughly enjoyed the experience of New York. She would have loved to live in the city but it was too expensive, so she lived in New Jersey near Johnson & Johnson, and stayed with friends in the city on weekends.

She met David at a party in Stanford, Connecticut hosted by a Northwestern MBA classmate. She had gone more to see her other friends than to find a date, much less a husband. It was not love at first sight. In truth, when David called she wasn't quite sure who he was: she'd met two McKinsey guys that night, and she wasn't sure which had been which. It took them three months to set up their first date, as David was working full time in Detroit for a McKinsey client and was never available. They met finally when David flew in just for dinner and went directly from the airport to meet her. The right McKinsey guy showed up for that dinner, and after a long courtship they were married in Vermont in 1989.

Before her first meeting with Gene, David warned her and even apologized in advance. At the time Gene was still very strong, very opinionated, and very authoritative. But as it turned out, Bertha was well-equipped to deal with a patriarch, coming, as she did, from a strongly patriarchal culture. When she met Gene, she was placating and slightly flirtatious, which Gene loved. And it wasn't all deference. Bertha found herself captivated by Gene's intelligence and old-world charm.

Whenever they met, Gene would interrogate her. He was very frank and very direct, as if he were bringing his office to the table and Bertha was the business of the day. He had to know what she studied, why, and where she was headed. He wanted her resume. She found that his accent put her at ease, as it reminded her that they were both directly connected to foreign cultures. At the time, Gene was always alone when he visited Bertha and David in New York. She didn't meet Betty until after she and David were already engaged.

The wedding party was held at the family's Vermont house, and that meant something to Betty, because Betty and Gene loved the house. Yet Betty didn't approve of Bertha, her background, her ethnicity, or her Catholicism. When Bertha would say she was going to Mass, it always seemed to be a problem. Later, one of the most difficult things about Betty and Bertha's relationship was the divergence of their views on child rearing. Bertha was of the belief that a child should be cherished, protected, and loved unconditionally. Safety and comfort were paramount. Betty felt that independence was important and, while she was hardly emotionally cold, she did feel that setting rules and boundaries was not just acceptable but necessary. For example, when Bertha's children cried, Bertha picked them up, loved, and consoled them. In Bertha's culture, mothers picked up crying children. Betty thought that Bertha was excessive and not willing to be tough enough. She was not shy about sharing her views with Bertha.

Initially, some of David's sisters also took a strong dislike to Bertha. It might have been her religious views, or it might have been that she was so strong-willed and not afraid to speak her mind. Or it may have been that she was beautiful, and there was some jealously. Their distaste for her may also have been related to Bertha's easy and even close relationship to Gene. After all, they'd struggled for their entire lives to reconcile themselves to who Gene was. How could Bertha swoop in and so easily establish a connection?

When Gene moved in with them, David was doing well, having embarked on what would be a long career with McKinsey & Company. Bertha became, in part, Gene's secretary, keeping up his Rolodexes and his correspondence, reading his mail, and getting out all the Christmas cards. For a while there was a flurry of calls from the Italian government asking Gene to come over and participate in discussions on taxes and on the divisions between the north and south communities on issues of security. There were invitations to symposiums in the U.S. from various think tanks, and there were a variety of speaking requests. But Gene couldn't possibly go, so Bertha quietly explained to the organizations why their requests could not be honored.

What Gene could do was talk about his past. Bertha sat with him and he remembered and talked. He would remember when he was five or six, how his brother Gino had wanted to play, and Gene had said, "I have no time for these childish games." Now Gene was sorry he had said that and was sorry he had never been interested in his brother. But the fact was Gene had never wanted to be a child. He talked about his love of learning, about how doing math brought him to life. He would often speak about the conversations he'd had with his father and recall doing math problems with him, how important that connection with his father was, and how when his father was dying, Gene sat with him and gave him a hard problem, which had occupied and cheered them both.

Gene would recall his youth and his time climbing the Alps and the feeling it gave him. He described the experience of climbing to a new level, one he'd never reached before, the feeling that filled him at the moment when he rose up to the final peak and the vista spread out before him. He also remembered his mother's apartment on Central Park West in New York and her dinners, that she was a terrific cook and that she also had a terrific cook, and the dinners and parties.

David and Bertha would take him to Vermont, which he loved. They pushed his wheelchair outside and he stood holding the handles and looking into the mountains. On Nantucket, they took him sailing, which he had done when he was young, and he sat in the front of the boat and you could see him remembering the joy of the past. It was as if, for the first time, he was taking time to remember, or maybe even taking time to notice in a way he never had before. Maybe this was the only way it could happen, when his body and mind finally slowed down enough that everything wasn't rushing past.

Gene on Nantucket beach (1993).

Of course, it was not all fond remembrances and sentimentality, and Gene had not, in essence, changed that much. Having him in the house was hard. He was demanding and he could still be unkind. David's sisters said that he was using Bertha, and maybe he was. He was certainly manipulative. He had, at some point, realized that this was the end, that unlike his bypass surgery, this wasn't something he could will himself back from. This wasn't something that could be fixed. This was simply age, and no amount of Gene Fubini could change that. He accepted the reality, but not easily, and not happily. If he was to be an invalid, it would be on his terms. He expected everything done for him, and everything was. But like his children showing him a good grade or any other achievement, nothing was ever enough.

Plenty of times he screamed at Bertha, and she screamed right back. She might have come from a patriarchal culture, but that didn't mean she was docile. They became like an old married couple. It was simple to understand the distance between Gene and his daughters. They had had a lifetime of him and he was their father. If it had been Bertha's father, she would have been the same way. But he wasn't her father, and she he did not have the same hold on her. She was not afraid of him.

Bertha and a weakened Gene in Boston (1995).

Gene now knew he was losing his capacities, but he loved when friends called, and even toward the end you could tell that there were many levels at which he understood national security. He never talked, even then, about such things. Bertha and David didn't have the clearances and even then he would not violate those codes of secrecy. When friends such as Dick Close or Bert Fowler came by, he would ask that Bertha and David to leave the room lest they overhear something of a classified nature.

Gene loved the pretty nurses and the beautiful dentist who came to check his teeth. When he was with these women he became the Italian gentleman. He sparkled when they came to care for him. Whenever they went to the hospital in emergencies, he refused to speak to anyone but the lead doctor, and every time it infuriated Bertha and David because he was so stubborn and, at times, elitist in his views. Underlings were fine, but to Gene you only dealt with the senior brass to get things done.

Finally, the shunts stopped working, and try as the doctors and nurses did to get the fluids under control, Gene slipped into a coma. After almost three weeks of a nearly unconsciousness state, with the family sure the end had come, he awoke, opened his eyes and said, "Where's my coffee?" He remained conscious, if debilitated, for another two years before his health began its final decline.

Gene died peacefully in his sleep on August 5, 1997 in David and Bertha's home in Brookline, Massachusetts. He was eighty-four years old.

18

Bill Perry, The Fubini Award

*T*here were many people, and Bill Perry was among them, who believed that no one in the history of the Defense Department had contributed more to the department than Gene Fubini. In a general way, over the course of more than forty years, Gene had immersed himself in the life of the department, serving on committee after committee, often as the motivating presence, in every aspect of the work of bringing technology into national security affairs. With his brilliance, there was little in the way of defense technology that he couldn't understand, and similarly there was nothing he could not and would not explain to anyone of any background. In light of the ever-increasing constraints on the appearance of conflict of interest, there will never again be anyone able to move as effortlessly and effectively as Gene Fubini did between academia, industry, and government. Yet Gene did that and did it with the integrity recognized and respected by everyone he encountered.

More particularly, he was among the first and the most influential proponents of electronic warfare, bringing it into the national security vocabulary through his unwavering and effective support, frequently against considerable opposition. He was also an early and ardent supporter of advancing military command and control; it was largely due to his sustained efforts—through administration after administration—that command and control evolved into command and control and communications, and then command and control and communications and computers, which has become the critical nerve center of modern warfare. He was a foundational visionary in, among other areas, the advance into space and the development of stealth aircraft. He had a hand in early computing and the groundwork for modern digital communications. Equally important, he served as an invaluable example, mentor, and friend to generation after generation of other men drawn to serve in the defense of their country.

In July of 1996, shortly before Gene's death, then Secretary of Defense Bill Perry issued this memo:

> Memorandum for secretaries of the military departments; chairman of the joint chiefs of staff; under secretaries of defense; director, defense research & engineering; assistant secretaries of defense; general counsel of the department of defense; inspector general of the department of defense; director, operational test and evaluation; assistants to the secretary of defense; director, administration and management; directors of defense agencies
>
> Subject: Establishment of the Eugene G. Fubini Award
> For Outstanding Service or Contributions to
> The Defense Community in an Advisory Capacity.
>
> 1996 marks the 40th Anniversary of the Defense Science Board. In recognition of that important milestone, the "Eugene

G. Fubini Award is herein established for outstanding service or contributions to the Defense Community in an Advisory Capacity. This award is being created to recognize extraordinary individuals who, like Dr. Fubini, have made a significant contribution to the Department of Defense and the national security through their outstanding scientific or technical advice."

By this same memorandum, I am also designating Dr. Eugene G. Fubini as the first recipient of this award for 1996.

Epilogue

$\mathcal{S}$hortly after my father passed away, while packing up his office in the Arlington Virginia office, I discovered a large silver plate that was given to my father many years ago. It was slightly bent from its inappropriate placement in the back of a study credenza and bore this inscription:

The Defense Science Board and Secretaries of Defense under whom he served salute the Honorable Dr. Eugene G. Fubini with our sincerest appreciation for his decades of faithful and exemplary service to the defense of the United States of America

The plaque, dated October 21, 1992, bears the inscribed signatures of former Secretaries of Defense Dick Cheney, Frank Carlucci, Caspar Weinberger, Harold Brown, Donald Rumsfeld, J.R. Schlesinger, Elliot Richardson, Melvin Laird, Clark Clifford, and Robert S. McNamara, as well as that of John Foster Jr., then chairman of the Defense Science Board.

To be honest, I'd never appreciated the full measure of this award, though the silver plate has rested on the mantel in my office for many years. My father had never displayed this award and I don't recall any formal presentation ceremony. As we well know, Washington, D.C. is a place that hands out awards and commemorations immoderately, but as I pondered this plaque I came to realize this was something with considerable weight: This single plate carried the signatures of ten Secretaries of Defense, spanning twenty-four years of service for both Democratic and Republican administrations. Each of these administrations had had vastly different agendas, different world circumstances, and major crises to respond to. And for each, my father had been of indispensable service. As a testament to my father's longevity and political objectivity, it was for me almost profound.

This is, succinctly, what writing this book has done for me: it has provided perspective. Perspective on my father's career and accomplishments and, even more importantly, perspective on who he was as person and a father.

We all know the cliché of the difficult father who, in his old age and with the daily battles behind him, mellows and connects with his friends and family in a way he never had before; this was not my father.

He remained, until his death, a beguiling, opinionated, loving, frustrating personality. When he first came to live with us he would try (until bluntly told not to) to sit in on meetings with me, discussing my clients and offering advice just as he had so freely at the Pentagon. He argued, debated, and was as demanding with Bertha as he'd been with my mom (although his overbearing attitude failed with my even tougher wife). Even at the end—literally near to death—he remained stubbornly, immovably himself: so secretive as to expel me and my lack of security clearances from the room if he was talking with an old Pentagon colleague. All of this was maddening, but hardly, after a lifetime, surprising.

Part of what writing this book has enabled me to do is embrace my father's work. As a child, and even well into my adulthood, his work was essentially the great unknown into which my father completely disappeared. It was the reason for the constant flow of colleagues who visited our various homes on the weekends, crowding out family time. It was the thing that drove him and defined him, and it was the source of his secrecy and inscrutability. The work on this book has laid bare much of what had never been seen before; it inspires in me not only something akin to awe, but also boundless respect for his abilities, his dedication, and his integrity. These days, such selfless, unmitigated devotion to a country and a cause not naturally one's own seems monumentally, almost heartbreakingly, rare.

But the other thing the book has helped me to do—and again, it wasn't something I set out to do, nor was it something I was ever aware I particularly needed to do—is bridge the gap between that which I'd longed for in a father, and that which I'd gotten. To one degree or another, I realize, everyone goes through this process with their parents, sometimes in smaller ways, sometimes in larger. We all have to make the leap to understanding our parents as people. We get the parents we get; the burden to make sense of it is ours.

His unusual personality that we, as children, found peculiar and off-putting, was seen as endearing by many of his colleagues. He seemed to know the answer to *every* math, science, or history question, and he seemed to have so strong a need to teach that every question was followed by a time-consuming dissertation on whatever the topic was; his colleagues saw his brilliance, foresight, and deep understanding of not only the technical but the practical. We saw a father who, while committed to the outcome of our efforts, was not at all concerned about, or necessarily even aware of, the process of adolescence and ups and downs of life's journey;

countless others saw my father as a caring, compassionate mentor willing to go to extraordinary lengths to help another. How to reconcile these two views? This effort has allowed a conversion of sorts.

For me, it happened while listening to interviews with my father's colleagues, when I read old memos and articles about my father, and when I began to assemble all the research into the book itself. Little by little, a sense of him formed in my mind and understanding. It wasn't the man I'd known growing up and into my adulthood. It was more than that. It was the dimension and depth behind that person. Somewhere in the process of writing this book, I stopped seeing him as a child does— simplistically and without texture or subtlety—and came to understand him from my own perspective as a professional, as an adult, and as a father of my own children.

I'm fifty-four years old now, and I've reached the second half of my career; I've accumulated accomplishments and achieved most of what I set out to do in my chosen field as a management consultant; I'm proud of what I've done. But at roughly the same age, my father was just entering the most productive and significant phase of his career. This is astonishing to me and, again, something I'd not appreciated before. I am also, like most everyone else, a product of my time. My approach to my role as a parent and husband is informed by the social mores I've known every day of my life. As the result of my new perspective, I understand that the same was true of my father. He was, in most ways and by today's standards, a difficult, demanding, and distant father. But I can only judge him fairly in the context of the times in which he lived.

I now understand that despite his failings he had pushed us children to have the same passion he had for academics and our work. He was the father of five girls, all of whom he demanded, cajoled, and in his way, supported to become accomplished professionals in their fields. Be it economics, satellite/space technology, the law, or veterinary medicine, each succeeded. He did this at a time when women were not welcomed in such fields. Yes, he used an approach that was borderline abusive, but he believed that gender was not a deterrent; rather, it was simply another obstacle to be overcome.

I came to dislike the expressions he used time and time again to get me to do more: "Always do three when one will suffice;" or, when job-seeking, "Never be interviewed; always do the interviewing." When faced with an immovable object, he would say, "Cooperate with the inevitable." He was not a normal father, true, but he instilled a love of learning, a desire for continuous personal improvement, and the simple notion that humility is the less traveled, more rewarding road—all foundational beliefs that stay with me today and which I now pass along to my children.

Some people and personalities are complicated; everyone knows that. But now I truly feel I understand my father. I finish this book feeling more personally enriched than I would have thought possible at its outset, and the most enriching thing of all may be how surprising the learning has been. In ways my father could and would never have explained, I have come to understand him now. It was nothing I expected, and that's what makes it truly meaningful.

Acknowledgements

*T*he idea for this book was first formed during the celebration of my father's life in fall of 1997 at a gathering at the Cosmos Club in Washington, D.C. At this large gathering, nearly a dozen of my father's closest friends, colleagues, and family members shared memories of my father, who had passed away early that year.

Among the speakers that day was Harold Brown. He was relating a number of my father's idioms and stories and at one point paused and, in an off-hand remark, said, "You know, someone should write these down."

At that moment, I thought that I would at some point undertake that task. Now, more than 12 years later, that task has been completed. It would not have been possible to undertake this project without the support of many individuals, all of whom need to be acknowledged for their contributions.

First and foremost is my wife, Bertha. Her willingness to take my sick, and later dying, father into our household was an act of unselfish love for him, my family, and for me. For nearly six years, Bertha incorporated my father into the family's daily routine, and when that became impossible to do without outside assistance, then the healthcare givers became a part of our family as well. With Bertha's encouragement and insistence, my father traveled to Nantucket and Vermont on vacation with us at a time when most in his condition would have been confined to a hospital bed. Bertha, in effect, became a geriatric specialist and developed a network of healthcare professionals that supported her and my father as his illnesses and needs multiplied. She was a fixture at Beth Israel Deaconess Medical Center during my father's long recuperations from many surgeries. All this while she was raising two boys and pregnant for a time with our daughter, Anna. Her support of my father knew no bounds and no words can convey my love and deep appreciation for her for the role she played in the final phase of my father's life.

Bertha was also essential in the effort to make this book a reality. Her contributions are too numerous to detail here, lest we take up too many pages and too much of the reader's attention. It is sufficient to say she has been supportive at every turn, encouraged the work to get this book researched, and tolerated the time away from our children that was required for it to be written. Her love and support of my father was complete and absolute. Her support of my effort to document his life was the same.

Bert Fowler, one of my father's closest and longest-lived friends, was essential to this book. Bert made possible many of the interviews critical to writing of the book. He read the manuscript on three separate occasions as it was developed. He has made sure that it was, to the best of his knowledge, accurate and portrayed people's roles and efforts appropriately.

Fred Dillen conducted well over 75 interviews and did most of the initial research for this book. Fred worked tirelessly for more than eight months on conducting these interviews and doing research in the Harvard, MIT, and Defense Department archives. He also pulled all available data from the Defense Department. Finally, Fred wrote the initial drafts and was critical to the development of much of the detail that underlies the narrative.

Larry Fahey took the final version of the manuscript and helped, with his editor's skill, to turn it into an enjoyable narrative. He helped me reorganize the chapters and ensure that the story was lively, readable, and emphasized the most salient points of my father's rich life.

Harold Brown—from his initial, off-the-cuff idea at the podium at my father's memorial celebration, through to his agreeing to write the forward to the book—has been an encouraging voice in this endeavor. Harold's friendship with my father was a rich and valued one, and my father called this friendship and collaboration one of the single most enriching parts of his life. I fondly recall my father saying that the smartest man he ever met was Enrico Fermi. The second most impressive mind was that belonging to Harold Brown. I see no reason anyone should argue with my father's view.

Finally, I want to thank my sisters and my cousin, Joyce. My sisters have been supportive of this effort but have also been careful to avoid putting their stamp on the ideas and thoughts in the book. I appreciate that my sisters have allowed me to characterize their thoughts and opinions. The sentiments expressed, I hope, are true. However, the accuracy of their feelings may not always be correct. Joyce has read much of the manuscript and added color and ideas on the part of the story that I am less familiar with, which deals with my father's brother and his family. Joyce has also been a wonderful sounding board.

Index

LaVergne, TN USA
25 November 2009
165226LV00002B/2/P